Family Practices in South Asian Muslim Families

Palgrave Macmillan Studies in Family and Intimate Life

Titles include:

Harriet Becher
FAMILY PRACTICES IN SOUTH ASIAN MUSLIM FAMILIES
Parenting in a Multi-Faith Britain

Jacqui Gabb
RESEARCHING INTIMACY AND SEXUALITY IN FAMILIES

David Morgan
RETHINKING FAMILY PRACTICES

Eriikka Oinonen
FAMILIES IN CONVERGING EUROPE
A Comparison of Forms, Structures and Ideas

Róisín Ryan-Flood
LESBIAN MOTHERHOOD
Gender, Families and Sexual Citizenship

Palgrave Macmillan Studies in Family and Intimate Life
Series Standing Order ISBN 978–0–230–51748–6 hardback
(*outside North America only*)

You can receive future titles in this series as they are published by placing a standing order. Please contact your bookseller or, in case of difficulty, write to us at the address below with your name and address, the title of the series and the ISBN quoted above.

Customer Services Department, Macmillan Distribution Ltd, Houndmills, Basingstoke, Hampshire RG21 6XS, England

Family Practices in South Asian Muslim Families

Parenting in a Multi-Faith Britain

Harriet Becher

palgrave
macmillan

First published 2008 by
PALGRAVE MACMILLAN

Palgrave Macmillan in the UK is an imprint of Macmillan Publishers Limited, registered in England, company number 785998, of Houndmills, Basingstoke, Hampshire RG21 6XS.

Palgrave Macmillan in the US is a division of St Martin's Press LLC, 175 Fifth Avenue, New York, NY 10010.

Palgrave Macmillan is the global academic imprint of the above companies and has companies and representatives throughout the world.

Palgrave® and Macmillan® are registered trademarks in the United States, the United Kingdom, Europe and other countries.

ISBN-13: 978–0–230–54927–2   hardback
ISBN-10: 0–230–54927–6   hardback

This book is printed on paper suitable for recycling and made from fully managed and sustained forest sources. Logging, pulping and manufacturing processes are expected to conform to the environmental regulations of the country of origin.

A catalogue record for this book is available from the British Library.

A catalogue record for this book is available from the Library of Congress.

10   9   8   7   6   5   4   3   2   1
17   16   15   14   13   12   11   10   09   08

Printed and bound in Great Britain by
CPI Antony Rowe, Chippenham and Eastbourne

My thanks to Margaret O'Brien, Clem Henricson, Fatima Husain and Tony Becher for their advice and encouragement; to the Economic and Social Research Council and Family and Parenting Institute for funding this research; to Hakim Mendjeli for his constant support; and most of all, to the parents and children who generously invited me into their homes and gave their time to participate in this study.

Contents

List of Tables and Charts

Series Preface

The remit of the *Palgrave Macmillan Studies in Family and Intimate Life* series is to publish work focusing broadly on the sociological exploration of intimate relationships and family organization. As editors we think such a series is timely. Expectations, commitments and practices have changed significantly in intimate relationship and family life in recent decades. This is very apparent in patterns of family formation and dissolution, demonstrated by trends in parenting, cohabitation, marriage and divorce. Changes in household living patterns over the last twenty years have also been marked, with more people living alone, adult children living longer in the parental home, and more 'non-family' households being formed.

There have also been important shifts in the ways people construct intimate relationships. There are few comfortable certainties about the best ways of being a family man or woman, with once conventional gender roles no longer being widely accepted. The normative connection between sexual relationships and marriage or marriage-like relationships is also less powerful than it once was. Not only is greater sexual experimentation accepted, but it is now accepted at an earlier age. Moreover heterosexuality is no longer the only mode of sexual relationship given legitimacy. Gay male and lesbian partnerships are now socially and legally endorsed to a degree hardly imaginable in the mid-twentieth century. Increases in lone-parent families, the rapid growth of different types of stepfamily, the de-stigmatization of births outside marriage, and the rise in couples 'living-apart-together' (LATs) all provide further examples of the ways that 'being a couple', 'being a parent' and 'being a family' have diversified in recent years.

The fact that change in family life and intimate relationships has been so pervasive has resulted in renewed research interest from sociologists and other scholars. Increasing amounts of public funding have been directed to family research in recent years, in terms of both individual projects and the creation of family research centres of different hues. This research activity has been accompanied by the publication of some very important and influential books exploring different aspects of shifting family experience. The *Palgrave Macmillan Studies in Family and Intimate Life* series hopes to add to this list of influential research-based texts published in English (both new texts and new translations), thereby contributing to existing knowledge and informing current debates. Our main audience consists of academics and advanced students, though we intend that the books in the series will be accessible to a more general readership who wish to understand better the changing nature of contemporary family life and personal relationships.

Harriet Becher's book *Family Practices in South Asian Muslim Families* is a very welcome addition to the series. While diversity in patterns of family organization and practice are now widely recognized, there are still comparatively few studies of the family experiences of different ethnic or faith minority groups in the UK. At a time when there is increased public and policy interest in Islamic ways of life in Britain, Becher's empirical study of south-Asian Muslim family patterns provides an insightful analysis of the interplay of multiplex factors on the 'doing' of family. While a major focus of the study is on the nature of parent–child relationships in south-Asian families, it extends well beyond this, drawing on the understandings respondents had of these relationships to explore the construction of family life, both inside and outside the household.

As the title indicates, the concept of 'family practices' acts as the core theoretical driver for the study. The analysis is concerned with the routine and everyday experiences of being in a family, with how these experiences are negotiated and managed, and with how they change over time. The focus is on agency and construction rather than on preset normatively-determined patterns of behaviour. At the same time, Becher is sensitive to the interaction of domestic/familial practices on the one hand and cultural/ethnic/religious practices on the other. As she argues, the family practices her respondents constructed can only be understood in the context of their religious and/or ethnic commitments and principles. Becher is able to illustrate the interplay of these processes very well through her examination of everyday family behaviour including food production, clothing, language and leisure. She also illustrates the gendered and generational dynamics of family practices, especially in the context of these south Asian families' migration histories and ethno-religious cultural commitments.

Becher's study is a multi-method one. Its starting point is a questionnaire survey of primary school age children and their parents drawn from 5 schools in an outer London Borough. Principally though the analysis is grounded in qualitative interviews with a subset of the children and parents who responded to this questionnaire survey. What is particularly novel about the research design is that it involves separate interviews with children and their mothers (or mother substitutes), and in some cases also their fathers. The great advantage of this for the study is not simply that it allows for family practices to be examined from the perspectives of the different family members, but also that it facilitates the focus on changing generational perspectives. Overall Becher provides a fascinating analysis of the nature of domestic relations and family life among south-Asian Muslim families in Britain, one which highlights diversity among these families, and not just their commonalities.

Graham Allan, Lynn Jamieson and David Morgan
Series Editors

1
Introduction

In recent years, there has been growing public debate about the impact of parenting on the social fabric, with increasing weight given to the idea that social 'problems' such as truancy, delinquency or youth crime can be linked to inadequate parenting (Gillies 2005). Accordingly, the Government has paid more attention to parental responsibilities, and given priority to 'enabling' parents in their role. These developments indicate an assumption that all parents will face difficulties of varying degrees at different times, and that some level of support or information should be available to assist them in bringing up their children effectively.

In spite of these developments, there has been concern that some groups of parents in Britain – for example, minority ethnic parents, disabled parents, young parents, fathers – may have less access to, or be less likely to use, such services. In 2001, the Family and Parenting Institute undertook mapping research into the provision of family services in England and Wales (Henricson, Katz et al. 2001). Data sources included questionnaire responses from statutory and voluntary family services, and interviews with commissioners and providers in ten local authority sample areas. One of the principal findings of the report was that few services, in fact only 2 per cent, targeted minority ethnic families. Service providers also reported difficulties in attracting minority ethnic families to generic services. Additionally, the report found that at both the national and local level, there was an absence of family services that were culturally appropriate for different ethnic groups.

The formulation of more culturally 'sensitive' services was identified as a priority by the authors of the FPI report, a conclusion that resonated with other researchers' findings (e.g. Butt and Box 1998; Qureshi, Berridge et al. 2000). However, it was suggested that in order to develop improved services, policy-makers needed more research evidence to inform them about family life and the needs of parents from different minority ethnic groups. The research knowledge that did exist was focused on a variety of groups, but the coverage was patchy, often out-of-date and lacked a specific emphasis on the place of ethnicity in contemporary parenting (Butt and Box 1998). Large-scale survey studies (e.g. Modood, Berthoud et al. 1997) provided valuable information about family formation and structure in minority ethnic families, but gave less insight into day-to-day family processes. This initial policy review identified a need to discover more about normative family life, at a qualitative level, among Britain's ethnic minorities: a requirement that is all the more pressing because of the growth of Britain's ethnic minority populations, both in terms of their absolute numbers[1] and their political and social presence. Concurrent with these demographic changes, Britain has experienced a cultural shift, with minority ethnic 'voices' gaining in prominence. The notion of Britain's ethnic diversity as an important source of richness has been used frequently in political rhetoric in recent years: 'We celebrate the diversity in our country, get strength from the cultures and the races that go to make up Britain today.' (Prime Minister Tony Blair, 2 October 2001).[2]

A parallel development that helped to shape the research was the increasing visibility of religion in British society. Over the past few decades – and contrary to the forecasted 'secularisation' of modern Western societies, which was expected to lead to declining individual religious commitment, and a decline in the prominence of religion in social life (Sherkat and Ellison 1999) – religious beliefs, practices and membership have begun to receive renewed attention in the public sphere. World events and public debates over the last 50 years indicate that religion remains variously a salient source of personal and social identity; a source of political mobilization or conflict; a resource to which people turn in times of need; and a source of social capital and integration into civil society. Significantly, the British Government reintroduced a religion question in the 2001 Census for the first time in 150 years, signalling the renewed importance of moral and religious values in society. The results revealed that almost four in five British people still align themselves with a faith group. In politics, too, religion has begun to play a more central role. In 2003, the Government broke with tradition by announcing the establishment of a ministerial working group 'to consider the most effective means of achieving greater involvement of the faith communities in policy-making and delivery' across government.[3] The resulting report included recommendations on how the government could better engage and communicate with faith communities, and work with them 'on the ground' to deliver services (Home Office 2004). In 2004, the government introduced protection against incitement to religious hatred, bringing legislation on religious offences in line with that on racial offences.[4]

Importantly, as Britain's cultural diversity has increased, the prominence of religion has not been limited to Christianity. Rather, there has been growing awareness and debate around the notion of Britain as a multi-faith society, and more generally an acknowledgement in the media, political and public arenas of the existence of contrasting cultural and religious value systems. The increasing salience of Islam is a notable example. Muslims make up the largest minority faith group in Britain (3.1 per cent of the population in England, and 8 per cent of those in London, were Muslim according to the 2001 Census). Events such as the Rushdie affair in the 1980s had brought British Muslims to centre-stage as a significant presence in public life. Early in the lifetime of this research, the dramatic events of 11th September 2001, when members of the Islamic extremist group Al'Qaeda hijacked and flew two passenger planes into the World Trade Centre Towers in New York, brought Islam to the forefront of public consciousness. Further terrorist attacks in London in 2005 brought the question of alienation from mainstream British society amongst a minority in the Muslim community further into focus. The ensuing reactions in Britain – seen by some (e.g. Van der Veer 2004) as akin to a 'moral panic' – helped to sharpen the debate about what it means to be a British Muslim. Muslim communities in Britain have become increasingly organized in their responses, with organizations such as the Muslim Council of Britain being established to co-ordinate their views. There have been responses from the academic community too, in the form of a number of recent studies looking at the lives of British Muslims (e.g. Modood, Berthoud et al. 1997; Shaw 2000).

This growing portrayal of Britain as a multi-cultural and multi-faith society has had an important impact on the nature of debates about family life. Discussions about what it means to belong to a family are taking place in a more self-conscious, global, context of contrasting value systems; 'The growing multi-ethnic and multi-faith character of contemporary Britain are creating new socio-economic and cultural contexts for negotiating what it means to be a father [or mother, or child]' (O'Brien 2003:121).

Over the last century social scientists have reported increased democratization of the father's and mother's position in the family, through the decline in patriarchal socio-legal structures and growth of women's rights (O'Brien 2003). The increasing secularization of family life has also been documented (Newson and Newson 1968; 1976). Alongside this, there has been a new emphasis on notions of children's rights and agency (e.g. James and Prout 1997), and parental duty and responsibility (O'Brien and McKee 1982). Yet despite these broad patterns, the growing diversity of Britain has brought an awareness of the existence of *contrasting* value positions on the roles of parents and children in the family. This shift can be seen as part of a more general revision of earlier 'grand narratives', and awareness that social change is not linear but uneven, with parallel sets of alternative values in existence (Giddens 1991).

Family practices

This book reports findings from a research study exploring family practices (Morgan 1996) in South Asian Muslim families in Britain. The aim was to map parenting belief systems, and everyday family practices, from the perspectives of mothers, fathers and children. The study paid particular attention to the role of religion in family life; for example, its influence on ideas about family roles and obligations, as well as its impact on everyday family routines and rituals. It also aimed to examine the process of seeking help for family problems, and explore the formal and informal support systems that are available to South Asian Muslim families in Britain today.

David Morgan's concept of 'family practices' (Morgan 1996) was adopted as a broad theoretical framework for understanding individuals' ideas and experiences of family life, both at the levels of individual action and social structure. Following Morgan's definition, this book views 'family practices' as a term capturing the way in which people 'do' family; that is, the beliefs, expectations and action surrounding parenthood, kinship and marriage. Such practices are active, everyday and routine, constructed by individuals, and historically, as significant in some way.

Morgan sees 'family' as an adjective rather than a noun, defining it as 'sets of practices which deal in some way with the ideas of parenthood, kinship and marriage and the expectations and obligations which are associated with these practices' (1996:11). He outlines the key features of his use of the term family practices as follows:

- It seeks to combine the perspectives of the actor and the observer: there has been recent privileging of the actor's perspective in social science, but it is important to acknowledge the perspective of the observer too, partly because the actor may not always define what they are doing as 'family practices';

- It conveys a sense of the active, in contrast, for example, to the term 'family structures', which suggests something static and concrete;
- It carries some sense of the everyday; so practices are 'little fragments of daily life which are part of the normal taken-for-granted existence of the practitioners. Their significance derives significance from the location of these practices within systems of [for example] parenting...' (Morgan 1996:189–90). These everyday aspects of family life have often been absent in family theorizing (Daly 2003).
- It conveys some sense of regularity; the meaning and character of family practices are in part derived from the fact that they are routine and repeated;
- Family practices convey a sense of fluidity – despite the feeling of fixity derived from their everydayness and regularity – because they are open-ended and could be described in a number of ways;
- Practices constitute major links between history and biography (Mills 1959).

'Practices are historically constituted and the linkages and tensions or contradictions between practices are historically shaped. At the same time practices are woven into and constituted from elements of individual biographies' (Morgan 1996:190).

Morgan gives the example of feeding children, which

'may be shaped by a whole host of factors, often felt as limitations or constraints. Expert notions on nutrition, previous feeding experiences, commercial and advertising pressures, gendered expectations, expectations located within particular classes, status groups or ethnic groups and external timetables all meet around the breakfast table. At the same time these influences and constraints are also resources which may provide legitimations for the adoption of one set of feeding practices rather than another' (Morgan 1996:190–1).

This approach highlights the perspectives of both the actor and the observer and accounts for a sense of regularity as well as fluidity in family life. Family practices additionally embody the relationship between self and society, since they encompass daily lived actions alongside beliefs and expectations, thus allowing an examination of how people integrate 'being' and 'doing'. The overlapping of family practices with other social foci such as gender, generation, religion or ethnicity enables an appreciation of the interrelatedness of such themes (Morgan 1999).

The concept of family practices, then, lends itself to a qualitative and exploratory methodology, in which social actors are invited to talk about their daily family lives, routines, rituals and obligations as they perceive them. For this study, family practices offered an attractive way of integrating both beliefs and behaviour, while accounting for the interrelatedness of family with key themes such as gender, generation, religion, and ethnicity. It also allowed an exploration of the interaction between structure and agency, through a focus on the negotiation of family tradition and change.

This study focuses on one aspect of family practices at the level of dyadic relationships (Parke 2004): the relations between children and parents. Within this framework, 'parenting practices' can be seen as the way in which people 'do' parenting; that is, the sets of ideas, actions and expectations surrounding the relationships between parents and children.

Research design and methods

This study examined family practices in one ethno-religious group in the UK. It was hoped that this focused approach would generate evidence relevant to the experiences of ethno-religious minority groups in general, as well as to the specific group studied. South Asian Muslim families were chosen because they constitute the largest minority ethno-religious group in the UK, yet relatively little research has explored family practices within these groups, especially from the various perspectives of individual family members (and the views of fathers are particularly underrepresented).

The aims of the study were:

• To map family practices from the perspectives of South Asian Muslim mothers, fathers and children, focusing particularly on the role of religion.
• To examine the nature and sources of help and support for parenting in South Asian Muslim families, in order to contribute to the Family and Parenting Institute's aim to develop more culturally sensitive parenting education and support.

The study focused on parenting in the middle-childhood years, 9–11 year olds, when the expectation of religious observance can become greater for children in many faith communities, including Islam (Husain and O'Brien 1999; Bose 2000). Researchers have argued that children at this age are capable of providing meaningful and insightful information, both to surveys and in interviews (Borgers, de Leeuw et al. 2000; Scott 2000).

The research design incorporated multiple methods and perspectives. The first stage, a questionnaire survey carried out in local state primary schools, was intended to provide some broad cross-sectional data, which would assist me in situating the views and experiences of South Asian Muslim families in the context of families in London more generally. By asking basic questions of children in the classroom, and also sending a questionnaire to their parents, I was able to gain comparative data on children's and parents' views of religion, family life, and sources of support, across a range of ethno-religious populations.

Fieldwork took place in five primary and junior schools randomly sampled from across the borough. The survey was conducted during a day-long visit to each school, during which all year five children (aged 9–10) present at school that day were invited to participate. Children completed a short questionnaire in a classroom setting and were given a separate questionnaire (linked by serial number) to take home for their parents. A total of 327 children (response rate 90–95 per cent) and 149 parents (response rate 46 per cent) completed a questionnaire.

The second stage consisted of qualitative interviews with mothers, fathers and children in South Asian Muslim families, and was designed to allow in-depth exploration of daily family life and parenting values among the population of interest. Twenty families fulfilled the criteria for follow-up, the child and responding parent having identified themselves as Muslim and South Asian, and the parent having agreed to being re-contacted and provided their contact details. All 20 families were followed up by letter and telephone call; 18 families agreed to participate. These families were diverse in terms of gender of the child, ethnic background, parental work status, level of religious observance and length of time in the UK. Forty-four interviews were conducted; the reference child participated in all 18 families, with 19 children interviewed in all as one family contained twins. Sixteen mothers took part; in the 2 remaining families, adult sisters who lived at home gave an interview instead, having been nominated by their families as the 'best person to talk to' about the reference child's upbringing. Fathers were present in 13 of the families and 7 of these took part in the study.

The interviews provided rich data on daily family lives, roles and obligations, belief systems and family resources for South Asian Muslims.

By interviewing up to 3 members of the same family, I was able to gain 'multiple perspectives' which were valuable in helping me to understand the complexity of individuals' experiences, even within the same family (Marsiglio, Amato et al. 2000). The inclusion and comparison of different family members' perspectives allowed a closer exploration of the dimensions of generation and gender. Past research has shown that maternal and paternal perspectives on parenting may vary (Parke 2004), as may the accounts of parents and children (Alanen 1990; Qvortrup, Bardy et al. 1994; Brannen and O'Brien 1996). The design allowed a particular focus on these different strands of experience.

The methods and fieldwork process used in the study are described in greater detail in Appendix A.

Outline of the book

The following chapters describe the findings that emerged from the study. Chapter 2 outlines the socio-economic and demographic context to the families' lives. Chapter 3 explores the ideological context: that is, the systems of beliefs and values that were important in articulating and constituting family practices. The subsequent chapters focus in turn upon different themes within family practices, to explore how these demographic and ideological contexts were played out. Chapter 4 investigates cultural expression and consumption, including aspects of food, dress, language and leisure. Chapter 5 examines everyday family and sacred practices in time and space. Chapter 6 shifts the spotlight to explore roles and relationships of mothers and fathers, while Chapter 7 analyses roles and relationships of children in families. Chapter 8 assesses the multiple resources and connections (both positive and negative) that families create and experience outside the household, including with extended kin, the religious community, neighbourhood and the wider world. Chapter 9 points to some potential theoretical and policy implications of the research.

2
Family and Demographic Contexts

This chapter sets out the socio-economic and demographic background to the lives of the parents and children in this research study: their family origins and settlement stories, parental work patterns, household structures, local community contexts and religious involvement. These factors provide an important structural context to family practices.

Each section within this chapter begins where relevant by exploring mothers' and fathers' accounts, and then moves to explore the same themes from the point of view of the children in the study. In this way, contrasts within and across gender and generation, as well as between different families, are included. Contextual data from the larger survey of parents and children are also incorporated in the analysis where useful. In addition, a summary table detailing key characteristics of interviewed families can be seen in Appendix A.

As outlined in the following pages, the families in the sample represent a diverse spread in terms of family origins, time in the UK, household composition, and economic, health and social status. This range is consistent with the wider existing demographic information on South Asians in the UK as reported in the 2001 Census.

2.1 Family origins and settlement

The parents' family origins reflected the diverse nature of South Asian immigration to the UK. The majority of parents were of Pakistani origin, although some came from India, while a few more had come to the UK as twice-migrants, their families having previously immigrated from South Asia to another country (for example, Kenya, Saudi Arabia, Mauritius) before settling in the UK. Their geographical origins were similarly varied; around half reported urban roots in Lahore or Jhelum (both in the Punjab area of Pakistan), or Indian cities such as Bombay, while the other half were of rural origin. These migration patterns are common to many contemporary South Asian families living in the UK (Shaw 2000).

Several parents had settled directly in Northeast London and had stayed there ever since; others had initially lived in areas such as Lancashire and had then moved to London, usually along with other members of their family – many of the latter group had relatives in other parts of England, as well as 'back home', adding an extra element of distance to family get-togethers.

The generational status of migrant families – that is, whether the parents were first-, second- or even third-generation settlers – is acknowledged to be an important factor in the family's experience of life in the UK (Dosanjh and Ghuman 1996; Husain and O'Brien 1999; Bose 2000). In this sample, too, the parents' generational status was influential. The interviewed families were divisible into two broad groups: *first-generation*, with both parents born outside the UK and having immigrated as adults (n=8), and *mixed-generation*, where one parent had immigrated as an adult, and one had been born or grown up in the UK (n=10). In the *first-generation* group of families, both parents had arrived in the UK relatively recently (for example, in the 1980s), and usually together as husband and wife. In these families the main household language was Urdu, Punjabi or Gujarati rather than English. Household décor and the clothes of family members were more often in a traditional South Asian style.

The second, *mixed-generation* group of families each contained one first- and one second- generation parent. Following the definition used by other researchers (e.g. Ballard 1994), second-generation was held to include those parents who arrived in the UK at a young age and were educated there, as well as those who were actually born in the UK. In either case, these second-generation parents had been living in Britain for much longer than the parents in the first group of families. They spoke fluent English, and were relatively familiar with the education system. Their own parents had usually come to the UK in the first wave of economic migration in the late 1950's and 1960's (see Henley 1986; Ansari 2002). Some described what has been referred to as 'chain migration', wherein a male family member came over to the UK for work and then began to 'call over' other male relatives to live with him. After a few years he would go back home and marry, then bring over his wife and any children to live with him in Britain. Family migration was therefore a drawn-out, transgenerational process:

> ... my dad came first and then he... he got one of my other uncle, younger than him, he called him over and my grandfather, my

mum's dad, he came. He, he and my dad I think came together.... Then my dad went back home to get married then he got married to my mum, then he brought her over in, I think '64, '63... (Khalid's mother)

Without exception, the second-generation parents had all themselves 'brought over' a spouse from Pakistan or India, thus creating the mixed-generation partnership. This appeared to be common practice, and was explained to me as a desirable way of strengthening family transnational links (see Shaw 2000, and section 2.3 below). In the group of families in this study, the second-generation parent was, with one exception, always the mother, but there was no indication that this was a wider pattern.[5] In any case, the consequent differences in parental familiarity with the UK (and with the English language) often meant that parents brought differing expectations and values to the partnership, which appeared to influence the dynamics of authority and control within the family, an issue developed in Chapter 6.

There were no families in the sample headed by two second-generation parents, a situation Smalley (2002) also encountered. Given the apparently widespread approval for 'bringing over' a spouse from the country of origin (and see Pankaj 2000 who comments on a lack of data but estimates that this trend is 'substantial'), it may be that such partnerships are at present comparatively rare. However, the number will presumably increase as more second-generation South Asian Muslims reach adulthood. It is likely that second-generation families will differ in their expectations and negotiation of family practices. One comparative study suggested that second-generation Punjabi fathers were more closely involved with their children (Dosanjh and Ghuman 1998).

The children in these families had their own stories of origin distinct from their parents' accounts. In the mixed-generation group, and even in the first-generation group with a couple of exceptions, their parents had all been in the UK for more than ten years – meaning that most of the children in the sample were born in the UK, as second- or third-generation British South Asians. This pattern reflects a relatively settled South Asian population, and indeed this was also apparent in the wider survey, where 86 per cent of the children surveyed had been born in Britain. As a result, the children in the interview sample had a unique trajectory within the family: they sometimes described them-selves as 'British Asian' or 'half English, half Pakistani', and for them, the family's migration was a part of the family story that they had heard about from older relatives, but had not experienced directly.

2.2 Parental marital history

All parents in the interview sample, with one exception, had participated in arranged marriages, in which their marriage partner was selected by their parents' families through a process of suggestion and negotiation, with their own parents or other relatives introducing them to a potential partner or, sometimes, a choice of partners. This pattern reflects the fact that arranged marriages continue to be prevalent among the British Muslim population, and especially among first-generation immigrants. In the fourth National Survey of Ethnic Minorities (NSEM), the proportion of Muslims reporting that their parents had decided on their marriage partner ranged from 40 per cent of those who arrived in the UK before the age of 10 to 73 per cent of those who came to Britain aged 25 or over (Berthoud 2000:17). Marital history rarely came up during the children's interviews. For this reason, the majority of this section draws on parental (and particularly maternal) accounts.

Where parents had had arranged marriages, it was usual for the couple to be related in some way; often as first or second cousins. As Chattoo, Atkin and McNeish show, this is very common in South Asian Muslim circles. Cousin marriages are traditionally seen to be desirable in that they keep the marriage within the *biraderi* (the extended kinship network), strengthen existing family ties and enable the bride's parents to be more confident that their child will be treated well by her husband and his family (Chattoo, Atkin et al. 2004). In this study getting married 'outside the family' was seen as a significant departure from the norm. As one interviewee recorded:

> Getting married out of the family's a very big thing. My youngest auntie, she, out of, there were my mum's sister, there were six sisters, all of them married in the family. But the last one, she's married out of the family. That was a very big decision for my grandma. She found it very hard to do that. (Rubina's elder sister)

Even those parents who had not married a relative had usually married a close family friend. Thus these arranged marriages remained, to a large extent, an alliance between two families rather than a contract between two individuals. Parents' own experiences of an arranged marriage informed their aspirations and expectations for their children's matrimonial futures, as will be seen in Chapter 3.

In a small number of families it was clear that the ideal norms did not fully correlate with observed practices. For example, Aisha's mother, who had not had an arranged marriage with her husband, even though both their families would have expected this, revealed that she had gone to Pakistan on holiday with her mother at the age of nineteen, had met a man, fallen in love and married him. Similarly, although Yasmin's parents had themselves had a traditional arranged marriage, Yasmin's eldest sister had met a Bangladeshi man at college and married him, against the wishes of her family. In both cases, the response from their families had been one of initial disappointment but eventual acceptance. To illustrate the point, Yasmin's sister remarked:

> I fell in love, got kicked out, come back, they weren't keen at first because it was a different culture, a different language… but now, they are alright with it now, they have to get used to it don't they. (Yasmin's elder sister)

Marital continuity was another area where observed practice did not always correspond with expressed values. Despite community norms which emphasize the value of bringing up children within marriage and which regard divorce with disapproval (Beishon, Modood et al. 1998; Pankaj 2000), not all the marriages had run smoothly. In four families (all arranged marriages), the parents were separated, to greater or lesser degrees of permanence, with the father living away from the family home. Each of the mothers concerned talked about the difficulties of being a 'single mother' with the accompanying disapproval from their community and the expectation that they would not be able to cope without a father-figure present, a theme that is considered further in Chapter 6.

In some of these families, contact was maintained between the father and his children. For example, in Khalid's family contact was regular and frequent: the children visited their father every weekend and he often picked them up from school or mosque and drove them home. According to the mother, the parents were on relatively good terms. In Munir's family the contact was more intermittent: his father came every few months and stayed for a few days each time. It was noteworthy that in this family the child's account contradicted the mother's; while she had told me they were separated, Munir insisted that 'he hasn't moved out, he has just gone for a long holiday'. In a more extreme case, Mehmood's father (who was second-generation, having been born and brought up in England) had left the UK the previous year and gone to Pakistan to seek work, while his (first-generation) wife refused to go with him, preferring to remain in England with the children. She described their contact as being over the telephone 'every few months'.

The lowest level of paternal contact existed in Amina's family, where the mother disclosed during her interview that the separation had been due to her husband's violence towards her and the children. In this family, the father lived nearby but rarely saw either his wife or children and offered no financial or practical support to the mother. Amina avoided talking about her father at all during the interview, but had written in the comments box on her questionnaire, 'I don't like my dad and he don't like me', indicating strong negative feelings towards him.

Yasmin's father was also absent, having died and left his wife a widow. Although Yasmin's mother also talked about the difficulty of bringing up children alone, there was an absence of the idea that they were being judged or disapproved of by the wider family or community, as in the case of the separated mothers. The implications of the father's absence in this case were clearly quite different.

The experiences of these families need to be seen in the context of an ethno-religious group in which marriage dissolution rates are comparatively low: NSEM data showed that 4 per cent of South Asians aged 16–59 were divorced or separated compared with 9 per cent of White British (Berthoud 2000). Similarly, in 1997–99 around 9 out of 10 Indian, Pakistani and Bangladeshi children age 0–14 were living with both their mother and their father, in contrast with three-quarters of White British children (Scott, Pearce et al. 2001). There are indications that levels of lone parenthood are increasing in South Asian Muslim communities (see e.g. Lindley, Dale et al. 2004). However, where community norms and attitudes are currently opposed to parental separation, the experience of this type of family structure appears to be relatively negative.

2.3   Locality: neighbourhood and household settings

The majority of the families in the interview study lived in terraced houses on quiet streets around the borough, close to the participating schools. The families represented a mixture of owner-occupiers (about two-thirds) and council tenants (about a third). In two cases, in both of which there was no resident father, families were living rent-free in a house owned by a relative.

According to the 2001 Census, the nine wards across which the families' homes were spread all contain higher than average proportions of Muslims (ranging from 15 per cent to 25 per cent) and South Asians (from 14 per cent to 25 per cent).[6] Parents in particular often commented on the large number of other South Asian Muslim families in their neighbourhood (see Appendix A). This high density of other Muslims in the locality was viewed by the large majority as an asset. Parents spoke of close links with their neighbours and neighbourhood:

> My next door neighbours they're like family, every Saturday, Sunday, we always go to this house, go to the kids, we're a close family. (Najma's mother)

Putnam (2000) has suggested that this kind of ethnic proximity in neighbourhoods can serve as a positive resource, since it constitutes 'bonding' social capital and helps to reinforce solidarity and reciprocity within communities.

However, neighbourhoods with high proportions of minority ethnic groups can also have negative aspects (Burton and Jarrett 2000), and it is worth noting that not all parents viewed their neighbourhood settings in a positive light. In particular, Adam's father felt that he and his wife did not get on with their South Asian neighbours, who disapproved because she did not cover her head: they were therefore keen to leave the area. Meanwhile, for Mehmood's mother their home on the 11th floor of a crime-ridden and run-down council block was a source of extreme stress and anxiety. Mehmood echoed these feelings in his own interview. The notion of the local community offering a resource or source of support to families, or conversely acting as a perceived source of threat or stress, will be explored further in Chapter 8.

Nearly all the families in the sample had been living in the same area for at least 10 years – that is, the whole of the reference children's lifetime – and in fact some of them had remained in the same house for the whole period. This residential history further reinforced the distinctive nature of the children's settlement stories when compared with their parents', since it meant that their lived experience was of a stable family setting, as opposed to one involving migration and change. Ahmed explained how, because he had been born in the local hospital and spent his whole life in the UK, he considered himself 'half English'.

> I only speak English, because I was born in [local hospital]. (...) I have been brought up half Asian and half English, haven't I, yeah (...) I am half English and half Pakistani because both my parents come from Pakistan. (Ahmed)

However, although the families had generally remained in the same small area, the composition of the household was more transitory in many of them, with cousins, aunts and uncles and grandparents having featured as long-term guests, and often being mentioned as household members by the children, even when they were not currently resident.

> *So who's in this family?*
> My sister, my little sister, my brother, my father, my mother, but sometimes in the holidays my grandfather and my, well, actually my dad's dad and mother come. (Ali)

2.4 Household composition

Demographic data on family size has consistently shown that South Asian, and particularly Bangladeshi and Pakistani, households in the UK are larger than average (for example, the Spring 2002 Labour Force Survey found that the average Pakistani household contained 4.2 people compared with 2.3 for a white British household). This difference is usually attributed to higher numbers of children per family, as well as to a preference for extended family households with three or more generations living together. Indeed, extended households have often been portrayed as a key characteristic of South Asian families. However, there have been suggestions that South Asian families are gradually moving towards the majority pattern in Britain of smaller nuclear households (Husain and O'Brien 1999; Berthoud 2000)

The findings from the survey reflected these wider statistical trends. When asked which other people they lived with, the children defining themselves as Asian or Asian British were much more likely than children from any other ethnic group to live in larger households: 47 per cent lived with five or more other people, compared with 7 per cent of White British children.

The 18 families in the interview sample were also relatively large. In fact, they were slightly larger than the Census norm for Pakistani households, possibly because of the focus on families with children rather than 'all Asian households'. Households in this study ranged in size from 3–11 people, with the median being 5 people. With the exception of the 3 extended families which will be discussed below, these large household sizes were due to the high number of children in each – including adult offspring still living at home who were present in 7 of the families. The number of resident children per family (including adult children) ranged from 1 family with only 1 child, to 1 with 7 children, with the mean being 3.6 children (see Appendix A).

Contrary to what might have been expected, there were no extended households in which the reference child's grandparents co-resided with the parents and children. However, in 3 families the household had developed in the past few years into a multi-generational, co-residential one, in what might be called a 'newly extended' family. In each of these families this had happened because adult sisters of the reference child had stayed living in the family home and had married, bringing their spouse into the household and then having children. These households contained 9, 10 and 11 people respectively. In 2 of the families the arrangement was said by the adults to be temporary, until the adult children were able to move into a house of their own. In the third, the adult child spent months at a time in Pakistan where her husband lived. However, these arrangements had often lasted for months or years and so had acquired a sense of permanence, particularly from the children's perspective. The children all talked about such arrangements with pleasure, particularly in terms of having nephews and nieces for companionship. Jamila, whose elder sister and her 2 children were shortly due back from Pakistan, said:

> We're going to be happy now, because my niece and nephew are coming and I'll have someone to play with. (Jamila)

These newly extended families, created by sibling marriages rather than the long-term presence of grandparents, consisted of an extended network that was horizontal rather than vertical, representing a variation on the 'beanpole' pattern observed in the White British population (see Grundy, Murphy et al. 1999).

Even among the remaining 15 nuclear households in the interview study, many families displayed strong links with local extended family members. A number of families had relatives living in the same street or within a few minutes' walk and were in contact with them several times a day. This pattern of kin proximity was referred to by both parents and children, but was perhaps more significant for the children, since it often took the form of shared childcare; that is, a grandparent would take the children to school, or get them ready for school, or the children would go to their grandparents or other relatives for a few hours after school each day. Another form of such contact involved play, as with Rubina, who played with her local cousins every day and at the weekends. Thus it was often the children who were experiencing the most prolonged contact with their local extended family.

These temporarily enlarged households and close local links indicate that households were to some extent permeable; that is, while they ostensibly contained nuclear residential households, in reality the family spread out to encompass more people than those living there permanently.

The reference children in the study were all aged either nine (six children), ten (11 children) or 11 years old (two children). These children could be seen as being at the borders of childhood dependency and adolescent autonomy (see Leach, 2003). They occupied a variety of places within the birth order of their respective families. There were 7 oldest children, 7 youngest children, and 3 'middle' children, as well as one only child, allowing an examination of the significance of birth order. It appeared that the children's place within the family had a strong impact on their experience of daily life as well as on their perceived role within the family setting. In particular where reference children were the youngest and had older siblings living at home, this had a striking influence on their experience of being parented – the older siblings were to some extent sharing the parenting role and educating the child in their own values and beliefs (sometimes in direct contradiction to parental values). Meanwhile for those children who were the oldest in their family, responsibilities for housework and sibling care were often salient themes. The impact of birth order will be more extensively covered in Chapter 7.

2.5 Family languages

There was some variation in the languages spoken by the parents in the study, and as might be expected, this was related to their generational status. Second-generation parents all spoke fluent English, usually as well as Urdu, Punjabi or Gujarati, depending on their regional origins. First-generation parents' English levels varied and were in some cases not fluent. I was unable to interview some parents for this reason. Since every family contained either one or two first-generation parents, this meant that in every household there was at least one adult whose first language was not English.

By contrast, since they had nearly all been born in the UK, all the children spoke fluent English. However, they usually spoke Urdu, Punjabi, or Gujarati to their first-generation parent, and to other older family members – though they had varying degrees of fluency in the latter languages.

Thus in most households, at least two languages were spoken as a matter of course. English was spoken at school or work, and between the children, as well as between second-generation parents and their children. The 'language of origin' was often spoken between adults, and between first-generation parents and children. Interestingly, although second-generation parents usually spoke English with their children, there were certain occasions when their language of origin would be used instead – for example, when disciplining them or when telling stories about their culture of origin or religion. This calls to mind a dimension of 'speaking' family practices which will be examined further in Chapter 4.

2.6 Education and work

The demographic picture (ODPM 2003; ONS 2004) indicates that British South Asians, and particularly South Asian Muslims, tend to be less economically active, and to have higher unemployment rates, than the white British majority. Women from these groups also tend to have a lower rate of economic activity than the national female average (Ahmad, Modood et al. 2003; ONS 2004). These broader patterns appear well reflected in the characteristics of the families interviewed. Between them, they embodied a range of socio-economic circumstances. Seven families were without paid employment, at least in England, including 2 families where the father was out of work due to language or health problems, and 5 where the father was absent. This means that around 40 per cent of the reference children were in households with no-one in paid work, just above the national average of 33 per cent for Muslim children (ODPM 2003), and significantly higher than the average for all British children (18 per cent).

In 6 families, the father was the sole earner. There were also 5 dual earner families in which both the mother and father were in work. In 3 of these the mother worked part time while the father worked full time; in the remaining two families both parents worked full time. This represents a lower proportion of dual earner households than the national average of 66 per cent (Collingwood Bakeo and Clarke 2004), but is in accordance with other recent data on South Asian Muslims in the UK, showing that 68 per cent of Muslim women of working age were economically inactive (ONS 2004).

The 11 working fathers in the sample had a variety of jobs. When coded to the ONS standard socio-economic classifications, there were 2 professionals, 1 father in an intermediate occupation, 3 small employers or workers on their own account, 1 father with a lower supervisory and technical occupation, and 4 in semi-routine and routine occupations. Three of the 11 fathers had jobs which involved overnight or shift work, a situation which impacted strongly on daily family routines, as will be discussed in Chapter 8.

Of the 5 mothers who worked, all but one were involved in childcare work such as fostering, crèche work or child minding, reflecting a wider tendency for women to be employed in personal service occupations (Duffield 2002). These jobs were on the whole restricted to the times when their children were at school, or ones which allowed them to care for their own children at the same time. The exception was Aisha's mother, who worked full-time as a personnel manager for a large supermarket chain. Her job sometimes involved long hours and she relied heavily on her extended family (mother and sisters) to help with child care, which has been found to be the most common pattern among South Asian parents in the UK (Scottish Executive 2004).

Of the 12 mothers who were not working, most had not worked since having children: some had previously worked in a range of sectors, including office work, retail and factory work. These mothers often called upon a discourse of 'being there' for their children as a reason for not working, or commented that their husband had used this argument: as will be argued in Chapter 6, this echoes South Asian Muslim cultural and religious norms.

Each family's work status affected their daily lives in ways that are perhaps not surprising. Workless parents tended to talk about the difficulties of providing for their children in the absence of an earned income. For those families where both parents were working, themes of busyness and juggling work-life balance were prominent during interviews with both parents and children. Where the fathers were doing shift work, both parents and children referred to complex arrangements to cope around these hours. Father-absence due to work commitments was a common theme, often raised by children, particularly where fathers were running their own businesses.

According to ONS (2004) British Muslims are more likely to be educationally unqualified (around a third), and least likely to have degrees (around 15 per cent of those born in the UK and 5 per cent born outside the UK), compared with other groups. Parents in this sample had attained slightly higher than average levels of education. Three parents (2 fathers and a mother in 3 different families) were educated to degree level. The remaining parents had nearly all left school at age 16 or 18 years. Predictably, the first-generation parents had usually been educated in Pakistan or India, while the second-generation parents had completed most or all of their education in England.

Children's attitudes towards and expectations for their future education and work trajectories were often markedly different from their parents' experiences. The majority talked about wanting to go to university and pursue a professional career, an ambition that was apparently encouraged by their parents, in that it was often echoed in parental accounts. In some cases children's expectations were informed by the activities and achievements of their older brothers and sisters, many of whom were at university. Indeed, older siblings played an important part in encouraging high educational and career aspirations.

2.7   Health

Demographic sources indicate that as a group British South Asians experience lower than average levels of health. For example, the 2001 Census found that Muslims, especially females, have the worst levels of self-reported general health of all religious groups. Similarly, Muslims run the highest risk of having a long-term illness or disability that restricts their daily activities – 24 per cent of females and 21 per cent of males, or approximately one-and-a-half times higher than average (ONS 2004).

Seven of the 18 families in the sample included somebody with a physical or mental health problem. In 5 of these, it was a child who had the illness or disability, including a child with diabetes, 2 with epilepsy, one with cerebral palsy and one with haemophilia. In a further 2 families, parents suffered from multiple problems including high blood pressure, depression and Chrohn's disease. These relatively high levels of ill-health reflect wider correlations between health inequalities and poverty (Macfarlane, Stafford et al. 2004).

Health problems suffered by individual family members can impact negatively upon other family members, causing disruption to routines, stress and stigmatization (Maughan, Brock et al. 2004). Indeed, children's issues were a recurrent preoccupation in parental interviews, especially when mothers talked about the anxieties and frustrations related to their children's wellbeing:

I am trying to cope but my brain gets tired or I get upset, he is on medicine and everything and you see your child suffering everything and you just stand there and you can't do nothing, it is really hard. (Tariq's mother)

Such family health problems can further compound the difficulties created by economic poverty, representing environments of multiple disadvantage for parenting (Ghate and Hazel 2002).

2.8 Religious involvement

When parents in the school survey were asked to indicate their religion, the most common answers were Muslim (38 per cent), Christian (35 per cent) and 'no religion' (18 per cent). This distribution is very similar to answers given by their children (37 per cent, 37 per cent and 19 per cent respectively). The proportion of Muslims is more than double the borough average, probably reflecting the location of the fieldwork and the younger age structure of the Muslim population.

The interview sample was drawn from those families in which the parent and child had identified themselves as Muslim in their questionnaires. Beyond this commonality, there was a range of levels of religious affiliation and involvement, with some variation between families in the perceived importance of religion. The majority of interviewed parents identified their family affiliations as Sunni Muslim,[7] although one family belonged to the Ahmadiyya movement.[8]

Religion has a number of elements including beliefs, practices and involvement (Hyde 1990). These elements, and their relationship with wider family practices, will be explored in detail in subsequent chapters. However, it is useful here to provide an initial description of families' levels of religious involvement in order to situate the data in context.

Religious service attendance is recognized as one basic indicator of religious involvement. The survey questionnaire collected individual information around religious affiliation and attendance and asked the same questions of parents and children, allowing a comparison of answers as shown in Table 2.1.

It seems that children across all religious groups were as likely, or slightly more likely, than parents to attend religious services once a week or more, but were also more likely than parents to respond that they went never or practically never. Parents were most likely to say they attended only for special occasions. This difference probably reflects some children's regular attendance at religious classes, such as church Sunday school or Islamic classes at a mosque, in the absence of their parents.

Table 2.1   Attendance at religious services

	Muslim children %	Muslim parents %	All children %	All parents %
Once a week or more	63	53	37	28
Less than once a week, but at least once a month	12	10	14	10
Less than once a month, but at least once a year	3	12	7	14
Only for special occasions like weddings or funerals	6	18	16	33
Never or practically never	15	8	27	14
Base	*115*	*51*	*327*	*138*

As could be expected, religious service attendance varied strongly by religious affiliation. In particular, Muslim children attended religious services or meetings much more often than children in other religious groups. More than 6 in 10 attended once a week, compared with 30 per cent of Christian children.[9] Of those with no religion, 31 per cent attended only on special occasions and 67 per cent never, or almost never (respective figures for Christians are 19 per cent and 24 per cent, and for Muslims are 6 per cent and 15 per cent).

These patterns were reflected in the interview sample. All the children attended *madrasah* (Islamic supplementary classes) regularly. These classes are primarily focused on teaching children to read the Qur'an, but also involve wider instruction on Islamic beliefs and practices. Levels of attendance among the reference children ranged from 2 or 3 times a week to twice a day. Attendance at *madrasah* overlapped to some extent with mosque attendance since many *madrasahs* are based in mosques and children attend mosque prayers during their lessons. Among their parents, mosque attendance was more variable; some fathers in particular attended mosque several times a day, while many mothers did not attend at all. There was a similarly large variation in religious observance at home, for example in terms of whether or not family members kept to prayer times. Yet despite these varying levels of expressed involvement, attendance and observance, their Islamic affiliation appeared to be an extremely important overarching factor for all families. These themes will be considered in detail in later chapters.

2.8.1 Religious involvement and cultural affiliation

It appeared that high levels of religious involvement were not always allied to high levels of affiliation with South Asian cultural identity or practices, but that families could occupy various contrasting positions on the dimensions of religiosity and cultural affiliation. While some were high on both dimensions, or medium-low on both, it was also possible to be highly affiliated to Islam but low with regard to South Asian cultural affiliation, and vice versa. Indeed, examples existed of families in all 4 of these broad categories:

Maintaining 'South Asian-ness' and being highly religious was typified by Tariq's and Farid's families, and to some extent Ali's and Jamila's. Both their South Asian cultural origins and their affiliation to Islam were highly salient. Both parents were first-generation immigrants and fathers played a strong role in the family's religious identity, particularly through taking their sons to mosque.

Maintaining South Asian-ness but only being moderately religious characterized Rubina's and Habiba's families, and to some extent, Najma's, Mehmood's, and Munir's. These families maintained many South Asian cultural practices, for example in terms of dress, food and language. However, religion was relatively less salient, prayer within the home was not systematically observed, and children often found it difficult to express how or why religion was important. Fathers' roles were not as strongly felt as in the previous group of families.

Appropriating 'Britishness' but remaining highly religious was illustrated by Yasmin's and to some extent Hasan's and Khalid's families. In some ways these families best fitted the term 'British Muslims'. They made a distinction between affiliation to Islam and South Asian cultural traditions (which they saw as less important). Religious practices such as prayer and eating *halal* meat were prioritized, but were reconciled with selectively appropriated and adapted British cultural practices (wearing jeans, eating non-South Asian food, discussing the acceptability of marrying a person from any national/ethnic background provided that they were Muslim, etc). The religious impetus often appeared to come from a second-generation family member (Yasmin's sisters, Hasan's father, Khalid's mother).

Appropriating Britishness and being low or moderately religious typified Adam's family and to some extent Aisha's and Amir/Ahmed's. These families demonstrated a high level of appropriation of British values and practices and low affiliation to Islam. They wore Western clothes, ate British food, often had both parents in work, sometimes gave their children British names (or names that sounded both South Asian and British), and expressed low affiliation to Islam (but nevertheless sent their children to *madrasah*, observed *Ramadan* and made occasional prayer or mosque visits). These were all mixed-generation families.

Religiosity, or intensity of faith commitment, is made up of several dimensions including adherence to religious practices (especially frequency of prayer), involvement with a religious community as indicated through mosque attendance, and more generally the extent to which religious beliefs are salient in family practices. It is important to note that even families at the less religious end of the spectrum still identified themselves as Muslim, and all observed at least some religious practice. 'Cultural affiliation' reflects the extent to which families maintained and nurtured their 'South Asian-ness', versus the extent to which they appropriated and re-negotiated 'British' traditions[10] and saw themselves as oriented towards being British or at least 'British Asian'.

Both these dimensions are too complex to allow their presentation as unproblematic continua along which whole families could be placed. Family members could differ in their personal positions and families could change their affiliations depending on the context (for example, during the month of *Ramadan* most families increased the intensity of their religious involvement). Indeed, 3 families did not clearly fall into any one position, mainly because of widely diverse levels of religious commitment among different family members: Amina was more religiously affiliated than her mother; Zabar's father was more religiously observant than his mother; similarly Bashira's mother appeared more religious than her father. Nor did families' positions on these dimensions constitute a typology. It would be more appropriate to refer to loose constellations of families sharing similar characteristics.

The second and third groups are particularly interesting because they challenge the assumption that being Muslim is aligned with being traditionally South Asian. In particular, the third group reflects recent emerging notions of high-Islamization (Bauer 1997) and the conceptual separation of religion and culture among some young British Muslims (Jacobson 1997; Husain and O'Brien 2000). The different characteristics evident in the family practices of these groups of families will be explored in subsequent chapters.

2.9 Conclusion

This chapter has set the socio-economic and demographic scene for the research, by summarizing the various 'stories' of the 18 families who formed the interview sample, as well as describing some characteristics of the wider survey sample. When compared to white British families, the sample embodies distinctive features that are common to South Asian Muslim families, including an extended family context (including some newly extended households) and locally embedded community; children's involvement in extra-curricular Islamic education; use of multiple languages; issues of poor mental and physical health; and a relatively high proportion of workless households.

Despite these commonalities, we have also seen that the families were diverse in terms of origin and settlement, marital history and household structure, education, economic status, and religious and cultural affiliations, reflecting the variety of South Asian Muslim populations in the UK. This diversity has allowed an exploration of some important cross-cutting dimensions, notably work and economic status, family structure, gender, and various combinations of religious and cultural affiliation. The following chapters will explore the multiple ways in which these dimensions of difference are reflected in family practices.

3
Family Beliefs and Values

Family practices involve family members' values and expectations surrounding roles, responsibilities, and goals for behaviour and development (Morgan 1996). These sets of cultural meanings, which Daly has referred to as the 'implicit theories that families live by' (2003:771), may draw on a range of sources, including cultural norms and religious belief systems.

This chapter analyses the values and belief systems that were evident when South Asian Muslim parents and children in this study talked about family practices, and examines how these belief systems might inform or shape daily behaviour. The focus is on family members' own perceptions of 'what matters' in family life,[11] and what these factors mean to individual social actors. Moral practices, reasoning and identities have often been thought of as (at least partly) located in family settings and relationships (e.g. Mason 2000). In this sense family practices can be seen as a key site for the working out of morality through everyday moral choices, and notions of morality are, in turn, particularly salient in family belief and value systems. Belief systems are viewed here as akin to moral 'narratives' (Finch and Mason 2000), in that they are not simply external discourses that are 'drawn upon', but rather are constructed through people's individual accounts of what matters to them. They make sense of their own experiences, aspirations and fears in the light of their perceptions of wider norms, assumptions and practices.[12]

Both quantitative and qualitative results are presented in the following pages. The questionnaire study collected data on perceived influences on parenting. The results give some contextual indications of the factors which parents from a range of ethno-religious groups consider to be important in bringing up their children. The chapter goes on to examine the range of value narratives expressed by South Asian Muslim parents and children during the qualitative interviews. Religion is discussed first as a central overarching belief system and one that will form the main focus of the analysis in subsequent chapters. A number of other belief or value narratives which intersect with religion are then examined. These include the negotiation of tradition and change; families' positions as ethnic and religious minorities; associated ideas of difference and sameness; and aspirations for social mobility. This existence of a range of belief systems is important because it highlights the way in which individuals may develop and engage simultaneously with several varying sets of cultural meanings, echoing the 'cultures as toolkit' concept proposed by Swidler (1986).

3.1 Perceived influences on parenting

We begin by considering some contextual quantitative data from the survey study which highlights the sources of influence that parents perceive as important for their parenting practices. In the questionnaire parents were asked to consider a range of factors, and to assess how important each was to 'the way you bring up your children'. A summary of responses for all parents is shown in Table 3.1.

Table 3.1 Perceived influences on bringing up children

	Importance for bringing up children				
	Not at all important	Not very important	Fairly important	Very important	Not applicable (no partner)
Own personal values	–	4%	19%	77%	–
Partner's personal values	–	8%	25%	64%	2%
Child's views	1%	1%	30%	68%	–
Own upbringing	3%	8%	32%	57%	–
Partner's upbringing	6%	14%	37%	40%	2%
School's suggestions	3%	6%	56%	35%	–
Own religious views	15%	22%	22%	42%	–
Religious leader's views	24%	28%	22%	26%	–
Other parents' views	15%	36%	40%	10%	–
What the experts say	13%	30%	44%	13%	–
TV/ Newspapers	22%	37%	31%	10%	–

Base: all parents (N=149)

The factors perceived as having the strongest influence on parenting were one's own, and one's partner's, personal values. These were rated as very important by the majority of parents, with less than 1 in 10 parents deeming them not very important, and no parents suggesting that they were not at all important. Similarly, the views of their children were seen as central; virtually all parents found them either very important (68 per cent) or fairly important (30 per cent). The parents' own family background was also viewed as a significant factor in parenting: the ways in which they and their partners were brought up were seen as fairly or very important by the majority of parents. Although the concepts captured by these measures are multi-stranded, they all reflect ideas to be discussed later in this chapter, concerning the maintenance, transmission and renegotiation of cultural traditions.

In terms of 'outside' influences, suggestions made by the child's school were rated as fairly or very important by most parents (possibly reflecting the imagined audience, since the questionnaires came via their child's school). Other parents' views, 'what you see on TV/read in the papers' and 'what the experts say' were held to matter much less. This relatively low attention (or at least perceived attention) to external factors suggests that parents were placing an emphasis on the personal and private aspects of moral negotiation, reasoning and choice, while acknowledging less of a role for the 'formal' discourses provided by the media and expert institutions (see Mason 2000).

3.2 Religious beliefs

As might be expected, the perceived importance of religious factors for bringing up children was strongly related to parents' religious affiliation. As shown in Chart 3.1, Muslim parents in completing the survey were significantly more likely than those parents identifying themselves as Christian to describe religious influences as very or fairly important[13]. Their views on the importance of other factors were not significantly different.

These data suggest that personal religious affiliation for Muslim parents is a relatively salient theme in their parenting practices. Indeed, as the more detailed breakdown in Chart 3.2 shows, the vast majority of the Muslim parents in the questionnaire study saw their own religious views as important in bringing up their children – indeed more than eight in ten (84 per cent) saw them as 'very important', while a further 11 per cent felt they were 'fairly important'. Only 1 in 20 (5 per cent) said their religious views were not very important – and

Chart 3.1   Influences on parenting, by religion

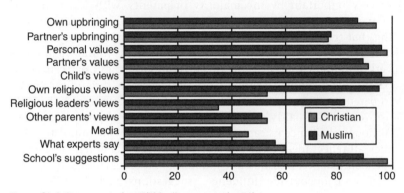

% citing each factor as either 'very' or 'fairly' important

Base: Christian parents (n=52) Muslim parents (n=56)

Chart 3.2   Perceived influence of religious views, by religion

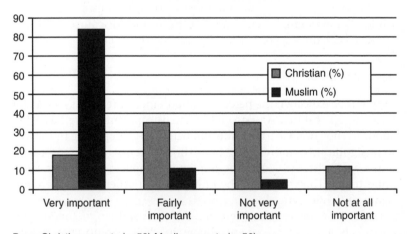

Importance of own religious views to the way you bring up your children

Base: Christian parents (n=52) Muslim parents (n=56)

none described their religious views as having no importance at all in bringing up their children. In contrast, Christian parents were more likely to find them fairly important (35 per cent), or not very important (35 per cent).

Chart 3.3   Perceived influence of religious leaders, by religion

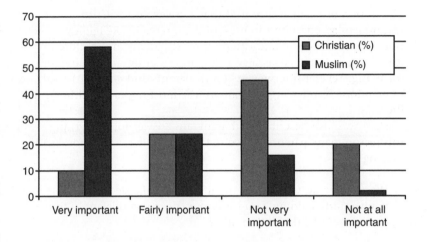

Importance of religious leaders' views to the way you bring up your children

Base: Christian parents (n=52) Muslim parents (n=56)

Similarly, as Chart 3.3 shows, the views of 'religious leaders' are seen as important by more Muslim parents: 58 per cent found them 'very important' (compared with 10 per cent of Christians) and a further 24 per cent 'fairly important'. Christian parents were most likely to find them 'not very important'.

These figures suggest that the role of religious values in parenting may be perceived as especially strong for Muslim families. They also indicate a relatively high degree among Muslim parents of trust and importance placed on membership of the religious community. Thus religious factors, in terms of both personal beliefs and values and social norms and expectations, seem particularly central to a Muslim concept of parenting. This pattern corresponds with recent North American work by Dollahite and colleagues, which has shown, for example, that highly religious families of all denominations consider fulfilling their 'sacred purpose' to be a central task in family life (Dollahite and Marks 2004).

The qualitative interviews allowed an exploration of how religion was important to South Asian Muslim parents and children. The interview data strongly reinforced the survey data in suggesting that religion was perceived to play a central part in family practices. Indeed, religion proved pervasive, even for those families who were at the lower end of the scale on religious affiliation and observance as described in the previous chapter.

3.2.1   Religion as central or pervasive

The notion of Islam as a central theme, relevant to all aspects of life, was present as a narrative in most of the interviews. Religion was mentioned spontaneously and often by most parents and children, typically being described as a 'way of life' offering a total framework for living. Several interviewees (both parents and children) used the same phrase in referring to Islam as 'the most important thing in my life'.

Islam was also described as having an 'answer for everything'. For this reason many parents looked to their religion as a basis for decision making.

> We follow the Qur'an in our life... to make decisions (...) once you've started, doing, you want to go deeper and Islam is, to me, is best way of life. (Khalid's mother)

In relation to parenting, Islam was perceived as a central source of nurturance and moral education. As one mother said:

> I think it is giving a child a really good start in life, a key thing they can base their life on. (Aisha's mother)

In some families Islam was imbued with a spiritual dimension, in that it was couched in terms of ensuring rewards in the afterlife. As Hasan's father put it, prioritising Islam was a means to 'invest for the life hereafter'. This orientation was linked with notions of generational transmission, since parents were not simply responsible for their own religious conduct but also for that of their children. The belief was also gendered, with mothers carrying particular responsibility – several interviewees referred to the expression: 'your mother holds the key of heaven', or alternatively that 'heaven is under your mother's foot', an issue explored further in Chapter 6.

Children's accounts, if sometimes less well articulated, also contained versions of the 'centrality of Islam' narrative. Although children invariably claimed that their religion was important, many found it difficult to say why. This quote is typical:

> I don't know. I, it's important to me like, cos look, it's, it's cos like, I can't really explain but it's important to me cos I mean like, I like,

I like my religion and I find it fun. I like, I like, I like doing stuff with my religion. And that's it. (Tariq)

Where children were able to say more about the centrality of religion, their comments often focused on the fact that Islam was important to their parents and must therefore be to them. In general these accounts indicated the pervasiveness of religion, in such a way that it was not considered or debated: it 'just was'.

Under this broad theme there was some variation both within and across families. An examination of the multiple perspectives within each family revealed that religion was sometimes more important to one parent than to the other. Hasan's father, who was himself highly religious, said of his wife:

She doesn't tend to enforce it so much. (Hasan's father)

Along similar lines, Adam (whose family was one of the least religious overall), commented that 'my mum takes it more seriously than my dad'. It was his mother who decided when her son and husband should be going to mosque. Indeed, in my interview with her, Adam's mother told me that religion was important to them, although they were not very strict, and said that they followed religious practices such as sending their children to Islamic classes and eating *halal* food. His father had given me a very different impression – at the outset of his interview he remarked that 'we're not really religious, hope that's ok'. He did not mention the children's Islamic classes at all. This difference between the parents has important implications for interpreting those studies of religion-family linkages that have used only one measure of parental religiousness (for a discussion see Mahoney, Pargament et al. 2001) – it would seem important to disaggregate the religious beliefs of individual family members in order to gain a fuller picture of such issues as the nature of religious nurturance experienced by children. While the relevance of Islamic belief to all aspects of life was a theme across families, the extent to which it was regarded as central could vary between individuals within the same family.

3.2.2 'We are not strict'

Alongside the basic 'centrality' narrative there existed an alternative, that of being 'not strict'. Often this counter narrative was present in the same interview accounts as the centrality narrative.

A few families still, they are very strict but as I said, we are not. So we try to be in the middle, (...) my sister in law, forget the TV, they don't have the TV, but their children don't even wear trousers and top (...) I don't like them having that all the time... (Hasan's mother)

Although she had also emphasized the fact that they followed Islam and prayed five times a day, this mother defined her family's position by marking the contrasts with stricter families (specifically her husband's sister's family), in order to demonstrate that they were not extreme in their own behaviour. Some children also showed an understanding of different levels of religious 'strictness'. Amina, for instance, made a distinction between being 'religious religious religious' and just 'religious', explaining that her family was the latter and so less strict in their observance of religious practices.

In general, it appeared that being 'not strict' was linked to notions of moderation and 'fitting in' with the wider society. As described in the previous section, Adam's father was at pains to emphasize that they were 'not really religious' and his wife also said several times during her interview that they were 'not strict'.[14] This account appeared to relate to the fact that they did not get along with other, more religiously observant Muslims in the neighbourhood who disapproved because the mother did not adopt traditional dress. He was also keen throughout to distance the family from 'fundamentalists and extremists' whom he considered to be getting Muslims in general a bad press (in this sense, his emphasis on not being very religious could be seen as a means of impression management, and may have been partly for my benefit in order that I would not associate him with the 'extremists').

Meanwhile, the narrative of being 'not strict' was also used to describe differences in values between different family members.

I am religious but I'm not religious to an extreme, like if I go out I won't put a scarf on my head, or on my neck, but my husband's always on my head about it, but I pray but I don't pray five times (...) I'm not strict religious you know or anything like that, but my husband is a bit strict religious. (Zabar's mother)

It was typically mothers who made this sort of comment about their husbands, often also describing a process of 'softening over the years' through which they had negotiated a middle level.[15]

Although, as might be expected, the theme of not being strict was most clearly represented in families low on religiosity, it was not confined to this group. Nor did expressions of non-strictness equate to a lack of religious affiliation or practice. One mother, from a family relatively low on religious observance, explained that even people like her would find it important to send their children to Islamic classes:

> You get some parents who are really Westernized, even they send their children, and like myself who do not know anything about Islam send their children to classes. Even people who the community say, you know, 'she's not a Muslim, she hasn't done what other Muslims do', even girls like that, when they've had their children they've always sent them to Arabic classes. (Aisha's mother)

Thus it seemed that where people created a narrative of being 'not strict', they were engaged in defining themselves as moderate or reasonable in contrast to others, rather than in disavowing the relevance of Islamic beliefs or practices.

3.2.3   Religion as a basis for moral reasoning

Given the centrality of Islam as a value system, it was common for family members to draw strongly on their religious beliefs while constructing and working through their moral choices. This was most apparent in the way that Islam was taken as a basis for judging good and bad behaviour, a process which occurred both implicitly and explicitly. Religious teachings informed family members' ideas of what was acceptable, and thus guided such parenting practices as limit-setting, rewards and discipline. Interviewees often explained how the moral benefits of following Islam gave you 'boundaries' and made you a 'good person'.

> If they learn this [Islam] now they won't do any silly things (...) like breaking into somebody's house, hurting people or stealing from old people. (Tariq's mother)

Parents often explicitly invoked religious guidelines as a means of instilling and nurturing desired behaviour in their children:

> ...as long as I have knowledge of my religion there are all good things, like not bad things to teach kids. Basic things like backbiting is not allowed in our religion and lying is not allowed and all, I tell

them two ways like in society it's not acceptable and as a religion is not acceptable, so that's all of these things. I will tell them that they've learned the religion as well, 'it is our religion but also that it is not good', that's how they learn, that it's in our religion as well. (Bashira's mother)

Being able to refer to the moral authority of religion was seen by some parents as a more effective means of teaching the distinction between right and wrong:

... they know that we are Muslim and it is part of our religion not to do things and it has a lot more impact then and it is not just mum telling them. It actually tells them why they shouldn't be doing things and what the consequences are if you do it and what can happen, so it teaches them what not to do and why not to do it. (Aisha's mother)

Aisha corroborated this when I asked what happened if she did something wrong:

...if we are being naughty they say that in the Qur'an it says you shouldn't do this and you should do this and you should listen to what they teach you... (Aisha)

For the most part children had internalized this notion of religion as providing a moral code. When asked what kinds of things a Muslim should or should not do their answers, referring to good and bad behaviour, were remarkably consistent. I was told that a Muslim should not tell lies, cheat, steal, argue, fight, swear, bully or be rude or unkind. By contrast, 'good' Muslims were obedient, respected their elders, helped, shared and were kind to people. Several children understood this as being linked with notions of reward and punishment after death:

If you do the wrong thing you go straight to hell. You don't go straight to hell but they count up on Judgement Day how much you have done and if you have done more good things you go to heaven and more bad things you go to hell. (Amir)

Thus when parents encouraged acceptable behaviour in their children, social nurturance also counted as spiritual nurturance.[16]

3.2.4 Religion in family practices

As we have seen, their religious beliefs and values mattered to all the families in this study, the centrality of religion to every aspect of life being a popular narrative – albeit one often juxtaposed with expressions of moderation and 'fitting in'. We have also noted that family members routinely drew upon religious beliefs and values in working out their moral reasoning, disciplining and judging the 'best way to behave'. Subsequent chapters will explore the range of ways in which religious beliefs and practices were tied up with the 'doing' of family.

3.3 Cultural tradition and change

Religion was only one of several important themes that were evident when parents and children talked about family practices. Issues concerning the negotiation of tradition and change, in respect of gender, relationships or family role expectations, and such practices as dress, food and leisure, also emerged repeatedly throughout interviews. These issues were related to the patterns of family cultural affiliation described in Chapter 2, where families were seen to take varying positions, from maintaining traditional 'South Asian-ness' on the one hand to adopting and developing aspects of 'British-ness' on the other. Family members' self-images regarding where they 'belonged' culturally were closely linked with their family practices. As explained in Chapter 2, orientations towards cultural affiliation were not straightforwardly related to religious affiliation, but the two overlapped in a variety of ways.

The following section will explore the narratives used by people to describe their strategies for maintenance and/or transformation of cultural tradition, and record how such values were negotiated within families. It is worth noting that while some authors (e.g. Chattoo, Atkin et al. 2004) have expressly linked tradition with structure, and change with agency, this interpretation would probably not make sense to the people interviewed for this study. Rather, the maintenance of South Asian traditions, and the adoption of new cultural practices in response to the British context, were both perceived and experienced as active processes involving choice, negotiation and constraint, and were not mutually exclusive activities. A number of possible strategies were employed by families, reflecting the values they placed on various cultural practices.

3.3.1 Negotiating tradition and change within families

A substantial number of interviewees described the process of dealing with different orientations among family members towards cultural maintenance or transformation. The collection of multiple accounts within families lends itself well to an exploration of these dynamics. Differences existed between parents, but also between generations, illustrating a theme that has been written about extensively (see for example Bhatti 1999; Bose 2000; Husain and O'Brien 2000; Chattoo, Atkin et al. 2004).

Several family members referred to the well-established expectation of conflict between first-generation immigrants and their second-generation children (see for example earlier work by Ballard 1979; Ahmed 1981; Anwar 1981; Anwar 1986; Anwar 1998). As one father explained, it is difficult for first-generation parents who immigrate to the UK to protect their children from assimilating what they see as threatening aspects of British culture.

> I think village types somehow, they haven't been out you know. (...) coming to this country, they see all these things because are getting, it's scary you know, "How can our girl be involved like this? And how can she walk with the male like that?" And things like that. So in a way they started imposing rules on her, putting things on her you know. "You're not going out now. You're not doing this, you think, your father's coming with you wherever you go." And of course a young child you know, she wants to be alone by herself, she wants to go in with her friends you know. So coming to this country they find very difficult. (Farid's father)

Such concerns seemed important to some parents, and particularly to first-generation parents. As another first-generation father commented:

> We worry about our children. When we came in this country our ideas were different, but they were born here, and I don't know, when they grow up, how they'll think and how their ideas will be. (Jamila's father)

A strategy which some parents adopted in response to this (especially where they themselves had differing attitudes) was to attempt to compromise – to be 'in the middle' – as described in the following section. Other parents attempted to shelter their children from outside influences (in particular, from 'bad habits' such as smoking cigarettes or drinking alcohol), but recognized that this might prove very difficult. For some there was a resigned acknowledgement that their children would probably be different from them.

> We're Asian. But our kids are not like that. They're whatever you are, same mind, same everything, because they are spending lots of time outside. (…) It's not good for our kids with the pressure now, it's no good. Because then they will be two-minded. I don't want them to be two-minded. Whatever they have to do they have to do school too you know. (Mehmood's mother)

From the children's perspective, the experience of being in a different world from their parents, as 'skilled cultural navigators' (Ballard 1994:31) between different spheres, was a theme that emerged fairly often. For these pre-adolescent 9–11 year olds, however, conflict with their parents was not yet salient – rather, its existence was remarked upon by their parents in reference to older children, or referred to in a hypothetical way, but not raised by the children themselves.

Differences between the desire for maintenance and the transformation of tradition also existed between spouses, particularly in mixed-generation families, where one parent had been brought up in England and the other had immigrated as an adult, bringing different cultural assumptions and expectations. In these cases their parenting beliefs could be quite different. For example, in Amir and Ahmed's family, the second-generation mother frequently found herself acting as a mediator between her first-generation husband and their children. When one son made female friends at school, she had to explain to her husband that this was 'all innocent' in order to assuage his worries. Like other parents in this situation, she referred to the 'cultural differences' between herself and her husband frequently during the interview.

Such differences were dealt with in a variety of ways. A number of mothers described a process of 'working on' their husbands over the years and often added that their partner had relaxed his ideas or was 'getting better now'.[17] Others, like Rubina's eldest sister, had been more forthright in expecting their husbands to change:

> You're supposed to change. Like they're, in, like back home they'll say that you know, women aren't supposed to work, they're supposed to be like housewives. My husband's got that type of thing as well 'cos he's from there. So, but I explained it to him, I go to him, "If you're living here, you have to change. You can't fit in to not

changing. So you have to change to fit in with everyone else".
(Rubina's elder sister)

He had subsequently agreed that she should go out to work in order for
them to afford to buy a house.

In some cases, however, these differences were irreconcilable:
in Khalid's family their daughter's wish to go on to further education caused his parents to separate. His mother agreed that her
daughter should go to a local university but the father left the
household.

My older daughter, she want to do, educate, that's what made me
and my husband, you know, split up. He didn't want her to, he
wanted her to get married, you know, tradition, you know, old tradition. But I didn't, I couldn't stand by him. (Khalid's mother)

As might be expected, in mixed-generation families it was usually the
first-generation parent who was keener on maintaining 'traditional'
practices, though this was not universally the case. In Hasan's family,
it was the first-generation mother who wanted to listen to the radio
and take the children to the cinema, while the second-generation
father was opposed to such activities. In this case the situation
was probably partly due to the father's strong religious affiliation.
The strategy for resolving this disagreement, according to Hasan's
mother, was one of compromise in terms of 'give and take both the
sides'.

3.3.2   Strategies for dealing with tradition and change

These differing perspectives within families concerning the value of
maintaining South Asian traditions, as against the perceived need to
change and 'fit in' with modern British society, resulted in a variety of
strategies that were worked out through relational practices. Often
more than one strategy was adopted by the same family (and indeed
the same individuals), depending on the context, recalling previous
discussions of situational ethnic identities (e.g. Madge 2001). However, in some families, their position with regard to tradition and
change was an important narrative that they created, and drew
upon, in conjunction with their religious beliefs, to inform their daily
moral and practical choices. It is noteworthy that, again, these strategies were a preoccupation of parents, but were seldom mentioned by
children.

Keeping South Asian traditions

One narrative emphasized the continuing importance to South Asians of their cultural roots. The significance of tradition was captured by Farid's father when he urged his children to 'carry on with the simple life'. The value of 'keeping tradition' was reflected in the perceived desirability of generational continuity, in that it involved the passing on of ascribed cultural norms for behaviour.

> ...if you bring them up nicely then they are going to be nice and they are going to be nice to their children and how they bring up children, from my parents, and respect your elders and talk to them. Even now if I am not in the house, if you see my daughter she's going to respect and welcome you and ask you for tea. (Tariq's mother)

'Respect' (*izzat*) was a key term that arose again and again in this context (and has also been discussed extensively elsewhere; see for example Shaw, 2000; Husain and O'Brien, 2001). The idea of showing respect for one's elders, for one's family hierarchy, and for one's peers, appeared to symbolize much that was desirable about 'traditional' South Asian Muslim practices. It encompassed the giving of hospitality, the obedience of children, and more widely the importance of the family's reputation or 'honour' in the community, which was affected by the behaviour of family members (and especially females). This was an aspect of tradition that was mentioned frequently by both parents and children, and widely seen as important to maintain:

> *You said that there were things that you had been taught that you would like to teach them, what are they?*
> Things like, we have got 2 girls, my husband, things like respect. My parents were really quite hot on respect, you know, you had to ensure that you were a respectable girl, things my mum and dad really believed in were, when you are out people don't know you for who you are, they know you for your parents, so it's how you mix in with the community; if you met an auntie you'd go out of your way to greet her properly, if someone spoke to you you'd speak back with respect, so things like that my parents taught us and I will teach my daughters. (Aisha's mother)

The continuing importance of respect was demonstrated by such practices as the use of traditional kinship terms for elders (for example, *papo* for one's father's older sister and *jutti* for one's father's younger sister). Amir and Ahmed's mother confessed that this was an aspect in which she felt she had failed: she was embarrassed when her children sometimes called their aunts and uncles by their names, since this showed inadequate respect for their age and place in the hierarchy. Other aspects of South Asian tradition described as important to maintain included values impinging on marriage and relationships, such as not having romantic or sexual relationships before marriage, and the desirability of marrying someone from one's own ethnic and religious group.

> ... I'm trying to say to her that in Islam we don't have boyfriends, we have a husband. You will stick to the husband's (...). But it's very hard, I say to my husband, (...).because she has a lot of friends who are not Asians. (Najma's mother)

It is probably significant that the aspects of South Asian culture that were emphasized in these 'keeping tradition' narratives were closely intertwined with religious beliefs and values. Notions of respecting elders, and of the necessity of marrying someone from one's own religion, also came up in discussions, especially with children, of what it meant to be Muslim. Other traditions, including aspects of cuisine, diet, language and leisure, were adopted or rejected less predictably (see Chapter 4), but were related to discourses of 'knowing one's roots' even among families of low affiliation to South Asian cultural practices. Even Adam's father felt that 'they should have a background of their background'.

'We try to do both'

Another narrative of tradition and change involved the establishment of a middle ground. This often arose in response to conflict within families, whose resolution called for different cultural expectations to be worked out through compromise. People referred to negotiation in their shared concern to accommodate elements of both tradition and change. Hasan's mother described how they compromised on the rules which were intended to govern the viewing of television programmes:

> Like watching telly, I tell them, they don't watch everything, if it is not suitable for children or something they won't watch it, if I tell them no. But like cartoon and things, ok, they are allowed and they

are allowed what programme I am watching sometimes and it's alright for them to watch. (...) I try to explain to them what I like and what I don't. So that's the way I, I go. (Hasan's mother)

Similarly, the mother who had described her children as 'two-minded' because they had experienced both inside and outside influences commented on how she dealt with the consequences:

You have to explain them everything. (...) They ask lots of questions, 'why we can't do this' and 'why we are not allowed to this'. (Mehmood's mother)

Another strategy for compromise involved establishing different rules for inside and outside the home. A graphic example was provided by Amir and Ahmed's mother who told me that in traditional South Asian Muslim culture one would always sit down on the toilet to avoid mess, and use water rather than toilet paper. She had taught her sons to do this, but had also taught them to do it in a different way (standing up to urinate) when they were at school.

'You have to change to fit in'

An alternative outlook emphasized the inevitability of cultural transformation, and valued the adoption of and adaptation to British cultural practices. This readiness to change was often acknowledged by parents in the context of adjustments in family roles. One first-generation father reflected on how children were different in Britain:

Coming to this country is very different to what our, when we were in our country religions-wise. Here children are more independent and things like that. Things we have done with our parents were quite different things. But the children here are more sort of outgoing and things like that. And sometimes gets very hard to get, control them you know. But so far I've been lucky with my kids. (Farid's father)

Meanwhile, his wife commented that the father's role in the family had changed. He was still a role model but not so dominant: his decision was no longer 'final', and family responsibilities were more communal.

Second-generation adults also noted discontinuities with their own childhoods. For example, Rubina's adult sister observed that the role of women had changed since she was a child:

> It always changes. I've seen it quite, like since I've been quite small, I've seen it change quite a lot with our family. When we were younger, it was a lot of like, what was it, it was, girls were more like you know, housewife kind of thing. Since I've been growing up, it's more like, you know, they're starting to spread out. It has changed. (Rubina's elder sister)

She felt this change was because people had seen 'how other people do it' and adapted their ways in response.

In some cases – especially in those families least affiliated with 'traditional' South Asian culture – cultural change was viewed in a particularly positive light, and accompanied by a desire for integration. As one mother said,

> I think that in terms of 20 years ago, we've different challenges in that our parents were fairly new to the country and the upbringing was completely different and the challenge for them was that they were bringing their children up in a Western society, (...) if anything's going on at school I always make sure they get involved in it, they have friends who are not just Asian friends and I encourage the girls to mix in and have different friends appreciate and understand people's backgrounds, so I think I've been really quite different to when we were growing up. (Aisha's mother)

This mother was keen to have a personal relationship with her daughters 'like friends as opposed to mother and daughter', in contrast to 'traditional' hierarchies.

It is important to note that an acceptance of cultural change as being inevitable did not necessarily equate with lesser religiosity. The point was clearly illustrated by Yasmin's family, where the adult siblings (who ran the household to a large extent) had a relatively strong religious affiliation but made a clear distinction between Pakistani culture, which they did not find it important to maintain, and Islamic practices, which they still perceived as central.

> The culture side is so different to Islam, the culture side is (whispers) you have to get married back home, Pakistani, and the Islamic side

is that you don't have to get married to someone who is Pakistani, it is better when you go outside the family. It is really different, very different, even like the culture side of it so different, the culture side of it is we don't wear this, we wear, you know those headscarf things old ladies wear, and the *shalwar kameez*, the Islamic version is that you cover your head and you have no hair to show and you cover, you wear the *jilbab* thing, the cloak thing. That. Even *shalwar kameez* are ok because you're still covering your body. But the scarf thing, the *dupatta* thing, that's not exactly covering your hair. So it's really different, everything is so different we didn't really accept the culture but we accepted our religion. (Yasmin's elder sister)

This provides a classic example of high-Islamization as identified by other authors (Halstead 1994; Bauer 1997; Jacobson 1997).

3.4 'Us' and 'them': being the same and being different

Difference and sameness were another pair of contrasting themes that emerged in the interviews. In some ways this narrative could be seen as related to the previous issue, in that it involved a debate centred on encapsulation versus assimilation (see Ballard 1994). It was typified by discussions of 'us' and 'them', and was fundamentally concerned with beliefs about distinctions or boundaries (recalling the work of Bourdieu 1984), reflecting the situations of the families in question as belonging to a minority faith and ethnic community. It seemed that there were two alternative narratives in play, one emphasizing their distinctiveness and the other promoting their normality.

'We are different'

The view of 'us' as distinctive was summed up in one father's description of how being Muslim put one inside a 'boundary'.

The boundary is still there, Islam is still there for you. Doesn't mean that you have come to this modern country, you give away your religion, you give away your veil and everything you know. It doesn't mean that. Still in the religion. (...) as long as you are in Islam, you know you got the symbol of Islam, and your mark as a Muslim, you should keep in your boundaries you know. (Farid's father)

This idea that as a Muslim from a different country you should recognize your difference and 'stick to your own' also emerged in other parental interviews. It was common for parents, in particular, to talk to me about 'our food' and 'your food', 'our clothes' and 'your clothes', conveying a strong feeling of distinction and simultaneously situating me as an outsider. Such narratives appeared to relate strongly to choices about cultural consumption (see Chapter 4).

Peoples' conceptions of where to place these boundaries did not always correspond with one another. As one first-generation mother told me,

> We are totally different. Our mind is totally different.
> *How is it different?*
> You know, we have more patience, we have more education, manners and this and that. (Mehmood's mother)

Interestingly, the distinction she was making here was not between 'Asians' and 'non-Asians', but as she saw it, between 'true Asians' like herself, and Asians who had grown up in Britain and had lost their 'Asian-ness'. As she went on to say, 'I don't like Asian people here'. Thus the boundaries people drew did not always correspond with the 'official' distinctions made by, for example, the Census. Peoples' sense of 'who belonged' was more complex than might first appear.

We are 'just like anyone else'

Alongside the indications of boundary-drawing discussed above, there existed an alternative discourse. It was often manifested in such throwaway phrases as 'they are just normal kids' (Adam's father), 'just like most households' (Hasan's father), 'we're just sort of, I don't know, a normal family' (Farid's father). However, it was also made explicit from time to time, through the expression of religious claims such as 'all religions are the same', 'God made everyone', 'we're all the same in God's eyes', which often arose in the course of emphasizing to children the importance of peace in a world in which 'politicians use the people, use religion' (Mehmood's mother).

> You know all religion is from God. So all this talk about different religion, I tell my sons and my children also that whatever religion, you have to respect them. (Farid's father)

This narrative was also drawn upon in talking about family roles and responsibilities, when parents used it to present their own values as 'normal'.

> I think it is the same in your culture as well isn't it? Like the parents' duties, you have to teach them good things... (...) Most of all mothers are doing the same thing and all fathers doing the same thing, whether Christian, black, white, Indian... I think most religions teach the same thing, not to lie and cheat. (Tariq's mother)

One of the most impassioned uses of this narrative came from a father who drew parallels between his own family and the British royal family, explaining that it was normal to love your daughters more than your sons – that even Queen Elizabeth feels this way, 'she's more near to Anne than her sons' – since 'that's the human nature'.

> Like, all over the world. Feeling, if you are British, if you are English, if you are American, if you are Indian, if you are Persian, if you are Arab, feeling is the same. Blood is the same. Colour is the same. My blood is red. Your blood is red. But face is different, colour is different. Feeling is same. Human nature is the same. (Jamila's father)

This was one of the few narratives discussed in the present chapter to which children also referred. A number of them, when talking about what it was like to live in their family, emphasized that it would be the same in any other family setting:

> ... it would be the same as in another religion, because if you are brought up in a religion you have your own duties to do and some are different some are same. (Munir)

School was described in similar terms – indeed it seems likely that these values, of treating everybody alike and respecting others' beliefs, had also been encouraged at school.

> *What's it like at school if you are Muslim?*
> Nothing because, I forgot my best friend's, well she hasn't got a religion, but like she will respect your religion but will treat you like any other person (...) and most of the people in my class are

Muslim, most of them are Christians, but one of them is Hindu, but they all treat you like you would treat another person, and no one in my class really wears, all the Muslims wear English stuff. (Aisha)

These beliefs concerning sameness and difference permeated family practices, but were most closely related to the connections families made and resources on which they drew outside the immediate household, which will be further discussed in Chapter 8.

3.5 Family aspirations

Aspirations comprised a final strand in the set of narratives about 'what mattered' to families: aspirations for education, careers, religious observance and their children's future marriages. The underlying thread was a strong desire for upward social mobility. In contrast to some of the other sets of beliefs and values discussed in this chapter (such as cultural tradition and change), aspirations also seemed salient to children. They were referred to by at least one person from every family included in the study.

3.5.1 The importance of education

In line with other research (e.g. Bhatti 1999), the value of education for their children was a particularly strong theme running through the interviews, with several parents labelling education as the most important part of being a parent. This was often linked with the idea of 'giving them the chances I didn't have', and the recognition that (higher) education was a means to achieving social mobility (Modood 2004). Education was believed to lead to a 'good job', which would be well-respected within the community. This usually meant some kind of profession (doctors, dentists and lawyers were particularly aspired to, though many parents then went on to say it should be their child's choice). This quote is typical:

The main thing is education I would like them to be a doctor or whatever they wanted to be, it is not up to me, I leave it up to them. When somebody see my children they will say so-and-so's son or so-and-so's daughter, oh she is a doctor or a barrister I don't want them cleaning, you know to confront me in the streets and say did you see this ladies' son or daughter in jail, I don't want that. (Tariq's mother)

Parental emphasis on education was usually demonstrated in practice through appointing tutors for their children, enforcing routine 'homework time', or more generally encouraging their children to work hard.

The emphasis on education was typically related to aspirations for social advancement. Parents wanted children to 'make something of themselves'. This was a theme raised especially often by fathers. Adam's father emphasized it repeatedly:

I'm trying to push him to make something of himself, and I've brought him up to believe that anything he wanted to have he's got to really work for it (...) sometimes you look down the road and there's a homeless person sitting down the street, you know, I say "look son he didn't do his homework" I know it's wrong but I've got to try and instil in him that he's got to work hard because life is hard out there. (...) My role is to ..... I don't know give them the best chance you can, make sure ... they have every opportunity to succeed... (Adam's father)

This father, like many other parents in the study, saw education as a 'way up' from or 'way out' of the disadvantages that he perceived other South Asians to face. The idea that they wanted a better life for their children was a narrative that emerged frequently.

[I want to] give them more education, you know, in a way that they would not suffer as I have suffered in my life, you know. At least they would have some kind of profession, even if they haven't got anything. (Farid's father)

Education, then, was seen as the key way in which children could get good jobs and thus, as one mother said, 'more respect'. Children had appropriated this aspiration. Several told me of their ambitions to become a doctor, dentist or vet, and many were acutely aware of their parents' values:

School is good and you can learn more in school if you don't play a lot and it's more hard and you'd better get higher levels in the tests and reading. (...) They [his parents] don't want me to be dumb like other children. (Zabar)

3.5.2   Being or becoming 'good Muslims'

Alongside educational and career ambitions, some parents harboured aspirations related to other aspects of their children's lives. As Aisha's mother said,

> ... one of the key things that Muslim parents want is that your children are brought up as good Muslims. It wouldn't be right if I didn't. (Aisha's mother)

This aspiration was sometimes advanced in contrast to their own lesser religiosity, representing an ambition to increase the level of family religious involvement through the generations.

> I don't want her to be like me. I want her to be more religious. I actually want her to grow up to be an Islamic teacher in an Islamic school. (Najma's mother)

In terms of rewards after death, this would have benefits not only for their children but also for themselves.

For some families this intention took the practical form of encouraging their children to become more involved in religious activity. Hasan's parents had encouraged their son to study to become a *hafiz*, someone who can recite the Qur'an by heart – an achievement they described as 'very special'. As his father commented, it was 'a bit more important, a bit more effort'. Achievements of this kind were talked about with pride. For some being a good Muslim was a more abstract goal, often to do with the importance, even in less religiously observant families, of marrying someone of the same faith.

> I think I would struggle if my daughters came home and said they were going to marry someone who wasn't a Muslim. (Aisha's mother)

3.5.3   'As long as they are happy'

A number of parents referred to their children's future happiness as their ultimate goal. In this context future happiness appeared to entail successful marital relationships. The idea came up several times in terms of letting children choose their own marriage partners, or only sanctioning a marriage if their child was willing. Ensuring that their children were themselves happily settled appeared to be an important goal to many parents.

> If you... have two daughters, and after that they grow up and marry and live with their husbands, you will go to paradise. That's the feeling in our religion. It's a very good feeling. (Jamila's father)

Meanwhile, the thought of children remaining unmarried was a source of concern for parents. Najma's mother, whose daughter was disabled, expressed her hopes that Najma would nevertheless have an opportunity to be happily married:

> I really do want her to have a chance to be married. I don't know whether she will. (Najma's mother)

Children, too, had internalized this expectation of marriage. In the course of conversation some referred matter-of-factly to their future expectations:

> ... when it's my wedding I am going to say to everyone that you can play around, kids you don't get bored like only old people can sit down and talk to each other. (Zabar)

3.5.4 Social mobility

As we have seen, aspirations for their children's education, future career, religious standing and a happy marriage were themes that seemed important to many parents (regardless of their own social or religious standing), and were also reflected in children's accounts. It is noteworthy that many of the aspirations expressed by family members were more broadly to do with social mobility. Thus getting ahead or making something of themselves, through working hard, getting good qualifications and attaining a professional career, were extremely common expectations of children. This theme has been highlighted by other writers on South Asians in the UK (see for example Bhatti 1999; Ahmad, Modood et al. 2003), and has been linked to increases in educational attainment, particularly among Indian children (Ansari 2002). For these families, educational success was also seen as a means of enhancing the family's 'respect' or its standing in the community.

The emphasis on social status was highlighted by some parents, both in terms of material possessions (as Aisha's mother said, 'I'm not going to have my daughter not wearing Nike trainers!') and in terms of social markers. The gradual adoption of Urdu over Punjabi, a finding also reported by Chattoo and colleagues (2004), was a striking example. Although many of the families in this area of North-East London counted Punjabi as their language of origin, Urdu was understood to be 'nicer' and so people were beginning to teach Urdu to their children in order to 'keep up with the neighbours'.

> ... nowadays it's like if you're talking to your child in Punjabi people will be looking at you, 'They're so rough they're talking Punjabi' and if you talk in Urdu it's more like, you know, it's like speaking in Cockney and then speaking fluent English, it's that type of difference. (...) I think most people tend to speak Urdu with their children now, they do ... because our next door neighbour used to speak Punjabi with her children and our children used to speak Urdu, so then they tend... then they changed, they started speaking Urdu as well ... (Zabar's mother)

Social mobility was aspired to in a number of different ways – both within the wider society (in terms of education and jobs) but also within the local South Asian community, where a family's standing could be judged in terms of their children's use of language and material possessions, as well as by their career achievements.

3.6   Conclusion

This chapter has explored the ideological context of family life in terms of the belief and value systems that mattered to people and the accounts they employed to talk about family practices. The quantitative survey data indicate distinctive patterns for Muslim families, with their religious value systems being relatively more salient to parenting than for non-Muslims. The qualitative interview data made it possible to further clarify the beliefs and values with which people engaged in their family practices. Following previous research (Dollahite and Marks 2004; Dollahite, Marks et al. 2004), religion emerged as a central theme. The pervasive nature of Islam was a frequently occurring narrative. Religion was perceived to be especially useful in offering a moral framework for making decisions, although there was also a counter-narrative at play which emphasized moderation and not being too strict. Another important narrative in talking about family life, particularly for parents, was the active negotiation of cultural tradition and change. Such negotiation typically involved intergenerational dynamics and beliefs related to valuing and 'passing on' South Asian cultural traditions on the one hand, while acknowledging cultural transformation (for example around family role expectations) on the other. Notions of being distinctive ('us and them'), versus being 'just like anyone else' were closely related to this. Finally, aspirations for social, educational and even religious mobility were important themes to many parents, and were also absorbed and reconstituted by children. This range of alternative and competing narratives reflected the variety of repertoires with which individuals engaged in their family practices.

4
Cultural Consumption, Cultural Expression

The multiple belief and value systems bound up with family practices in South Asian Muslim families in Britain were explored in Chapter 3. This chapter will explore how such value systems are enacted in the context of daily family practices, with a particular emphasis on what families *do*; what they eat, how they dress and how they choose to spend their free time. Activities related to consumption have been identified as being poorly represented in the available research on families – what Daly (2003) has referred to as the 'negative spaces' in family theorizing. These aspects of daily family practice are, Daly argues, pervasive and important in understanding the ways in which families live their lives, and warrant more attention from family scholars. He further suggests that 'material things' and consumption help to construct meaning, shape values and beliefs, mediate relationships, and that they are part of the process of 'identity work and dream management' in families (2003:778). The idea that material family practices contribute to family identity construction is related to the wider argument, originally proposed by Pierre Bourdieu, that tastes and preferences in consumption tend to express and reinforce one's position with respect to social and cultural boundaries (Bourdieu 1984).[18]

This chapter selects a number of areas of consumption that intermesh with family practices, and explores how they are negotiated within families. The choices made, and who makes them, reflect the ways in which families draw upon, reinforce and rewrite available value systems and identities. In the context of family practices, food, dress, language and spare time activities (particularly watching television) in are considered in turn. As will be suggested, these cultural practices were often sites for the negotiation of tradition and change, and in particular represented the ways in which families chose to remake Islam. It can be argued that through their eating, dressing, speaking and spending time, families were 'performing' their religious, social and cultural identities, so that the physical 'doing' of religion was closely intertwined with the 'doing' of family. Furthermore, the practices of cultural consumption formed the key channels through which families articulated the values of sameness and difference.

4.1 Food: eating family practices

Food and meals have been viewed as key areas of consumption through which social and cultural boundaries of inclusion and exclusion are defined (see for example Douglas 1984; Brannen, Dodd et al. 1994; Chattoo, Atkin et al. 2004). Indeed, as Morgan (1996:165) points out, the interaction between food and class is employed by Bourdieu as a central illustration of his theory of distinction. In the present study, families' choices related to food and the organization and performance of meals also emerged as important expressions of how they 'placed' themselves culturally and religiously. As Chattoo and colleagues found (2004:28), the set of values represented by the phrase 'you are what you eat' was especially salient for South Asian Muslim families in Britain.

4.1.1 Performing ethnicity

Through an ethnographic study of Iranian women in England, Harbottle (1996) explores how ethnicity can be 'performed' through specific food consumption practices. The women she studied applied Iranian cooking techniques to 'transform' British food (which was perceived as inherently dangerous) and therefore to safeguard their families' health and maintain their ethnic identities. Harbottle concludes that daily food consumption practices provide an important and accessible way to reinforce, modify or transform identity, and that women have a key role in this process.

For the South Asian Muslim families in this study, food consumption practices were comparably significant in defining their social identities, and particularly in developing the distinctions they drew between 'us' and 'them' in a minority context. It was striking that the majority of both parents and children voiced a distinction between what they called 'Asian food', 'home food' or 'our food' (which included rice, curry and food cooked with Indian spices) and 'English food' or 'your food' (such as pasta, fish fingers or chicken nuggets). However, rather than confining themselves exclusively 'Asian food', it was normal for families to eat a combination of both:

> She sometimes cooks Indian meals and sometimes just ordinary English meals, fish, eggs that sort of thing. (Amina)

The impulse to eat English food often came from the children (especially in first-generation families). Tariq's preferences were typical. When I asked what he ate after school he said 'Normal home food. Like rice and curry', but went on immediately afterwards to comment that his favourite food was pasta. As this remark suggests, children's favourite food was often not traditionally South Asian, and thus where families occasionally or regularly ate English food, this tended to reflect children's influence in persuading mothers to cook dishes from 'outside', drawing particularly on their experiences at school. Such accounts recalled wider commentaries around what is often called 'pester power' (Gunter and Furnham 1998):

> At the moment we have chapatti going on, we've got rice going on, we've got a vegetarian dish going on and we have got like a chicken dish going on and then they want pizza! (Yasmin's elder sister)

Parents and children commonly engaged in negotiations to establish the rules for what would be eaten and how often. Weekends were sometimes treated as special occasions. In families less closely affiliated with South Asian traditions (such as Adam's), parents might find time to cook 'proper' South Asian food only at weekends. Alternatively, children such as Hasan might be allowed 'one English meal' as a treat at the weekend. Similarly, Amina's mother and her children had made a pact that they would eat 'our own food' three times a week, and that for the rest of the time they would have meals which the children preferred, such as fish fingers: her own mother actively disapproved of this arrangement, however, illustrating the multiple divisions that could exist within families.

Like Amina's grandmother, a number of parents (in contrast to their children) expressed a belief that South Asian food was somehow better or more 'proper'.[19] Khalid's mother, for example, rationalized that although her children liked pizza and pasta, in reality they only wanted 'Asianized' versions:

> ... if they wanna have English stuff or Italian stuff, pasta and stuff, my children they love pasta and pizza and stuff like that but they

don't wanna outside one, they want me to make them cos I add chillies and all my other ingredients as well, so that makes it spicy. (Khalid's mother)

A few families, and especially those with relatively low South Asian affiliation, rarely ate South Asian food. As Adam's father commented:

... sometimes I cook, sometimes she cooks, but we can't always do it because we're both working and we get too tired so generally it's fish and chips or ... something like go to like... what we do is go to either Sainsbury's or Tesco's or somewhere and buy fish fingers... and put them in the oven, usually that or spaghetti or the usual stuff, no curries I'm afraid... (Adam's father)

In referring to fish fingers and spaghetti as 'the usual stuff' this father was emphasizing his affiliation with British culture and 'normalness' as he had done elsewhere in his interview. However, he also cited the pressures created by work as another reason for the reliance on English ready meals, implying that if he and his wife had had more time they might have done things differently.

Across all families, however, South Asian food was universally eaten on special occasions such as religious or family celebrations. Even Adam's father acknowledged that his wife would cook 'special food, mostly like chicken biriyani' for religious festivals or on 'special days'. This provision during family celebrations of 'special' food, together with the question of who was invited to share it, had the effect of symbolizing families' increased (re)connection with their cultural traditions.

4.1.2 Performing religion

Meanwhile, 'performing' religion through food was a separate process only partially intertwined with the performance of ethno-cultural identities. For the main part, religious eating (and, importantly, religious non-eating)[20] involved following the rules for eating *halal* (permitted) and avoiding *haram* (forbidden) foodstuffs (eating only meat consecrated in a particular way; a strict proscription on pork, including any food product containing traces of pork, such as gelatine, and a ban on alcohol). Strict adherence to these guidelines (at least within the home) was the norm in all families, regardless of whether the food consumed was 'Asian' or 'English'. Indeed, the presence of religious guidelines could be used to legitimate the redrawing of rules around food so that

English food could be seen as acceptable, as Khalid's mother put it, 'so long as it's *halal*'.

Children in general displayed an awareness of religious food restrictions, albeit with varying levels of comprehension. All were aware of the proscription on pork, but there was some confusion over other elements:

> We're not allowed to eat pork. And we can eat any *halal*, we can eat chicken but only *halal* chicken, beef, *halal* beef, and we can eat, well, it wouldn't be nice to eat the, birds, but we can, we can eat turkey. (Ali)

Similarly, Amina said that Muslims were 'not allowed to be alcoholic or drink wine'. Indeed, when asked what it meant to be a Muslim, diet was one of the first things that most children mentioned (alongside reading the Qur'an and praying):

> *How should you behave if you are Muslim?*
> When you do the Qur'an you have to learn the *wuzu* [ritual ablution], wash yourself before you read the Qur'an, and you can't eat pig or any meat that is made from pig or gelatine, that's it. You can't eat snakes or rabbit or bird.
> *What, like chicken, chicken is a bird?*
> Yes but we eat a *real* chicken. (Amir)

The fact that Amir constructed *halal* chicken as 'real' chicken echoes Harbottle's (1996) finding, that religiously consecrated food is seen as somehow better or more authentic. Similarly, Khalid's mother considered eating *halal* a more 'nutritious' diet.

The performance of religious eating incurred an awareness of boundaries, both in terms of inclusion and exclusion. Yasmin's elder sister talked of Yasmin learning about it as normal:

> ... here around every corner there is a *halal* shop, even when it comes to sweets we can't eat gelatine, pork or stuff, and my sister knows that she has to read the labels before she buys it. It is just gelatine or alcoholic stuff, other than that it's alright, it's not a major thing in our life. (Yasmin's elder sister)

By presenting it as 'not a major thing', with a shop 'around every corner', Yasmin's sister indicated that by eating *halal* food they were situating themselves as members of the local Muslim community. Jamila, however, found religious restrictions difficult because they excluded her from such activities as eating at McDonalds, and so made her aware of the differences between herself and her non-Muslim friends.

> It is really hard because like McDonalds burgers and that, when you see it you want to taste it but you can't. (Jamila)

As these accounts suggest, the strict observation of religious rules about eating was important in reconstituting the family as Muslim (both in relation to the South Asian Muslim community, and as distinct from non-Muslim others.) Adam's father, who was one of the least religiously observant individuals in the study, was the only one who admitted to having broken these proscriptions, and even then only partially and guiltily:

> But then again I won't eat pork. But I might have an occasional drink sometimes with a friend but I don't really... I feel guilty about it sometimes but... (Adam's father)

It is also important to note that the performance of religion through food, although an everyday process based on the continued attention to *halal* and *haram*, was especially salient at certain times. The consumption (and non-consumption) of food as an expression of religion was most important during the holy month of Ramadan. During this period, the requirement to fast from dawn to dusk meant that one's relationship to food was defined entirely through religious practice. During Ramadan in particular it could be said that food *was* religious practice, illustrating the importance of cyclical sacred times in shaping the relationship between consumption and religion in family practices. These issues will be explored further in the next chapter.

4.1.3   Performing family relationships

So far, the discussion has been concerned with exploring how the practice of eating is bound up with the processes of cultural and religious expression. Leading on from this, the relationships between family members were also partly constituted through food, since the preparation of food, how and when it was eaten, and with whom, were activities in which religious and cultural values around gender and generational divisions were brought to bear.

Morgan (1996) has commented that food is a particular symbol of women's care work in families, and indeed the responsibility for preparing nutritious food for family members was prominent in mothers' perceptions of their roles, as Bashira's mother suggests:

> ... these kinds of decisions I make. Because diet should be, you know, balanced diet. Kids like potatoes, keep eating, don't eat anything else, no meat nothing, so it's not good. So I try to give them a balanced diet, kebabs, chicken, stuff. Cooking – my duty (laughs). (Bashira's mother)

In these households the preparation of food was almost invariably undertaken by women. Children were aware of this, and all mentioned cooking when describing 'what a mother should do'. Some of them perceived a mother's predominance in decisions over food as a symbol of her power in the house – as with Aisha who, when asked who was the boss in her house, said that her mother and father both were in different ways: her mother because 'whatever she is cooking, no-one is saying "let's have this", she will just cook it'.

In most families, the father's role was restricted to a responsibility for material provision (literally, bread-winning), and ideally the presiding over meals as the 'head of the household'. Only in Najma's family did the father routinely prepare the food – he remarked that this was because 'Najma likes it when I cook', while her mother explained that he was a better cook than her, having been forced to learn while living in an all-male environment.

> It is mostly him, but then he's a good cook. He lived in Saudi Arabia for ten years, working there, and it was all a man's thing so they had to do everything. (...) It's just handy for me. (Najma's mother)

She went on to say, though, that 'my husband said Najma has to learn, because she might not get as good a husband [if she can't cook]', indicating that they still found it important to ensure that their daughter was ready to fulfil culturally-informed gender roles.

Children could be seen to have played a role in affecting decisions over what was eaten: as remarked earlier, a number of them effectively persuaded their mothers to cook more English food. Mothers and children tended to agree that, although the mother was officially in charge of cooking, what she actually cooked rested on her children's preferences:

> I know what they want. (...) anything they want, anything. I try to do it for them. If not I promise that I'll do it tomorrow. (Ali's mother)

Sometimes, birth order and family dynamics meant that one sibling had more say in what the family ate, as with Khalid who, as the youngest, was allowed to choose what he wanted to eat:

> [Khalid's] the one who chooses and everybody eats that anyway. So sometimes my older one she complains 'Why does he have to choose every time?' (laughs) – when she doesn't like it but they don't mind actually. Yeah. And he tells me that he doesn't like, that's he's in my secret, he goes 'I don't like nobody else's food, even no nanny's, and no auntie's, only yours'. (Khalid's mother)

Here practices concerned with food served to define and reinforce family relationships. The emotional bond between this mother and child was moreover reinforced through sharing the 'secret' that he liked her food the best.

The ways in which meals were arranged was also revealing as to beliefs about family relationships. There was some emphasis from parents (echoing wider discourses), on the desirability of a 'family meal' in the evening. In practice roughly half the families routinely ate their evening meal with everybody present. There was an emphasis on the importance of talking together and discussing the day, usually raised by parents and particularly stressed by working fathers:

> When I get in at that time, we have dinner, all the family together. And after that we discuss what's happening, done in the day, that we've done this and this. (Jamila's father)

In one group of families the members did not always eat dinner together, especially where there were older siblings present, or one parent was working long hours, so that time constraints imposed on ideal preferences. Eating together was nevertheless viewed as a desirable goal. Hasan's father tried to 'fill in' at weekends.

> Because it's not that I don't want to, it's because of pure timing and stuff yeah. (...) It's probably the weekends when we normally tend to eat together, you know, try and fill them, just try to fill in. (Hasan's father)

Family meals were a setting in which to promote 'good manners' and deter undesirable behaviour: Farid's father tried to discourage talking about work or school at the dinner table, because this ran counter to his conception of family life as separate:

> I don't talk about my job here or about my colleagues, about my manager, about how my days have been at work. I don't want to bring that home. Because if I bring that at home on my table, my children are gonna learn from me, say 'Daddy's talking about work. I'm going to talk about my college, I'm going to talk about my school.' And they will gradually, and everything's just gonna be mixed up and there's not going to be a family life.

In some households the chosen style of eating reflected cultural traditions. When I ate a meal with Bashira's family, we spread a cloth on the kitchen floor and ate sitting down, scooping up the food with our fingers. Such practices would have been in sharp contrast to the way in which Bashira ate meals at school, underlining for her the distinctiveness of her family's cultural practices.

Practices related to sharing food generally convey messages about who 'belongs'. As is described in Chapter 8, members of the extended family helped to define religious festivals by their presence at shared meals, and in turn *who* was invited and *who* attended such meals helped to define the boundaries of 'family'. Similarly, the sharing of food was a part of the reciprocal exchanges in which families engaged with the local South Asian Muslim social network, as Amina's comment demonstrates:

> I like my mum's cooking, we give some to our neighbours then and they enjoy it as well. Sometimes they give food to us. So it's like we give to them sometimes and then sometimes they give to us. We enjoy taking different foods. (Amina)

4.2   Dress: wearing family practices

Clothes, alongside food, also served as markers of inclusion and exclusion, conveying messages about an individual's position with respect to South Asian-ness and Muslim-ness. Rules for acceptable dress varied across families depending on their levels of cultural and religious commitment and also varied according to the situation. Clothes also constituted a site of negotiation within families and across generations: for instance, children had a certain amount of agency in choosing what they wore (see Chapter 7). There also existed important gender issues relating to decisions about clothes.

4.2.1   Wearing South Asian clothes

Traditional South Asian clothes were commonly worn at home in the families in this study, especially by girls and women. Most wore *shalwar kameez* (baggy trousers and tunic) as well as a *dupatta* (scarf) around their shoulders and sometimes over their head. Men and boys more often wore English-style trousers and shirts (although a few wore *shalwar kameez*). These clothes met the cultural and religious standards of modesty in covering the body, and also the head for women.

The use of South Asian clothes depended to some extent on context. They were universally worn on special occasions and for family celebrations, such as weddings, funerals or *Eid*, and in these situations symbolized an increased affiliation to South Asian tradition. They were also worn by all children for Islamic classes, and to mosque, signifying the association of South Asian clothes with Islamic values. Indeed, they were often mentioned as an aspect of being a Muslim, especially by women and girls.

> ... being a Muslim mum, my religion is wearing certain clothes, a head scarf (Jamila's mother)

In all contexts South Asian clothes were considered to be 'respectable' and were seen positively by parents and children, especially from the more religious families.

> It's good, and I am proud that we wear these kind of clothes. When I wear [English clothes] it doesn't suit me. (Jamila)

Some types of South Asian clothes were liked better than others. Hasan's mother, on her recent trip to Mecca, had bought her sons long tunic-style garments which could be put on straight over their school clothes, and which they apparently preferred to the more traditional-style *shalwar kameez* as they were seen as more fashionable.

4.2.2   Wearing 'English' clothes

The use of English clothes also depended on the situation. Fathers (and some mothers) wore them to work, and most children wore them to school. This was presented as a means of helping them to 'fit in'. As Hasan's mother commented:

> I don't like them having [South Asian clothes] all the time because they have to live in this world, they go to school, they have all, not only Muslim friends, all ... you know, all kind of friends, so I think they should fit in everything, that's why. (Hasan's mother)

Thus English clothing served to identify children as being the 'same as anyone else' and to facilitate relationships outside the family.

The wearing of English clothes (or more precisely the non-wearing of South Asian clothes) was to some extent an indication of relatively low South Asian and religious affiliation. For example, each time I visited Adam's and Aisha's families all the members were wearing English-style clothes. Aisha's mother, in the context of a discussion about trying hard to 'integrate' her children, remarked:

> I don't sew Asian clothes myself, I find it easier, I mean I buy English clothes and the girls have never worn Asian clothes to school (Aisha's mother)

Similarly, Adam's father supported his wife in her decision to wear tracksuits despite disapproval from other Muslims in the community:

> ... I just tell her to ignore them, I tell her it's nothing to do with religion and it isn't, it doesn't say anywhere in there, and I've read it in English, that you have to wear a tent, *burkha*, that's just a cultural thing nothing else.... It does say you've got to be covered up but you can be covered up in tracksuit and top, init? (Adam's father)

Similarly, Amina's mother used religious guidelines in the Qur'an in deciding that her daughters should be allowed to wear jeans. She considered them to be acceptable because one's legs were 'still covered', and let her children choose between 'our clothes' and 'your clothes', even though one of her more religious aunts strongly disapproved. These examples illustrate how Islamic rules were distinguished from cultural norms and re-interpreted to derive respectability for English clothes. With this logic English clothes were acceptable so long as one was 'covered', thus legitimizing cultural change (despite inter-generational disapproval). Such reasoning did not, however, convince Yasmin's mother. Even though Yasmin herself was desperate to wear jeans (something her two eldest sisters considered acceptable on Islamic grounds), her mother refused, asserting that 'you are a Muslim, you have to wear the *shalwar kameez*'.

4.2.3 Gender issues and *hijab*

As previous research has suggested, there were different dress standards for male and female family members. For women and girls, the require-ment to dress modestly (usually equated with wearing South Asian clothes) was part of a larger set of cultural and religious values defining sexuality and gender relationships, in which girls were viewed as an embodiment of the family's honour and were subject to relatively more community surveillance than boys (Chattoo et al. 2004). In this context, English clothes for women were associated with the 'per-missive' white culture that was believed to encourage promiscuity (Shaw 1994). Men and boys had fewer choices to make: for them, English clothes had fewer moral connotations (see Chattoo et al. 2004).

Gender differences in the meanings ascribed to clothes were symbol-ized by the headscarf or veil (*hijab*), one of the main aspects of *purdah* (religiously prescribed gender segregation) which requires the 'covering up' and protection of women, making this a particular issue for mothers and daughters.

> *Are there certain ways you should behave if you are a Muslim?*
> Yes, you should wear certain clothes and not to show your body. (Habiba)

The observance of religious requirements for covering one's head varied across families. Many women would wear a headscarf when outside the home, and in religiously observant families a headscarf was worn inside when non-related men came to visit.

> ... a woman has to cover her head when she sees men around. What they say is, you don't have to cover your head if you see men

around, your own family like your dad, your brothers, but then when it comes to your cousins, you have to start covering your head when they come round. (Rubina's elder sister)

The most rigorous observance occurred in Yasmin's family (who were relatively high in religiosity). Because two of her adult sisters lived at home with their husbands, all the teenage and adult sisters kept their heads covered when either of their brothers-in-law was at home. This meant that one teenage sister had to wear the veil in bed, since lack of space required her to share a bedroom with one of the couples. A significant minority of women, however, did not wear a headscarf at all, a practice associated with low religious affiliation. For example, Zabar's mother refused to wear one even though her (first-generation) husband wanted her to.

Wearing the headscarf was also related to women's age and generation. Some, like Najma's and Farid's mothers, had started wearing one only since they had married, illustrating how accepted practice could vary over an individual's lifetime. Similarly, the majority of girls in the study, at age 9–11, did not wear a headscarf except for Islamic classes, when they wore a tight scarf that covered their hair completely. Although a number had experimented with wearing one on other occasions, some mothers considered their daughters to be too young.

> Aisha talks about wearing the scarf now and I said 'not at this stage', because I am a bit frightened if you have got a scarf on and children are running around... so I said to her 'not now', but when the time comes we will talk about it and I will encourage her... (Aisha's mother)

There was the expectation, among both mothers and daughters, that they would start wearing a headscarf more frequently when they reached puberty.

> ... this girl [at school] tried but she couldn't because it felt so weird. I tried myself but I found it really hard so what I did I thought I would leave it until [local secondary school] if I get in and I will start wearing it then. It won't be that hard because there, there will be lots of people wearing it whereas in our class there is only one person that wears it.

Does it matter if you don't wear it?
Well you should but when you are about 14; if you are under you should try to do it but when you are 14 it is compulsory.
So until you are 14 it is kind of up to you is it?
Yes, but they say you should do it when you are younger to get the practise. (Aisha)

In general, the extent to which girls wore a headscarf was the outcome of negotiations between mothers, daughters and other female family figures. The multiple considerations that could come into play during the process are illustrated by this dialogue between myself, Bashira (aged 9) and her mother. Bashira told me that she wore a scarf to school because she liked it. Bashira's mother, who was nearby during the interview, entered the conversation.

It keeps me warm, and if I don't wear it then sometimes when the wind is blowing my hair goes all over the place.
So you think it is practical?
Yes, so when I grow up I won't say I don't want to wear it. Because like my sister, when I was her age I started wearing it every day, but she doesn't wear it because she doesn't like it, well she does like it but her friend doesn't like it.
So you started wearing it when you were 7?
Yes.
Who decided that you were going to wear it?
My mum and dad.
Mum: She did it herself!
First I wore it one day and then I left a day then I wore it.
Mum: I told her to take it off but she don't. She doesn't want to!
Because in school if I take it off everyone's going to start staring at me.
Mum: She has got her own reasons; I said 'you shouldn't wear it every day', I said it was up to you because you are not big enough to wear it, but she said 'no I've got used to, I have to, I want to wear it'. She just, surprises me sometimes, she wants to wear it. She got used to it so much she's not old enough. And now she thinks I've decided!
No, because I didn't know how to wear it then you said it once then I started.

> **Mum: Yeah, I said 'only on Fridays, wear it on Fridays' and then you started wearing it. Then I said 'take it off' and she said no. Even when we're going somewhere women only, I say take it off, she says no.**
>
> *(...)*
>
> *Does it mean that you are more religious if you wear it?*
>
> No you just want to wear it. It's your choice if you want to wear it.

This dialogue illustrates the complex processes of negotiation between family members in making decisions about girls' dress. Bashira's account suggested that her mother took the initiative in suggesting that she should wear a headscarf (at least on Fridays), but her mother claimed that Bashira herself decided to adopt the habit, although she considered Bashira to be too young to do so. That Bashira continued to wear the headscarf regularly suggests that she had a certain degree of agency, although it is difficult to tell to what extent her mother influenced her in the decisions. It is also evident that the reasons Bashira cited for wearing a headscarf – namely that it kept her warm and stopped the wind blowing her hair around – and for not wearing it – peer pressure or simply not liking it – are very different from the 'official' reasons.

Such inter-generational differences in attitudes were in some cases linked to Islamization among the younger generation of Muslims (see Bauer 1997; Jacobson 1997), as became evident in a few families in the study. For example, Yasmin's two eldest sisters had started wearing a headscarf even though their parents did not approve:

> I didn't really learn it from my parents, it was really strange, I was supposed to have learned it from my parents, but they hated it when I started wearing this, most Muslim parents would absolutely love it, they'd think 'oh my daughter is so...', these were like pulling it off, 'stop wearing it'... (Yasmin's elder sister)

She went on to say:

> It is quite strange because in mosque youngsters are wearing the scarf and the elders ain't. I see that quite a lot. And they don't like it if their daughters are doing it even though Islamically

you are supposed to be doing it and you should be happy that your child is doing it but you would rather have the culture side, because they are scared of what their neighbours and their relatives might think. (Yasmin's elder sister)

In talking about 'the culture side' Yasmin's sister was referring to the *shalwar kameez* and looser *dupatta* preferred by her mother (which did not completely cover one's hair, and which according to her was not Islamic enough). Yasmin herself had begun to ask about wearing a scarf outside mosque because she saw her older sisters doing so, but like other girls in the study she had been told that she was too young.

... she says 'can I?', but I say 'you are not wearing it now' and she says 'go on' but if she wants to wear it outside one day then I would, but I don't like it when kids wear it at that age because it is too much for their mind, they dehydrate quickly, and I don't think it is right, you're not supposed to make them wear it at that time anyway, they have enough to learn. So Yasmin wears it when she goes to mosque but after that she doesn't really wear it. (Yasmin's elder sister)

4.3   Language: speaking family practices

In Chapter 2, it was noted that at least two languages were spoken in most families as a matter of course, while a third language, Arabic, was read in a specifically religious context. The complex meanings conveyed by which languages were spoken, in which context, and with whom, imply an interesting dimension of 'speaking' family practices. As will be argued, the use of language was a form of cultural expression which enabled individuals and families to establish inclusion within South Asian Muslim social and family networks, symbolized the passing on of cultural traditions, promoted the adaptation of 'Britishness', and allowed the fulfilment of religious goals.

4.3.1   Speaking English

English was spoken at school or work, between children in families (siblings, cousins and South Asian friends), and often between second-generation parents and children. Some children would also reply in

English to first-generation parents and other relatives who addressed them in Urdu, Punjabi or Gujarati.

> They understand Urdu but they can't speak Urdu even. If I speak to them in Urdu, they reply in English. They don't reply in Urdu, they can't think. (Mehmood's mother)

Being able to speak English was an important asset outside the home. While all children and second-generation parents were fluent, English was a particular issue for first-generation parents who, if they did not speak the language, were limited in what they could do:

> ... I wanted to learn, because when I go to the bus I don't know what to say to the driver, it was quite embarrassing to go out without speaking, I needed to go out all the time, it's no life. So I went to an adult education centre. (Bashira's mother)

Bashira's mother now spoke excellent English and this allowed her to interact with other people, particularly mothers at her children's school. Parents who had not learnt English often had to rely on other family members for help in making decisions.

> It's got to be with my auntie as well, the one that opened the mosque, cos she's very...well every decision my parents have made, cos they're not educated themselves, they can just, they can speak English but not very good, so they take a lot of decisions from her, they speak to her. (Rubina's elder sister)

Differences in the levels of spoken English between different family members could thus affect the power balance within the family (see also Husain and O'Brien 1999): in Yasmin's family her adult siblings had effectively taken over the decision-making. Where family members could speak good English, as in the case of Zabar's grandfather, this added to the respect accorded them in the community and could also enhance their earning potential:

> My dad's got his own business (...) and he's a councillor as well and he's quite, you know, he talks proper English and everything so he's quite well known... in our local area. (Zabar's mother)

The ability to speak English was also seen as useful in parenting; for example, Amir and Ahmed's mother commented that it was lucky she spoke English as it allowed her to answer the questions her sons asked about being Muslim in Britain (for example, when they saw Muslim actors kissing on television and wanted to know if this would be counted as a sin). In these various ways, English was identified with positive notions of assimilation and change.

4.3.2 Speaking the language of origin

The language of origin for most families was Punjabi or Urdu (or a mixture), though Najma's, Tariq's and Farid's families were all of Indian origin and spoke Gujarati (serving to recall how language marked out ethnic differences). Most children spoke their language of origin or at least understood it, albeit to varying levels. These languages were often spoken between adults (including between first- and second-generation spouses), and between first-generation parents and children. They were seen as a 'good thing', mainly because of their association with cultural continuity and social and familial networks, although there was also a notion that they were associated with greater commitment to Islam (see also Chattoo, Atkin et al. 2004):

> I think my mum takes [religion] more seriously than my dad... I don't know that, but I just think.
> *What gives you that impression?*
> Cos my mum speaks to me in Urdu. (Adam)

That Adam associated his mother's increased use of Urdu with a stronger religious commitment reflected that she was indeed more closely affiliated than his father with both Islam and South Asian tradition. The fact that he conflated cultural and religious symbols of expression suggests that he experienced the two as difficult to distinguish.

Although second-generation parents usually spoke English with their children, there were certain situations in which their language of origin would be used instead. Urdu, Punjabi and Gujarati was usually spoken with older relatives and members of the local community:

> Normally me and my children we speak in English but sometimes, you know, we are, when everybody's around and when parents especially and stuff, we speak Urdu with Punjabi mix. (Khalid's mother)

In this context, the use of the language of origin was a mark of respect. It also implied a common bond, thus helping to sustain social networks, and to denote group inclusion. To have failed to teach one's children Urdu or Punjabi meant having denied them the chance of interacting with other members of the community. As Aisha's mother remarked:

> ... the girls' Punjabi is really, really poor, if they have a conversation with my mum they would really struggle, but because my mum is used to how they speak whatever they want to tell her she will understand, but if someone came into our house who could only speak Urdu or Punjabi there is no way my daughter could have a conversation with them, so I feel a bit guilty about that and may be I should have done a lot more in terms of that. (Aisha's mother)

Aisha's mother went on to say that she had realized the full importance of this omission when she visited Pakistan. Her own Urdu was very poor and she felt like an outsider. This indicates that the language of origin, spoken on visits 'home', was important in building the connection with Pakistan or India.

The notion of language as a marker of inclusion and connection, and a delineator of national or ethnic origin, was related to the view that the language of origin symbolized of the 'passing on' of tradition. This is illustrated by the contexts in which parents used it with their children. Adam told me that his mother would always speak in Urdu when telling him stories about their religion or their culture of origin. Amina's mother usually spoke in English but would switch to Urdu when disciplining or scolding her children. These practices may have derived from their own experiences of being parented, and were thus related to the passing on of cultural norms. This linguistic process of passing on was considered to be important, and parents voiced regret when their children did not speak the language of origin well. For example, Amir and Ahmed's mother lamented that her children used to speak 'lovely Punjabi', but had been losing it since they started at nursery. Parents used a variety of strategies to ensure that their children would learn some Urdu, Punjabi or Gujarati. Hasan and his siblings were sent to 'ethnic language classes' on Saturday mornings, while Aisha's mother was delighted when Aisha expressed an intention to learn Urdu at secondary school.

However, despite the argument that the language of origin was strongly linked with cultural roots and the passing on of traditions, it should be acknowledged that this relationship was flexible enough to be strategically altered or combined. As described in the previous chapter, in some Punjabi families Urdu was being deployed to achieve upward social mobility:

> ... with the children at home we speak Urdu, and between ourselves we speak Punjabi because I speak Punjabi... at home we spoke Punjabi and then... we had children we started speaking Urdu with them, my sister she speaks Urdu with her children. (...) nowadays it's like if you're talking to your child in Punjabi people will be looking at you 'they're so rough they're talking Punjabi'... (Zabar's mother)

This comment supports the view that the language in question was not used simply to label area of origin, but was perceived as an indicator of social status, and could thus be manipulated or re-imagined.

4.3.3 Arabic: speaking religious practices

In the families in this study, Arabic was an additional language used exclusively in a sacred context. The majority of parents could read it – and indeed it was vitally important to be able to do so in order to fulfil one's duty as a Muslim, to read the Qur'an and to recite prayers.

> One thing is like we pray in Arabic. We don't pray in our language. If you can't read [Arabic] you can't learn how to pray. Like we have to recite certain parts of the Qur'an. If we don't learn how to read we can't learn them by heart so we don't know how to read it. (...) So it is important to pray exactly and read exactly. (Bashira's mother)

Learning to read Arabic was accordingly one of the main reasons for sending children to Islamic classes (and indeed a couple of the less overtly religious families actually referred to them as 'Arabic classes'). However, not all the children made the distinction between Urdu and Arabic: to take a case in point, Rubina told me that she read the Qur'an in Urdu. It may be that for children such as Rubina (whose family was strongly affiliated with South Asian tradition but not particularly high in religiosity) religion was not easy to distinguish from cultural or ethnic practices.

For parents, however, reading Arabic and using the correct pronunciation was seen to be a matter of some importance. A few mothers explained that the 'original' Arabic pronunciation of the alphabet was 'better' than the Urdu one in religious terms. Several parents used this criterion in choosing their children's Islamic teacher:

> I chose this one because a lot of people when they read Arabic read it in a Urdu way and I don't want it in a Urdu way I want it in an Arabic way, I want it the proper way, the proper Arabic way, so that's why I particularly chose her. It's rare people who do that. (Yasmin's elder sister)

However, most parents and children could not understand the individual words (though they usually had an idea of the general meaning). Language was not used here as a channel of communication but rather as a ritualized means of fulfilling one's religious duty: as Khalid's mother said 'you can get reward for it but you don't understand it'. Reading the English translation was an optional extra that was not covered in Islamic classes. Actually understanding the Arabic words would signify that one was especially learned in a non-traditional, active sense. Such practices are not the norm in South Asian Islam and have been associated with high-Islamization (Bauer 1997). For the families in this study, speaking (without necessarily understanding) Arabic was a significant requirement of their religious participation.

4.4   Islamic leisure: television

The final section of this chapter explores aspects of leisure or 'spare time practices' (Southerton 2004). Other authors, particularly those allied to the sociology of consumption, have followed Bourdieu's work in arguing that spare time practices are shaped by cultural orientations, and are an expression of cultural capital and social networks (e.g. Longhurst and Savage 1996; Longhurst, Bagnall et al. 2001; Southerton 2004). It has been argued that differing tastes for leisure help to establish mutually recognizable distinctions between social and cultural groups. In the context of South Asian Muslims in Britain, spare time practices are interesting because many mainstream British leisure activities (drinking alcohol, watching television and films, listening to music, visiting non-*halal* restaurants, clubs and bars) may be frowned upon by highly religious Muslim families. Indeed, in strict interpretations of Islam there should not be any leisure time: free time is instead used for prayer.

The families in this study used various strategies to negotiate the tensions between mainstream leisure opportunities and religious requirements. One alternative was to adopt 'British' leisure activities – such as children attending after-school clubs or parents drinking in a pub with colleagues. This could be done carefully enough to remain within the boundaries of family interpretations of Islam. Another approach was to appropriate and adapt leisure practices to create what might be called 'Islamic leisure'. These themes are explored below using the example of television viewing.

4.4.1 Selective adoption

Selective adoption involved participation in British spare time practices, without adapting such practices, but filtering out the least acceptable. Television is a particularly interesting aspect of leisure, partly because it is ubiquitous in modern British households (99 per cent owned a television in 2002/3[21]) and forms an important part of popular culture and social currency for children (Gunter and McAleer 1997): 8–15 year olds watch an average of 133 minutes per day.[22] Yet television would be considered unacceptable by strict Muslims; as Najma's mother explained,

> In Islam TV is a pastime. Unless it's for news. But otherwise you're supposed to use your free time for praying. (Najma's mother)

Despite this, all households in this study had a television set and watched regularly (though some cited friends or relatives who did not). The way in which television was used, however, provides a good example of the strategy of selective adoption.

Some parents and children avidly watched soap operas such as Eastenders or Coronation Street. Children tended to enjoy watching cartoons and other children's programmes. Yet most parents voiced concerns over the content of British television programmes as 'un-Islamic', in that they involved such unacceptable themes as violence, portrayed sexual relationships, and were believed to encourage unacceptable behaviour. Children reiterated these ideas in their interviews. As Aisha explained,

> Like you shouldn't listen to music but I have got a habit and all my family do it, it's hard but if you practise it will become easy. (...) and like you are not allowed to watch TV.
> *A lot of Muslim people watch TV and listen to music don't they?*
> Yes.
> *So does it matter?*

> Not that much but you should try not to, because it gets into your mind and makes you act like your favourite characters. (...) like if you are like Bart Simpson you could just pull your trousers down. (Aisha)

In response to what they saw as the possibility of exposure to undesirable content, several parents had placed restrictions on children's viewing. Some had banned programmes such as the Simpsons. Two mothers had forbidden their children from watching Eastenders after there had been a storyline involving rape (although one continued to watch the programme herself). Others restricted viewing to the family or children's channel, or dis-allowed television (or at least non-Asian channels) after a certain time, often 8pm or the 9pm watershed.

> ...when they're watching TV I'll always keep coming in to watch what they're watching, I don't let them watch TV in the evening or anything, 'cos they used to watch East Enders first but I've stopped them, I don't... I used to watch because I was, you know, addict but I watch it when it's repeated in the evening, I don't watch it in front of them 'cos .. I don't want them to watch ... violent programs or anything that's wrong. (Zabar's mother)

As Zabar's mother indicated, another strategy was the constant surveillance of their children's viewing habits, also undertaken by Mehmood's mother:

> I have to sometimes ask 'what are you doing, what are you watching', (...) I ask 'what are you doing, why don't you watch the Discovery channel'... (Mehmood's mother)

A number of parents told me that they would change the channel if something undesirable came on – for example, kissing or gay relationships. This move was then discussed with the children, so that if they were holding the remote control when something unacceptable came on, they knew they too had to change the channel.

> ...when I was watching my favourite programme when things come that I, that my mum doesn't like so she, she, she tells me to change it and I change it. (Ali)

In these cases mainstream leisure activities were followed, but with a high level of selectivity so that they could be reconciled with parents' criteria of acceptability in religious terms. As in the example of Eastenders, some parents had different standards for themselves and for their children, and it was notable that parents seemed to exercise most control in this area.

4.4.2   Adaptation: A specifically Islamic leisure

The adaptation of leisure practices to render them more specifically Islamic (or South Asian) was a wider-ranging strategy used by some of the families in the study. Unlike selective adoption, this involved the active remaking of spare time practices, and the production of Islamic versions. This practice can once more be illustrated through the example of television. Many families had cable TV with South Asian or Islamic channels such as ZeeTV, which showed a range of programmes in South Asian languages, from Indian soap operas to religious programmes. Children were encouraged to watch South Asian rather than British channels. Zabar's father insisted that the family watched Asian channels after the watershed:

> ... in the evening it's like him, you know, we'll watch the Asian channels we're not allowed to watch the English channels, if there's anything religious on he'll sit down and watch it, make us watch it as well, 'You listen to this and...' (Zabar's mother)

Thus apparently 'non-Muslim' practices such as watching television could be appropriated for uses that were more acceptably Islamic, such as watching religious programmes and Asian TV channels. Watching this type of television had additional benefits in that it could form part of the children's religious education (as it did in Zabar's family), assist with learning the language of origin, and more generally help families to feel connected with South Asia. It could be said that this form of interaction with specifically Islamic/South Asian television helped to construct and reconstruct local identities in a diasporic context, a finding confirmed by Gillespie's research with South Asians in Southall (Gillespie 1995).

This example illustrates suggests the notion of a specifically Islamic leisure, forged by family members in the context of their experience of (and reaction to) wider British leisure practices. Such practices involve the appropriation of elements of British culture and their reinterpretation to conform to Islamic guidelines. Aspects of British leisure that did not fit in with Islam and were not adaptable were usually simply avoided (for example, Hasan's father had vetoed going to the cinema on religious grounds).

4.5 Conclusion

This chapter has explored family beliefs and values as translated into material practices – what could be referred to as eating, speaking, wearing, and watching family practices. Examples from just a few areas of cultural consumption have illustrated how religious beliefs and values, interwoven with cultural norms and expectations, shaped the patterns of cultural consumption in which these families engaged.

The choices made about practices of consumption marked the families' membership in South Asian and Muslim social networks, and represented the passing on of cultural traditions, ultimately serving to construct a family identity that was specifically Muslim and South Asian. Such choices also helped to denote varying levels of distinctiveness from non-Muslim, non-South Asian 'others'. Practices of cultural consumption accordingly reflected the complex positionings, inside and outside boundaries, with regards to cultural affiliation with South Asian traditions, appropriations of Britishness, and levels of religiosity. Such boundaries could be manipulated according to family affiliation and context.

Material practices relating to food, clothes and language were also sites of negotiation within families, revealing as to gender and generational divisions. In particular, there were some examples of children's agency (which will be further considered in Chapter 7).

The means by which families were able to distinguish themselves as both South Asian and Muslim through their distinctive cultural practices, tastes and knowledge, recalls sociological work on class distinctions in modern Britain as constituted through 'cultural capital'. It is also related to the wider debate centred on the idea (originated by Bourdieu, 1984), that cultural practices are markers of underlying group distinctions. Bourdieu focused on social class (which he defined as groups of individuals occupying similar positions in social space), arguing that lifestyle and consumption are symbolic of class relations. He emphasized consumption as a marker of variation and distinction rather than as a source of identity or solidarity (Longhurst and Savage, 1996). The present chapter has applied these ideas to ethnic and cultural forms of social stratification, in terms of both distinctions and identity/solidarity, and has further contributed to the debate by looking at consumption from a religious perspective – a relatively undeveloped area. The examples of cultural adaptation cited in this chapter can be situated within wider debates on cultural change. For example, the argument that there is growing 'cultural omnivorousness' in British society (see e.g. Warde, Martens et al. 1999) suggests that renegotiations and changes in these families are part of a wider pattern of transformation.

This chapter has been concerned to portray religion as a central means of shaping the texture and fabric of daily life, and has shown that for the South Asian Muslims in this study, 'doing religion' was part of 'doing family' (and vice versa). In fact, rather than material practices simply reflecting family beliefs and values, it was through material practices that family beliefs and values were understood and constituted.

5
Time and Everyday Family Practices

This chapter will examine how mothers, fathers and children described their family practices at the micro-level; that is, the detailed day-to-day routines and rituals that together make up the rhythm and texture of family life for South Asian Muslims in the UK. Like cultural consumption, time and space have been identified as 'negative spaces' which warrant more attention from family researchers (Daly 2003). Examining the 'here and now' of family life (and the attendant notions of past memory and future aspiration) for different family members allows an exploration of the way in which their practices at the level of the everyday are related to the ideological value systems they live by. The category of 'everyday life' has incidentally enjoyed something of a renaissance in contemporary social thought (Bennett and Silva 2004). Morgan (2004) suggests that the everyday consists of a number of elements, including 'talk-about-ables' – special days and life events – as well as the more mundane and ordinary 'not worth talking about' daily routines. It also captures notions of normality.[23]

The focus for this chapter derived from questions about the relationship between sacred time and family time. As Daly and Beaton (2004) comment, notions of time are useful to family theorists for a number of reasons. Time, they suggest, reflects dimensions of agency and control within family life, since the lived experience of time involves interplay between individual choices, the negotiated schedules of family members, and the organizational constraints of work, consumption and other institutions. Looking at time also allows an appreciation of multiple perspectives, priorities and experiences from within families (for example through recognition of contrasts between 'his time' and 'her time' – see Daly 1996). Finally, and most pertinently here, Daly and Beaton suggest that people's meanings and use of time reflect underlying cultural values.

Notions of time have, accordingly, begun to receive more attention from family researchers, with much work exploring family members' experiences of family time.[24] For example, Daly (1996; 2001a) has reported that parental experiences of time involve a constant discordance between their idealized goals of 'togetherness', and the reality that there is 'never enough' (see also Gillis 2001), so that family time is often viewed as a source of guilt. Annette Lareau's ethnography of American children's lives (Lareau 2000; Lareau 2004) focuses on the ways in which children, especially those from the middle classes, are experiencing increasingly overscheduled daily routines. The emerging emphasis from much of this empirical work is that of time pressure or time deficits in the modern family (Southerton 2003).

Alongside notions of family time, writers such as Eliade (1959), have highlighted the dimension of 'sacred' time and space, representing a mode of being that is distinct from 'profane' (or secular) time and space. Participation in religious activities is seen to involve stepping out of ordinary time/space and into sacred time/space. Experiences of distinctively religious time and space can be perceived as a key aspect of religious involvement.[25] In the context of Islam, sacred times may be particularly salient in everyday life because of the special demands of regular and routine prayer, and the requirement for children to spend time learning to read the Qur'an. Over a longer time perspective, too, the wider family calendar may differ for Muslim families since the Islamic calendar has its own months and sacred days. Thus Østberg (2003:141) refers to Islamic ritual as representing 'qualitatively different time and space' in children's lifeworlds.

Acknowledging the ways in which family time at the beginning of the 21st century is being increasingly problematized on the one hand, and recognizing the significance of sacred time and religious calendars for religious observance on the other, leads to the questions: how are the dual demands (or ideals) of family time and religious time negotiated and experienced by members of South Asian Muslim families? Do the expectations of religious time present just another demand on family time, or is sacred time experienced differently? Are there gender and generational differences in the experience and performance of sacred and family time?

5.1   Talking about daily routines

5.1.1   Family time

Both children and parents in this study were asked to describe their 'typical' day, from waking up until bedtime. The extent to which the resulting descriptions of domestic time echoed a 'time scarcity' discourse was striking. People, especially parents, described the characteristic 'time crunch' reported in other studies (e.g. Daly 2001b).

> It normally works out, like most households in a mad rush trying to get things together and get out... (Hasan's father)

Later, this father reflected on his feeling of being constantly busy:

> Just tend to be sort of one thing after another. The demands on time are being stretched everywhere...(...) Although unfortunately not enough time for sport or that activity range. We really do sometimes kind of miss that. Then you've got to say to yourself 'Well really you know, you're doing your best in other ways.' And obviously you know there's only so many hours in the day isn't there, at the end of the day. (Hasan's father)

Pressures were present in the morning due to the need to wake everybody up, provide breakfast and packed lunches and get the children to school, and parents to work on time. Mornings were temporal 'hot spots' (Southerton 2003) involving a great deal of family 'care' work, especially for mothers, in terms of needing to wake, dress and feed their children. The children themselves spoke of the generally stressed nature of morning time, referring to elements of struggle in waking up and arguments over being late. This 'time crunch' was, unsurprisingly, most extreme in households where one or both parents worked, and less problematic in workless households.

After school, family members arriving and leaving – especially in the larger households – contributed to a sense of chaos or even stress, which Larson (2001:92) has termed the '6 o'clock crash'. For example, Yasmin's elder sister (in one of the newly extended households) said:

> ... it is all quiet until three o'clock again and then it goes chaos again, it's mad. First my daughter comes home, five minutes later Yasmin comes home and then fifteen minutes later my [other] sister comes home from [school] and then five minutes later my brother comes home, it's all crazy (...) so they come home and everyone is screaming who wants to watch TV and what they want to watch and what they want to eat because they don't want the

same thing so you have to cook different things. (Yasmin's elder sister).

Weekends, in contrast, were temporal 'cold spots' (Southerton 2003) during which time was kept free for interaction with significant others. Parents portrayed weekends as making up for the rest of the week by allowing more time for leisure (the contrast being especially clear for working parents), with an emphasis on 'time together', including family meals and socializing as a family.

> ... I tend to be involved around the house more when, at certain times, yeah. And obviously at the weekend's a core time, yeah. And I try to sort of catch up with them as much as I can about what's happening in school, what's happening outside... (Hasan's father).

Weekend timetables were more free-flowing, meaning that children's time was generally less structured and they experienced less parental surveillance. They tended to view weekends as times of play and fun.

5.1.2   Sacred time

An extra dimension present in the interview data, which has rarely been explored in other research on family time (a notable exception being Østberg 2003), was that of sacred or religious times in the day: those times that were expressly to do with religious practices or participation. This includes prayer at home or mosque, and also, for children, attending religious education classes, often every day after school, in which they practised reciting the Qur'an in Arabic. Within the context of Islam, prayer is accorded particular importance, since one of the five Pillars of the Islamic faith is a requirement to observe five prayers a day – at dawn, noon, mid-afternoon, sunset, and night. The times of these prayers follow the movement of the sun, and therefore change seasonally as the times of sunrise and sunset change. Each prayer, or *namaz*, follows a ritual consisting of specific words and actions, and must also be performed in a specific position, since the person praying must face in the direction of Mecca. Ritual ablution or *wudu*, which consists of washing the head, arms and feet in a certain order, must be carried out before praying in order to purify the body. Prayer carpets are usually used in order to ensure that the prayer is carried out somewhere that is clean. 'How to pray' properly following these protocols is something that Muslim children are expected to learn, and is thus a central part of religious nurturance in Islam.

Sacred prayer time was in some interviews explicitly mentioned as part of the family's 'typical' day. In others it was not initially spoken about, but emerged after more detailed questioning. This difference appeared to reflect contrasting levels of religious observance and affiliation, with members of the most observant families explicitly referring to prayer while describing their daily routines.

In both contexts, the existence of sacred or prayer time, when first mentioned, was generally presented as being compulsory. I was often told simply 'we pray five times a day'. Interviewees portrayed the sacred prayer times as structuring the rest of their lives. In this, they were echoing the formal message of Islam; it might be said that they were referring to a discourse of 'what good Muslims do'. Whether or not family members actually observed these prayers strictly or leniently (an issue that will be discussed later), the prioritizing of prayer time over other domestic or external constraints was a strongly expressed value. As one father told me emphatically:

> Of course we are strict on the five daily, because this is the word of God you know (...) we got five pillars of Islam and this is the first pillar of Islam.... (Farid's father)

This father referred to the belief that prayer is the 'word of God' and must therefore be followed. Other interviewees voiced a variety of reasons for prayer, which included receiving spiritual benefits in this life or in the afterlife – in this view, prayer was an investment that would pay off at a later time. By contrast, retribution in the afterlife was a theme that appeared to resonate particularly with children:

> If you don't read them [prayers], you get something called *gunar* and that means that when it comes to Judgement Day I will go to hell for doing that. (Amir)

Mothers, in particular, claimed that they derived emotional or health benefits from this periodic 'stepping out' from the dictates of secular time pressure:[26]

> It seems complicated but it's so, you know, relaxing and peace of mind and everything, if you don't, if I don't do that, I've got habit on doing five times (...) if I don't do that, then I don't feel peace in my life... (...) I'm not on my normal behaviour sort of things, makes

me, you know, irritating and stuff. (...) I used to be getting, I was so
ill and I stopped my medications, you know, blood pressure medications. After ten years when I've started Islam, you know, doing
all my prayers and stuff and everything seems okay now. (Khalid's
mother)

As will be seen later in this chapter, there were important gender
and generational differences in the performance of sacred prayer
times.

Madrasahs, or Islamic classes, can be seen as children's sacred times,
since they are often described as being held at 'mosque' (regardless of
whether in fact this venue is an actual community mosque, or just a
house or room used to teach Islamic classes) and involve prayer and
reading the Qur'an. The majority of the children interviewed gave a
clear impression that they understood *madrasah* as in some way sacred
(referring to it as 'holy', decreed by God, or bringing spiritual reward).
This view of Islamic classes as sacred or spiritual was also conveyed in
the survey data: when asked what the 'best thing' was about going to
religious meetings or services, two-thirds of Muslim children referred to
an aspect of spiritual activity (making comments such as 'I like to say
my prayers and to remember God') , compared with only a quarter
of Christian children (who were more likely to refer to having
fun or seeing friends, with comments such as 'I get to see my friends
there' or 'I go there to play'). It is important to note, however,
that there were other feelings at play that might not be seen as 'sacred'.
For example, children commented that madrasah was 'like school';
that the time went slowly and it could be boring, and also that
one of the best things about it was being able to see your friends.
Thus, while Islamic classes have been categorized here as forming
an element of sacred time, they may have been experienced in
diverse ways by the children themselves, not all of them purely
spiritual.

5.2   The relationship between sacred and family time

5.2.1   Sacred time structuring family time

Family time was seen to be organized by sacred time in a number of
ways. Most apparent was the way in which the daily timetable was
punctuated by prayer times. Prayer was supposed to be the first activity
on waking, and the last before sleeping, and thus played an explicit
part in morning and evening routines.

This interaction was most evident in the highly religious house-holds, a number of which had a special radio in the kitchen or living room connected to a local mosque and set to play the call to prayer throughout the house at the appropriate times (it was silent for the remainder of the time). I observed this while I was interviewing Bashira. Her mother immediately stopped what she was doing, rearranged her *dupatta* (shawl) so that it covered her hair, and went into another room to pray while the children continued as before. While I was struck by this introduction into the domestic space of the external order and structure from the mosque, the entire episode was treated in a matter-of-fact way by both parent and children. It was clear that the same process occurred several times a day. In this instance sacred timings were imposed or imported from outside the family, and domestic timings were submitted without question to the demands of religious prayer time.

Especially in the most religiously observant families, this regular punctuation of family time with religious time meant that their religious affiliation remained constantly salient for family members.

> Anything we do it is always about Islam, about our religion, even when it comes to, because we have to pray five times a day so it is always like 'oh get ready', it only takes about five minutes to pray really but because it happens five times a day we have to do this and when they come back then they get ready for mosque and then we talk about it why you have to go mosque and why you have to pray, and when they come back. So there's always something going on with the religion in this house. Especially when it comes to *Ramadan* and then it is 'why this' and 'why that'. (Yasmin's elder sister).

Religious activities replaced more secular activities to varying extents – for example, extracurricular activities for children (Islamic classes meant correspondingly fewer other clubs), socializing (with members of mosque) or other leisure pursuits. This had the effect of increasing the duration of religious time, and decreasing that of family time.

> *So what is it like being in your family?*
> Don't know, I'm not normally at home.

No? Where are you normally?
I go to school in the morning and then I come home for an hour and then I go to the mosque and then after that then I go to another mosque as well. (Hasan)

His mother, talking about getting him and his siblings ready for Islamic classes, said:

Well, it's usually rushing. They want to watch telly as well because that's the time when, you know, their, their favourite programmes are on the BBC, so they want to watch that as well. So they do watch about ten, fifteen minutes of that while they're eating and then I off, I have to off the telly, they won't, and then three of them sit to pray and I have to listen to them, one by one. And then about four twenty-five they're off. (Hasan's mother)

As this quote indicates, the rhythm and structure of these children's daily lives differed from their non-Muslim classmates, since they were additionally constrained by the need to attend Islamic classes after school. They usually had only half an hour or so to relax, eat something and watch television before having to get ready (a ritual-ized process which included changing into traditional Islamic dress and performing ritual ablutions) and go to their classes. The scenario recalls the highly scheduled lives of Annette Lareau's American middle class children (Lareau 2004), whose activities had been initiated by parents, to fulfil a perceived duty to develop and educate their children (with only a limited sense of 'the child's choice').

This structuring of family time by religious time was to some extent a gendered experience, since it tended to be only men who would visit the mosque for daily prayers. In one group of families fathers often took their sons with them to pray at mosque, but were less likely to take their daughters. This gender difference echoed the wider survey, which found that 60 per cent of Muslim boys 'often' went to religious services or meetings with their father, while only 19 per cent of Muslim girls did so.[27] For the men and boys in question the necess-ity to pray at a certain time was a clearly defined event. Sacred time was more rigid and involved physically 'stepping outside' the family sphere.

How did families perceive this apparent shaping of family time by religious time? In most families sacred time was not in fact experienced as an imposition on family time. Rather, sacred activity was viewed as an integral part of domestic and family life, as much part of the routine and as important as meals. Children's 'home-work' tended to include both schoolwork and homework for religious classes. Similarly some interviewees, particularly children, would initially forget to mention prayers when first describing their typical day, in much the same way as they forgot such details as meals or cleaning their teeth (see also Østberg, 2003). The resulting impression was that they were so automatic as not to be worth mentioning. From this perspective, sacred time did not structure family time, but was embedded in its production.[28]

5.2.2 Family time determining sacred time

The relationship between family time and religious time went in both directions, since there were ways in which family time could be seen to impose on and shape religious time. As interviewees explained more about the five prayers, it almost invariably transpired that despite having at first described an ideal of praying five times daily, most people did not in practice follow the requirements strictly. That is, there was a discrepancy between ideal and actual behaviour in nearly all households. This interview quote from Rubina's eldest sister is typical:

> *You said about learning the prayer as well. Is that something that you do and the kids do at home or...?*
> Everyone does.
> *Everyone does?*
> Yeah...(...) Early in the morning, there's one just before midday. There's one after midday. One just before sunset. And one in the evening. There's five.

But a few minutes later she went on:

> ...it's supposed to be compulsory. It's supposed to be five. But because, the way I see it is in the olden days cos they had so much time on their hands, they had nothing like, you know, you had to go and work, you had to earn, that's when they used to be able to do it. Now you have to fit it into your lifestyle. Like now that I've got a small child, I can't do it all the time

on those times. So I end up missing quite a lot of it. (...) when you're at a very young age, it's very hard to get them to do it. They prefer not to do it. So it's usually just me and my mum. My dad goes to work so he can't do it. (Rubina's elder sister)

What emerged here was a notion of religious time as flexible or fluid. People gave a variety of explanations about who could acceptably miss prayers and in what circumstances. A common theme was the interaction of sacred times with other constraints imposed by secular family times. For example, interviewees said that mothers engaged in caring or domestic work were excused from praying; that it was not compulsory for children who had not reached puberty – and in any case they found it difficult to wake in time for the dawn prayer and usually lacked the facilities to pray at school; and that parents earning money for their families were excused if their workplace did not make the necessary provision. While five daily prayers was the ideal requirement, in reality religious requirements must fit in with the other demands of modern family life: that is to say, sacred times had to be negotiated in the light of domestic and external demands. Families also had an element of flexibility imposed by the seasonal variations in the times of dawn and dusk; some were less likely to observe sacred times in the summer, since the prayers were so early that they found it difficult to wake up.

The leniency over prayer times was predictably most apparent in those families considering themselves of low or moderate affiliation to Islam. In one such family, Amina explained to me that only 'religious religious religious' people needed to pray five times:

They should do it at least three times a day as they are adults. If they can't if something happened that they couldn't then that's OK. Only religious religious religious people do five times a day, other people just do it a few times a day. Especially if you have five children or something and you are a lone parent and not a religious person you at least pray one time a day. My mum does that. (Amina)

Since sacred times are negotiable within other time constraints, prayers could be treated flexibly, rather than being at set times or not taking place at all. It was possible to 'catch up' on prayers if one missed the specified time.

> If you pray on right time it is really good but if you are really busy before the second praying time you pray at any time. (Tariq's mother)

Tariq's father had to change the times of his prayers to fit in with his breaks at work. Along comparable lines, some parents and children told me it was permissible to join two prayer times:

> Sometimes we join them because it gets late, and we don't realize the time. (Ali)

To some extent, then, the degree to which sacred time was fixed or negotiable depended on the level of family religiosity – that is, the priority which families chose to give it. It was also contingent on one's position within the family in terms of age and generation. Children's sacred times were accorded a substantial degree of flexibility (though this would change as they reached maturity), highlighting the more general point that an individual's (or family's) position in terms of the flexibility or rigidity of prayer was not fixed, but rather could vary across the life course as circumstances changed. For instance, several mothers commented that their adherence to religious practice had either increased or decreased with the onset of motherhood (see Chapter 6 for further discussion of the conceptual linking of motherhood with religious duty).

The experience of sacred time was also related to gender. For women, prayer time was often more fluid and more personally dictated, in that they were more likely to pray alone at home – offering an interesting link with the concept of a gendered sacred space. The women in the participating families probably prayed more often than their husbands because they were less likely to be working and accordingly had more opportunity to do so. It is also worth noting who determined the relative priorities accorded to family and religious times. Interestingly, although it was men who were expected to engage in the public practice of religion at the mosque, women were often the ones doing behind-the-scenes 'religion work' in terms of ensuring that the children prayed and went to religious classes. In a few families it was also the mothers who prompted their husbands to visit mosque, indicating that power balances within the family might be more complex than traditionally assumed. Having said this, the role of some fathers in taking their children (especially sons) to mosque was significant in some families, reflecting wider research suggesting that paternal religiosity may be linked with increased father involvement (Dollahite 1999; Bartkowski and Xu 2000; King 2003).

It was clear, then, that sacred time did not straightforwardly structure family time as it first appeared to do from people's idealized accounts. Rather, the two were intertwined or even integrated to varying extents. Sacred time provided one important source of structure for family time, but was accorded varying levels of priority depending on family religiosity (note, however, that as explained in Chapter 2, this was not necessarily correlated with adherence to 'traditional' South Asian culture). Although interviewees spoke about the importance of compulsory prayers, sacred time was often in effect constructed as flexible in the light of other domestic demands rather than immobile in respect of religious doctrine.

5.3 Special days: longer-term time

We now move away from the everyday, to discuss sacred time in the longer-term. Sacred celebrations and holidays are important aspects of religious affiliation and observance in most religions (see e.g. Jackson and Nesbitt 1993) and Islam is no exception. Since the Islamic calendar differs from the Georgian calendar, having its own months and years, this is an important marker of difference from 'mainstream' culture for British Muslims: it offers an alternative time frame for delineating the year. The way in which family members, especially children, talked about their 'special days' was revealing as to the temporality of family practices – that is, the way in which they were imbued with time, both linear/irreversible, and cyclical/renewable (Adam 2000) – and also as to how these 'special' times helped to build family identities. This section will first consider Fridays, then the month of *Ramadan*, and follow this by an exploration of how families engaged with non-Islamic special days.

Fridays are significant in Islam, since they denote prayer day, during which special prayers take place at mosques. Indeed, Friday was widely referred to by both parents and children as a 'special day'. For most families, prayer (and especially prayer in a mosque) was more likely to be observed on a Friday, and was also seen as bringing more benefits than prayer on any other day, since to say a special prayer (the *Juma* or Friday lunchtime prayer) would bring forgiveness and protect one from

bad things happening for the remainder of the week. In some less religiously observant families Friday was the only day of the week when
members visited the mosque to pray, or even prayed at all. As one
mother commented, people were 'more religious on a Friday'. In some
families the celebration extended beyond prayer in mosque to include
a special meal or bath. Thus Fridays were used, especially by parents, to
reassert their religious affiliation and to compensate for missed prayers
during the rest of the week. However, although they understood it as
'special', a number of children remarked that for them, Friday was not
different from any other day: since the prayer took place while they
were at school, their experience of this 'special day' was less intense.

The month of *Ramadan* was more universally viewed as important.
When parents and children were asked about special days and celebrations, *Ramadan* was almost invariably the first that was mentioned.
Ramadan, or the 'holy' month, entails fasting between dawn and dusk
for thirty days, culminating in the festival of *Eid-al-fitr*, which is celebrated with food, presents and prayer. In addition to fasting, Muslims
are expected to pray, to read the Qur'an and to donate to charity.
Fasting during *Ramadan* is one of the five pillars of Islam, and emerged
from the interviews as significant in a variety of ways.

Firstly, *Ramadan* was explicitly seen as a 'special' time during which,
in addition to fasting, other aspects of religious observance were given
added importance.

> In *Ramadan* they have facility in school as well. People who don't
> pray the whole year pray in *Ramadan*. They try to pray five times.
> (Bashira's mother)

So even where people (including children) did not usually adhere to
sacred prayer times, during *Ramadan* they would make more of an
effort. Both parents and children expressed strongly positive feelings in
relation to *Ramadan*, including happiness, enjoyment and a feeling of
achievement and 'inner strength'. Even more so than Fridays, *Ramadan*
was anticipated and enjoyed as a means of reconnecting to Islam and
reaffirming one's Muslim identity.

Secondly, the month of *Ramadan* offered families the opportunity to
reconnect and reinforce links with extended kin and the wider community. As Jamila explained:

> We go to my cousin's house and all our family are there and
> we eat there and we fast and after that we just watch TV, the

children go there and the grown-ups there, then after that we eat. (Jamila)

Thus the performance of fasting was treated as a social event. The communal element was even stronger during *Eid-al-fitr*, the celebratory festival which ended *Ramadan*. *Eid* was usually the children's favourite festival and several referred to it as being 'like Christmas'. It involved visits to the mosque for men, a special meal with family and friends, the giving of presents and the wearing of new clothes. These links did not stop at the local community but were also global. At the broadest level *Ramadan* was seen as connecting people with the experiences of the poor and hungry around the world.

Thirdly, the activities carried out in *Ramadan* served to sharpen and clarify the Islamic identity of individuals by reinforcing their links with the *ummah* or worldwide community of Muslims. As Werbner has pointed out:

'the sacrificial lambs slaughtered on *eid* are consumed in parallel feasting events convened by British Muslims throughout the whole of Britain. At the very same moment, hundreds of thousands of animals are slaughtered and consumed in the valley of Mina in Saudi Arabia as the culmination of the annual pilgrimage to Mecca, and in parallel rituals throughout the Muslim world. It is on these occasions that ethnic and diasporic subjects are constituted' (1996:155).

Finally, *Ramadan* was held to be significant in the family context because it provided a barometer of the children's growing maturity. Fasting is not obligatory until children are around 13, but most were encouraged by their parents to try it, and to increase the number of days on which they fasted as they grew older (although many were not allowed to fast on school days because of the practical difficulties). Children aspired to keep as many fasts as they could manage, and often reported proudly the number they had achieved the previous year or talked about their aspirations for undertaking more next time. Parents also spoke of their children's fasts as achievements. Hasan's father's account is typical:

[They don't] start doing it till about eight or so, yeah. And even then it's almost just like a slow movement you know, one, then possibly a couple, then half a dozen and so forth right. And actually Hasan has been doing it for a few years now. That's because he wants to do it. I think he could do it all this year. (...)... it's him wanting to do it, yeah. It's the actual attitude really you know. You see your parents do it, you want to do a bit, you get into you know, what the role, you know the cycle. And they physically want to, you know, move in that direction as well, which is great you know. It helps them, it motivates, and it boosts their, you know to have achieved it. (Hasan's father)

This progression to maturity articulated through increasing fasts is an example of how cyclical sacred time (represented by the annual fasting) can also carry elements of linear time.

As noted above, parents and children, and especially the latter, sometimes drew parallels between Islamic sacred days and Christian (or British) holidays such as Sundays or Christmas. In this sense, their own family practices were being articulated in the context of 'majority' festivals. There was some evidence, however, that a number of these families were engaging with and reinterpreting non-Muslim festivals in the light of their own faith values. Birthdays, for example, are not celebrated in Islam, but – as other researchers have also found (Larson 2000; Smalley 2002; Østberg 2003) – parents often made concessions to their children's wish to copy their friends from school, holding birthday parties, giving presents and providing birthday cake. This practice was sometimes kept more closely within the bounds of traditional South Asian practice by restricting the party to include extended family members rather than friends. One child described a birthday party along these lines, as being 'a bit like *Eid*'. Similarly, some families recognized Christmas because the children celebrated it at school, but would usually take the opportunity explain why they did not celebrate it as a Muslim festival. Werbner (1996) has suggested that Christmas in the UK consists of the performance of 'nation' through gift-exchange, but that this performance excludes non-Christians (and specifically, ethnic and religious minorities), causing them to redefine themselves by their non-participation as 'internal stranger-citizens'. She suggests that they experience Christmas as 'a kind of embarrassing realization of their otherness' (Werbner 1996:153). In this study, some families would seem to have dealt with this by presenting *Eid* as an alternative Christmas equivalent, or by buying into such aspects of Christmas as allowing their children to take part in a nativity play or make Christmas cards.

5.4   Conclusions

This chapter has explored the performance of family routines and rituals, and the relationship between sacred and domestic time. It has been argued that religious time did not conflict with family time and space or vice-versa. Rather, the two were intertwined and jointly nego- tiated; produced through a pragmatic interplay between religious values and ideals (such as wanting to pray five times a day at set times) and family or social aspirations (such as wanting to have 'family time' and meals together, or meet the demands of school or work). Sacred times were important, punctuating secular life to varying extents, but were ultimately treated as flexible. It would seem, further, that sacred time and space were usually perceived as integral to domestic life rather than as an intrusion or constraint – a welcome release rather than as another ingredient of the 'time crunch'. Similarly, sacred space was fluid in its ability to permeate domestic space, especially for women. Sacred time also had particular significance in the longer term: Islamic 'special days' such as Friday, the month of *Ramadan* or the festival of *Eid,* can be seen as punctuating secular life and marking a reconnection with family, community (including the global com- munity), religion and tradition.

As suggested by Daly and Beaton (2004), an examination of time and space illuminates South Asian Muslim family practices in a number of ways. Family uses of space and time reflect the cultural values of family members, as well as their social contexts in terms of work, education and the leisure requirements of the wider culture (Daly and Beaton 2004). As this chapter has argued, religious considerations may also play an important role for contemporary South Asian Muslim families in the construction and performance of family times and spaces.

It was also noted that the experience and enactment of sacred space and time, and their relationship with family space and time, differed for men and women and for adults and children. Exploring this vari- ability in individuals' experiences of family time and space – as well as in the levels of agency at play in negotiations around them – can con- tribute to understanding the dynamics of gender and generation within families, a theme pursued further in the following chapters.

6

Parenting Roles and Relationships

This chapter and the next will examine family roles and relationships as an aspect of family practices in South Asian Muslim families in Britain. The main concern is to examine the expectations and obligations for mothers, fathers and children, and in particular to investigate how they are bound up with the wider belief and value systems discussed in Chapter 3. Data from the qualitative interviews with parents and children is used to compare the multiple perspectives of family members, highlighting the complex strands of divergence and convergence within family experience.

Accounts of family roles and relationships contain a number of inter-related elements including norms or expectations (what I believe a father 'should' do); desires or aspirations (what I wish my father would do); and perceptions of actual practice (what I believe my father actually does). Theorizing about family roles has been similarly disparate, depending on whether the focus is on personal identities (being a father), or on individual practices and their impact on other family members ('doing' fathering) (see for example Woollett and Marshall 2001, on approaches to motherhood as identity and mothering as practice). The following sections draw upon a variety of disciplinary perspectives. Following role theory (see Chatters and Taylor 2004), religious and cultural meanings are viewed as central in defining family role identities (the expected practices associated with certain statuses). The analysis also draws on recent work on identity theory (see Henley 2004) which sees identities as multiple and fluid, and as being co-constructed within the family through interactions between family members.

This chapter analyses parents' roles, exploring first the multiple narratives about mothers' roles and responsibilities, then fathers', and finally those relating to co-parenting, including power and decision-making, divisions of parental labour and divisions of religious labour. The notion of a parental duty to ensure the transmission of religious beliefs and practices is found to be central. Chapter 7 then examines the various ways in which children are perceived, including beliefs about their responsibilities and notions of their agency.

6.1　Mothers' roles

Mothers', fathers' and children's accounts all portrayed strikingly convergent representations of motherhood. Mothers' roles and responsibilities were seen to be several and varied, as is captured by Najma:

> *What should a mum do?*
> Give us food. Tell a child off... if they do something wrong. The mum should tidy up everything, and she should sometimes watch TV, cook every day, and work. Or dad work. (Najma)

As Najma's comment indicates, domestic work – cooking and cleaning – and caring work – including nurture, physical maintenance, management and daily discipline – were constructed as central aspects of motherhood. Additional themes within mothering included loving, teaching and playing, and more generally 'being there'. Mothers' work outside the home was a more ambiguous concept. The following sections explore these elements both as idealized norms and as practice.

6.1.1　Mothers and domestic work

The association of mothers with domestic work was dominant in most interviews, conveying a shared understanding that 'putting the food on the table' and doing the housework were key responsibilities for a 'good' mother. These roles were acknowledged by the mothers themselves, and attributed by other family members:

> [my husband] calls me 'queen of the house' (laughs) because he wants me to work in the house and look after the kids... (Bashira's mother)

This image reflects a wider conceptual association of women with domestic work in many societies (Morgan 1996), as well as corroborating research evidence that women still do the majority of housework in practice (see Morgan 2003). More specifically, the linking of mother-hood with domesticity is in tune with South Asian Muslim ideas about gender roles (Lau 2000). According to Najma's father, in Islam a mother:

> ... can't go outside working. Her job is house is clean, cooking, and my daughter's clothes is clean, washing, ironing, everything. (...). Wife's responsibility inside. (Najma's father)

Maternal, paternal and child accounts tended to concur in the claim that mothers in these families did the majority of the house-work and cooking. While accepting this as 'ladies' work' (as Jamila's mother put it), some mothers nevertheless described it as a burdensome duty, espe-cially when undertaken with little help from their husbands:

> ... I take the children to school, to mosque, bring back and all the time I go downstairs and upstairs and my legs get very tired. And clean the house and the cooking, everything I do, then go to do the shopping and bring the shopping home. It's a lot of work. Sometimes go to bank, builders coming. Everything I do. (Jamila's mother)

Some first-generation mothers, such as Mehmood's, considered life to be harder for women in the UK than in Pakistan, since in Pakistan they might have servants to help and would themselves do just a 'bit of cooking and that's it... here they have to do everything'. Mehmood's mother also pointed out that when mothers worked outside the home as well, the demands of domestic work would be particularly heavy: indeed, those mothers who were working corroborated this claim. Adam's mother provided a relevant example, having to pay a high price for her domestic duties. Her husband admitted that 'she has it a bit tougher than me' and as a result she no longer had time to pray as often as she wanted to.

> Before, when I was single, I prayed five times a day, and holy Qur'an as well, at the moment it's too much for me. If I have spare time then I read, then I pray at night, not five times though because days go very quickly. (Adam's mother)

Children had strongly-held perceptions of mothers as being asso-ciated with domestic work. Nearly all of them immediately mentioned cooking and cleaning when asked 'what mothers do'. As Yasmin said:

> She cares a lot about us. She cooks and washes up and washes our clothes and cleans the house and everything. (Yasmin)

Ahmed, in turn, made an explicit connection between mothers' domestic tasks and wider aspects of gender difference, indicating that he understood his own gender identity in the light of his parents' practices. When asked what a mother should do in a family, he replied:

> I don't know, cos I ain't a girl... maybe clean around the house, do all the work around the house and maybe take the children out somewhere while the dad's just sit home or something, do some stuff, I don't really know what else. (Ahmed)

6.1.2 Caring mothers

In addition to their widely recognized commitment to domestic work, there was a universal view in every family in the study that mothers were responsible for nurturing and caring, a claim also found in the academic literature (Arendell 2000).

> The mother is the one that actually nurtures them more than I do; I can only be there on the peripheries as it were, yeah. Only be there at certain times, yeah. But the core work is done by her. (Hasan's father)

Again, this division of labour is confirmed in other research in both the UK and North America (Coltrane 2004). In the families participating in this study, mothers and children formed 'relationships of care' (Gordon, Benner et al. 1996, cited in Arendell 2000) that were exemplified in a number of maternal practices, including physical maintenance, management, surveillance and discipline.

Physical maintenance included the provision of food, clothes and hygiene, all of which were perceived to be maternal responsibilities (in contrast to fathers' responsibilities 'outside', discussed later in this chapter).

> ... she will take responsibility of the child that he is properly nourished and properly fully clothed and things like that (Farid's father)

For the majority of mothers (particularly those who did not work), such activities were a major focus of their everyday lives:

> ... *what's the most important part of being a mother?*
> Well caring for them, caring for them, because most of my time is spent caring for them, when they're not at home I'll be cleaning a room or something or ironing their clothes... (Zabar's mother)

In most families, mothers also took on what could be described as a 'management role' in the care of their children. They were usually the planners and the 'sorters', as Aisha's mother explained:

> ... the girls know that when there's something to organize, when there's something to sort out, they'll come to me, they won't go to their dad, mum will sort it and what will happen, what we need to do, even things like trips, it's 'mum we are doing this or doing that', 'we have got parents' evening, can you make it'. (Aisha's mother)

Several children also acknowledged this facet of their mother's activities, and mentioned the part their mother played in scheduling their days – waking them up, getting them to school on time, picking them up, and sending them to bed.

> [A mother should] make sure everyone's awake in the morning. Make sure they've gone to school on time... (Adam)

This management role was also constructed as mothers' main area of power and authority in the family. A number of children remarked that it was their mother who made most decisions about their food, clothes or bedtime.

A further aspect of the mothers' caring work comprised monitoring their children. Zabar's mother saw this as an important part of her obligations.

> ... you have to take notice, I do take notice of my children, what they're doing at school, what club they're going to, who's come round, what friend they're sitting with, who's house they've gone to, what they're doing there, even when they go to my mum's I'm always worrying about who they're going out with... (Zabar's mother)

This constant surveillance was seen as symbolic of a mother's care and concern. Similarly, mothers emphasized daily discipline and rule-setting as part of their caring activities – an aspect of the mother-child relationship that was also mentioned by children:

> *What do you think a mother should do in the family?*
> If [the children] are doing something bad tell them off or if they ruin something or somebody tell them off or if they don't listen tell them off... Try and make them clean stuff. (Khalid)

There was also a gendered division of parenting in the exercise of discipline, in that mothers were primarily involved in day-to-day discipline while fathers tended to be brought in for more 'serious' matters. This pattern has been found in other studies of UK families (e.g. Valentine 1997), and is explored in more detail later in this chapter.

6.1.3   Mothers 'being there'

Many mothers (and especially those who did not work) drew on a discourse of 'being there' for their children, reflecting the more general image in modern North America and Europe of 'good mothers' as 'always there' (Walzer 2004). For example, Amina's mother referred to herself as 'the rock', and commented that being there was the most important part of her mothering role, whereas for working mothers such as Aisha's, the realization that she was there less than 'other mothers around here' was a constant source of guilt. This discourse relates to the construct of availability discussed by researchers as an aspect of parental involvement (Lamb, Pleck et al. 1987). As Tariq's mother said, 'your children needs you, if something is wrong they need mum'. Farid's mother linked this with Muslim tradition.

> In our religion, the mother is always there. (Farid's mother)

Such constant presence was an expected sacrifice for mothers.

> ... the mother has to sacrifice lots of things. I think she should. Otherwise you can't bring up your children properly. If you ignore your children when they grow up they will ignore you. Really. They will ignore you. (...) I don't do anything. Normally I try to finish my work while they're at school or at the mosque. When they

come I have to focus on their needs. I join with them, that's it. I join with them, I do everything, and sometimes they help me as well. (Mehmood's mother)

Most children in this study spent more time with their mothers than with their fathers. Mothers as 'always there' were sometimes placed in contrast to fathers, whose other duties meant that they were often not able to be present.

6.1.4   Loving mothers

When it came to emotional work (Arendell 2000), mothers and children were more likely than fathers to mention the affective aspects of mothering, and particularly the image of mothers as gentle and loving. This aspect of their role was explicitly linked with religion by some mothers, such as Tariq's, who when talking about the guidance given by Islam, said:

how you bring up your children it is really important. You have to be gentle with them, do your duty as a mother. (Tariq's mother)

Similarly, Khalid's mother remarked that Islam called upon mothers to 'be kind to your children, teach them gently'. Children (and particularly daughters) presented similar views on being able to rely on their mothers for help and protection.

What should a mum be like in a family?
Very protective, she should.... help people, (...) if someone says something to you she will stick up for you and she'd sort it out
What does it mean to be protective?
Like if you have hurt yourself they will help you, and if something is harmful they would say like 'come here'. (Aisha)

Beyond this, motherhood was seen as both a source of personal fulfilment and a key aspect of personal identity. Najma's mother commented that 'my whole life revolves around my daughter', while Habiba's mother asked:

If you don't have children, what kind of life can you have? (Habiba's mother)

Zabar's mother, too, argued that there was no 'worst thing' about being a mother, since having someone to care about gave her life meaning:

> ... you've got something to do, you've got somebody to care about, somebody to think about, and I don't know really I don't think there's any ... reason or meaning of life 'cos I think you need... like you need somebody to care for and you need somebody to care for you. (...) as I'm a mother I wouldn't change it for anything, so I think it's quite nice, there's no regrets... (Zabar's mother)

One of the main ways in which the ideal of loving and protective mothering was expressed was through the open sharing of feelings. A number of mothers mentioned this as desirable – for example, Aisha's mother said 'I want to have a relationship with my girls where they can come and speak to me about anything', while Hasan's mother described how her children would share confidences with her in a way they would not with her husband:

> ... what's happened in school, which teacher told them what, which friend they have spoken to, all three of them come and tell me. So sometimes my husband tells as well that they are, 'they're your reporter'. Because even for two hours if my son would go with my husband outside, he would tell me everything, 'Dad spoke to me about this, we went there, we, we met this person, we did this' everything. But if they are with me, they won't come home and tell their dad. (Hasan's mother)

However, this openness was not typical practice in every family. Yasmin's elder sister said of their mother, 'she is more like the cook and clean up, to actually give advice or be there for you, she is not really like that kind of person'. Similarly Jamila said of her mother 'I don't talk to her that much because she is cleaning the rooms of the house', while Zabar also implied some discontent when he pointedly said:

> [Mothers should] help children at home, help them, don't concentrate on other things like the phone and people out there, looking out the window or at the TV, concentrate on them. (Zabar)

Furthermore, depending on the context, talking and sharing was not always desirable. Amir and Ahmed's mother remarked on how she was 'always there to talk about things', but when her eldest son had wanted to discuss relationships with girls she had had to arrange for his father to speak to him because it was 'culturally inappropriate' for her.

Perhaps surprisingly, the negative aspects of emotional work were not often mentioned by mothers or children. There were some descriptions of mother-child conflict (particularly between Zabar and his mother):

> ... sometimes we are angry with each other because she's all the time telling me off and I be very angry with her, and my dad said 'if you are angry our God won't be very happy, you mustn't be angry with your mum, your dad will hit you', that is my last warning and if I do it one more time I will get punished a lot. (Zabar)

Zabar's father's reported comment highlights the fact that child-parent conflict did not sit easily with Islamic representations of family relationships (as characterized by respect and kindness), which is possibly why such conflict was not much discussed. When mothers expressed frustration, it tended to be prompted by excessive domestic work. Some children similarly perceived too much housework as impeding their 'fun' relationships with their mothers:

> [she should] play with us but she doesn't get time to do that, because she is too busy cooking and washing the dishes... (Bashira)

6.1.5 'The child's first teacher'

Although mothers' duties concerning domesticity, caring and loving were sometimes explicitly linked with Islam, it was in connection with teaching that religious responsibilities were most strongly affirmed. Farid's father explained how, in Islam, the mother was seen as 'the child's first teacher':

> She will have to look after the children, teach her the way, the first steps of Islam (...) she would teach him like stories, simple stories (...) So this is the first school, before he goes outside and wandering around you know, and goes to nursery, this is the first school he starts from here. So that's the mother's responsibility sort of thing. (Farid's father)

He went on to say that children should learn from their mother how to pray and follow Islam:

> ... they should take all the sort of, all the advices and lessons from the mum, you know. Because after all, she is more at home with the

children than the male figure. (...) They should stick with her; they should listen more to her whatever she says in the house (...), the mum would show them how to pray and things like that. (Farid's father)

Mothers in these families were often the ones who told religious stories, taught children how to pray and to perform ritual ablutions, and helped with their Islamic school homework. Accordingly, they played a strong part in their children's day-to-day religious nurture, as Hasan's father recognized:

... she's there a lot more in the evening than I am. So definitely her prayers and her motivation and her outlook will, is fundamental you know. (...) before they go to the [*madrasah*] in the afternoon, late afternoon, normally the actual, you know making sure that they know, have done their exercises as it were, have done their homework... (Hasan's father)

The emphasis on the mother's role in teaching religious practices was symbolic of a wider value, that of religious transmission as a central parenting 'project' for both mothers and fathers. It was common for mothers to describe the explicit passing on of religion as one of their most important responsibilities:

... the parents have to teach them, in mosque they learn it but it's not as much as you teach them at home, but with us our parents taught us everything (...). I think parents have got a big responsibility, I think whatever religion you are to teach your children the religion, the values and to respect it. (Zabar's mother)

The notion of religious transmission was something that children themselves also understood.

Do you learn those things at mosque or from your mum and dad or someone else?
From my mum and dad, because they told me, my dad know a lot from his dad and his dad learns from his dad, that's my dad, his dad, over there. His dad learned it from his dad. (Zabar)

In this sense, religion could be seen as being constructed in families through relational practices (Finch and Mason 2000). We will return to this theme later in this chapter, when the role of fathers as religious 'coaches' is discussed.

Linked to this was the idea that Islam assigns to mothers the responsibility to teach their children good behaviour (as derived from the Islamic moral code) or as Tariq's mother put it, to 'teach them good ways'. Khalid's mother, too, described her responsibility to

> ... teach them to be honest, truthful, respectful to other religions and be kind to other persons and stuff. Yeah. And if you teach them they will never go wrong, they will respect everybody. (Khalid's mother)

Although this was sometimes seen as a joint responsibility, Farid's father presented the mother as the main proponent of moral education.

> Respect the elders in the family and things like that. (...) Don't raise your voice when you speak to your parents and things like that, all those things like that. So that's mother's steps, she would take that side of things you know. (Farid's father)

Motherhood was seen as bringing renewed religious connection for women. Several mothers commented that they had become more religiously observant since having children.

> [before being a mother] I used to skip [prayers] and you know, that's a big sin in Islam because first pillar of Islam is praying, five time prayers is first pillar of Islam. So, I started thinking, 'if I'm doing that wrong and my, what I'm, what kind of mum am I to my children?' (Khalid's mother)

The sacred importance accorded to the mother-child relationship in Islam was also frequently mentioned:

> We say that the heaven is in, under mum's foot. So a mother is very special to the children, that's why. So if they're very close to me and if they listen to me a lot and that's why, in our religion we say that he's got the heaven, that's why. Because a mother has to go through a lot of hardships, not their dad, that's why. So before, in Islam, it's the mother then it's the father. That's how a mother is very important for the child. (Hasan's mother)

The expression, 'heaven is under your mother's foot' was one I heard across a number of interviews. A similar expression was that 'your mother holds the key of heaven':[29]

> There's more respect for a mum as well. And I don't know how I can put this, but there's a word in the Qur'an that says (...), that means the mum is holding the key of the heaven for you. If you follow your mum's step and if you listen to your mum respectfully and respect her, she will take you to the heaven. So this is what Islam says about mum... (Farid's father)

6.1.6   Mothers taking on fathers' roles

There were certain ways in which, particularly from the children's perspective, mothers could legitimately 'take on' paternal roles. This possibility was most commonly discussed in the context of the father's absence, when mothers were seen to acquire paternal roles by default.

> *So who do you think is the boss in this house?*
> My dad, because he is the man of the house. Mostly my mum is because my dad is not here, so she is like the man in the house cos no-one else is here. (Amir)

Since Amir's father worked long hours and night shifts, he saw his mother as being 'like the man' in taking on decision-making responsibilities while his father was away. Similarly, Munir (whose parents were separated according to his mother, although Munir told me his father was 'just on holiday'), said that his mother would 'take over' his father's responsibilities in his absence.

> Like the father is taking all the responsibilities and suppose he goes on a holiday and the responsibilities are free and my mum takes over. (Munir)

Mothers' working was another activity which was seen as an example of women 'helping out' men, rather than as a task for women in itself. Particularly in families closely affiliated to South Asian cultural practices, paid work was legitimized as a temporary and pragmatic solution to financial problems.

> Although Islam doesn't forbid you from working independent, is the father's or the master of the house decides whether my wife is to

go to work or not (...) Sometimes she would help herself, help him sort of temporary until you know everything's settled down. So in that way, the burden is a bit less on the father. (Farid's father)

6.1.7   Good mothering

The model of good mothering constructed by family members in this sample closely resembles the ideology of 'intensive mothering' that has been identified as prevalent as a normative standard in North America (Arendell 2000). Motherhood was ideally exclusive, child-centred, involving, and time-consuming. Being a mother gave one's life meaning and purpose. Mothering practices were multifaceted, but with a strong emphasis on domesticity, allocating to mothers the principal responsibility for childcare and work within the home. The affective aspects of mothering, including loving, talking and supporting, were also regarded as central, while other roles, such as work and leisure, were peripheral. The mother-child relationship was furthermore imbued with sacred significance. Religious duty was seen to pervade all mothering activities, but especially in the role of a child's first teacher. Thus perhaps contrary to expectations (since stereotypes may be that only fathers are engaged in religious parenting practices), Muslim mothers in this study were constructed as having an important and active religious role.

6.2   Fathers' roles

Mothers' roles overlapped and contrasted in a number of ways with the responsibilities of fatherhood. The ways in which fathers, mothers and children talked about fathering give rise to a range of themes, from traditional notions of breadwinning and authority, to 'softer' practices of fun, loving, caregiving and 'being there'. The corresponding practices reflect several of the aspects of father involvement identified by other researchers (e.g. Lamb, Pleck et al. 1987; Pleck and Stueve 2001; Townsend 2003; Parke 2004), including responsibility, availability/accessibility and engagement/interaction.

   As the following sections show, the fathers in this study were involved with their children across a range of domains. Achievement-oriented activities (Parke 2004) and fun were particularly important; physical nurturance and caregiving less so in many families. Religiously prescribed fathering duties – especially concerning religious transmission – were also of significance. In addition, some interesting contrasts arose from the comparison of multiple perspectives within families, where fathers' perceptions of their roles did not always accord with mothers' and children's accounts.

6.2.1   The breadwinning father

The idea of material provision as a key fathering responsibility was recurrent during interviews. The father's obligation (to work outside the home) was seen as contrasting with, and complementary to, the mother's (to work inside the home). This ideology of the father as breadwinner echoes wider research highlighting 'the continuing importance of 'the provider' role' for fathers (Morgan 2003:382), and is in line with other studies of 'traditional' South Asian Muslim representations of fatherhood (Husain and O'Brien 1999; Lau 2000). This theme was raised by all fathers, but was particularly stressed by fathers from families high in South Asian cultural affiliation, and first-generation fathers such as Najma's:

> Husband and father is a responsibility. Husband's job is go outside, work, if your wife needs anything, clothes, food, anything, you provide because your wife is home. Wife's responsibility inside. My responsibility is outside. (Najma's father)

However, even second-generation fathers, and families in which mothers worked, held the view that fathers were more responsible for managing money.

> I just generally tend to pay the bills, look after the money, that's about it really. (…) I think I'm better at handling money than she is, so... and the kids look at me if they want to buy stuff... (Adam's father)

Their father's breadwinning role was also raised by many children. In response to the question 'what should a father do?' Amir's and Mehmood's answers were typical:

> ... make money, that's it really (Amir)
> Um, work. Work, sleep, um, that's all. (Mehmood)

In general this issue was raised in the initial discussion of what fathers 'should' do, but was subsequently related to accounts of what happened in children's own families.

6.2.2　Father as 'head of household': power and authority

Parallel to the notion of the father as breadwinner, was a narrative that accorded him the most power and authority as the 'master' or 'man of the house'. Like the breadwinning father, this theme closely relates to traditional religious and cultural notions of family hierarchy and patriarchy (again see Husain and O'Brien, 1999; Lau, 2000). Farid's father illustrated the point:

> ... when you start a family, the master of the family, as I say, would be the father, decider, the decider would be the father. Father would decide for the children, for the woman in the house, the living of the house, all sort of things you know. Father's responsibility to look after the children. (...) the core responsibility is the father's responsibility. I mean the sickness, the medicines, things like this, is the father's responsibility. Until the children are grown and got married. (Farid's father)

Farid's mother, like many other mothers, made a similar comment in her interview. In common with several mothers and fathers, she went on to link this model of fathering to Islamic teachings, thus invoking religion as a rationale.

The above quote supports the idea that ultimate responsibility for the family's general wellbeing rested on the father. It was also linked to the belief that he had ultimate authority for making family decisions. Hasan's mother gave an example of how this worked, when discussing the differences between her own and her husband's roles. She was required to ask his permission to do things with the children, but he was not obliged to ask hers:

> It is different because ... if I do something by myself, he wouldn't like it so it's like I have to ask him everything I do. But I think for husbands it's, they don't need, they think that they don't need to ask a wife.
> *Can you give me an example of the sort of thing you mean ...?*
> (Pause) Can't think of any. (Pause) Ok, if I, I did want to take them to the cinema and one day we were quite bored at home and they said that 'All my friends go and we want to go to watch as well.' I asked my husband 'Can I take them?' and we were going out for a walk, I was going and we phoned from outside, to ask him that 'Can we go to watch a movie?' he said 'No, you can't' so, well I have to ask him everything. And, but if he wants to take them

to see my in-laws, he thinks he doesn't have to ask me. (Hasan's mother)

A third aspect of fathers' power and authority was their perceived role in disciplining children. Several mothers, including Zabar's, confirmed that they would leave discipline to their husbands because the children were more likely to obey them:

> ... [Zabar] doesn't listen to me, he ends up being rude to me and fighting so then I let my husband deal with him. My husband's okay: he won't hit him, he'll just tell him off, he'll sit him down and talk to him and make him understand. (Zabar's mother)

Even where mothers were in charge of day-to-day discipline, there was a residual sense that fathers should deal with the more serious breaches.

> ... my wife generally takes care of discipline, day to day discipline. Obviously there are some aspects of his behaviour or whatever, or his, you know, non-behaviour, yeah, then she'll come to me, and I'll see if I can bring it up with him further and ask him the right questions and see what's happened, yeah. If it needs a bit more of a man, you know, I'll be there. (Hasan's father)

Hasan's father's belief that serious discipline 'needs a bit more of a man' reflects how strongly fathering models were influenced by culturally-informed assumptions about gender.

The idea that fathers had the most power within the household was aligned with the corresponding demands of responsibility, disciplinary duties and authority in decisions, and was also a strong theme in children's representations of their fathers. Both the twins Ahmed and Amir remarked independently that a father's job was to be 'the man of the house'. According to Ahmed this meant that as a father 'you can do anything you want'. Aisha likewise described a father as 'the head of the family':

What should dads be like?
They should be the head of the family and they should look after everyone and they should make sure everyone is happy, and

if anything's out, tell him, and he will look after it and stuff. (Aisha)

At this point Aisha was referring to the theme of paternal responsibility. Munir similarly said of his father, even though he was not currently living at home, 'he has to look after everybody'. Other children also described their fathers as taking a central role in family decisions. As Aisha said, 'my dad would be like the boss of what's going to happen, the rules and stuff'. Fathers were also portrayed as the major dispensers of discipline – 'he tells us not to do stuff' as Rubina expressed it.

Various reasons were given for the father's authority position. Ali and Bashira both maintained that it was because he was the oldest or 'biggest', whereas Najma suggested that it was a matter of ownership, because 'he got the key of this house'. Farid, however, linked it to the fact that 'my dad goes out and knows lots better, and my mum is at home', illustrating the connectedness of paternal authority with bread-winning and a presence outside the home. Whatever the reason, children were very unlikely to report that they disagreed or argued with their fathers.

The perception of a father's authority was just as predominant, or even slightly more so, in families in which the father was a first-generation immigrant. This suggests a closer affiliation with South Asian cultural practices among the families in question (see Chapter 2), but contradicts the claims of some researchers (see Pels' 2000 study of Moroccan fathers in the Netherlands) that where the father lacks language skills or familiarity with a country the traditional role hierarchy could be reversed. For the families in this study the traditional role hierarchy was still a strongly-held value. This representation of fathers could be seen to reflect a patriarchal model in that it entails 'the dual domination of children and women' (McKee and O'Brien 1982:21); however, as will be seen in the following sections, patriarchal notions were tempered with other, markedly less patriarchal themes such as care and involvement.

The themes relating to breadwinning and paternal authority could be seen as a culturally and religiously informed version of the responsibility element of fatherhood that has been identified by researchers such as Lamb et al. (1987), while the requirement for making significant (rather than small day-to-day) decisions could be seen as representing a managerial role (see Parke 2004). The models of fathering held by fathers, mothers and children were not, however, limited to responsibility but were combined with other themes. Some fathers in particular held more active notions incorporating the provision of care and involvement. These are explored in the following sections.

6.2.3 Fathers as coaches

A father's role in what Parke (2004) has called 'achievement-oriented' activities was a key theme in the interviews. The idea that a father had a role in motivating and encouraging his children's success – religiously, morally and academically – was salient in most fathers' representations. Ali's and Hasan's fathers both believed that a father was more important than a mother in this respect. The practices of coaching and encouragement on the part of fathers can be viewed as particular types of paternal engagement (Lamb et al. 1987).

Fathers' responsibilities as 'religious coaches' were seen as central, reflecting the importance accorded to the generational transmission of religion. Although mothers were often the parents who taught day-to-day prayer and helped with Qur'an reading, fathers also presented themselves as having a distinctive and important role in reinforcing their children's religious upbringing.

> [reminding his son to pray] If I'm around, then obviously my presence is there, then I can reinforce it. Then if I'm not around, then obviously you know my wife may not be, shall we say, not undisciplined, but maybe not sort of put it as regularly, as I may do if I'm around, yeah. **She might not reinforce it as much as I do, yeah. That's the difference between being mother and being the father of a household right, from a religious level.** Just making sure that he knows that he needs to do, not forcibly, but remind him to do things that he should be. (Hasan's father – emphasis added)

Hasan's father went on to talk more generally about how important this transmission was:

> *... is it important to you that your children are growing up Muslim?*
> Definitely it's important, yeah. It's very important. That's something that we believe is the means by which their conduct in this life will have an effect on their life hereafter. So you know for us to actually show them that direction, that guidance is a means by which they themselves will have salvation

in the future, yeah, so if that, that's how important it is, yeah.
(Hasan's father)

Farid's father similarly remarked upon how he would constantly
remind his children when it was time to pray.

Fathers, then, took their part in religious transmission by encouraging their children to pray and observe other religious practices (such as
fasting). Additional strategies included teaching about religion, which
according to Zabar's mother was her husband's domain. Some fathers
placed a further emphasis on modelling:

> ... him seeing me going to the mosque every evening, he knows
> I'm doing this, so that's sort of underpinning him actually yeah.
> So by me sort of doing it, you know, obviously I go out in the
> morning while they're still asleep, but hopefully before they leave
> for school you know they see me praying or reading the Qur'an or
> something, that will remind them in the future that 'My dad used
> to do it.' yeah. (...) that will maybe hopefully remind him that this
> is something he should be undertaking as well. (Hasan's father)

The wider understanding that a father acts as a role model for his children
(Daly 1993) was here being applied in a specifically religious context.

As noted in Chapter 3, religion was seen as central in providing a moral
code for behaviour. Accordingly, another aspect of paternal responsibility
for religious transmission, alongside that of mothers, was the moral
upbringing of the children – 'to teach them how to be a good person', as
Ali's father put it. Farid's father spoke of the importance of being heard
'as a father' when he showed his children how to 'carry on' traditional
cultural and religious practices such as showing respect.

> So I really want my family to, you know, to look at as me, you know,
> to hear me as a father. And just to become, just to show them how a
> simple life you can still carry on, in the modern way you can still carry
> on with a simple life. (...) You talk with your family, you talk with
> your mother with respect, you talk with your father with respect.
> (Farid's father)

The representation of fathers as moral coaches was also acknowledged
by mothers.

> ... he teaches my children like my daughter and son, they know that if
> they want anything they mustn't steal anything from anybody at

school and not to borrow from school, he says 'tell me, and when I have the money I can get it for you'. And not to do bad things to people... (Tariq's mother)

Tariq's mother went on to add 'and I agree with him', signalling her support for her husband's commitment to this activity.

Fathers as coaches were also closely involved in promoting their children's academic and career success – a goal that was mentioned by virtually all the fathers in the study. To Adam's father it seemed crucial element in his fathering identity, in that he raised it repeatedly throughout his interview:

What do you think is the most important part of being a father?
The most important part is .... making sure he's successful, and I'd die happy if I can get that he's (....), don't end up on the dole or something, as long as he's trying to make himself successful, whatever field he chooses ... like all of them, yeah I'd be happy with that. (...) I believe that my religion teaches me to get... make sure I have a good education and that I work for a living and that's what I try and stress to him... (Adam's father)

As this comment implies, the emphasis on educational success was perceived by some fathers as part of their religiously-defined fathering duty. It was also strongly linked with aspirations for social mobility, as discussed in Chapter 3. Indeed, a recent research review indicated that South Asian fathers may be more likely than mothers to take responsibility for home-school communication within families. The same study suggested that fathers' involvement in their children's learning can have substantial positive impacts, which may partly explain high educational attainment in some groups of South Asian children (Goldman 2005).

6.2.4 Fathers 'being there'

For one group of fathers in the interview sample, availability or 'being there' was an important aspect of their fathering (it is possible that the fathers who did not agree to be interviewed may have differed in this respect), reflecting the findings of academic research and the subject matter of public debate (Hobson and Morgan 2002). Hasan's father emphasized the need for involvement and availability in his description of his role.

What do you sort of see as your role, being their father?
I mean sort of presence, yeah, direction, just you know making sure that I'm involved really, yeah. (...) I don't, I just don't leave

everything to my wife, you know, leave her to get on with it. I'm there. And I think it's important for them to see me there as well. You know the father sort of like role is important to the hub, yeah. (...) I'm sure they appreciate that, you know, it makes a difference. (...) my father was there. It's important for me to be there. For them too as well, at the same time. It's that presence. If you aren't around, you wouldn't be able to have an impact, yeah..(...) So you know it's, I'll hope it's, looking back I hope I was a hands-on sort of parenting, fatherhood sort of role, yeah. (Hasan's father)

Hasan's father demonstrated his 'hands-on' fathering approach by his presence and by attending 'special events' and 'taking an interest' his children's friends, school and Islamic classes. Hasan himself was conscious of his father's availability:

Who do you reckon you spend most time with in your family?
My dad. He takes me to school and he takes me to the mosque as well and on the weekends he plays with us. (Hasan)

The importance to these fathers of 'being there' was evident in the efforts they made to fit family time into their demanding working lives. Tariq's mother told me how his father, despite working long hours and overnight shifts, made sure that he phoned home 'to see what they're doing', and booked his time off work to coincide with school holidays so they could 'be all together'.

However, while most interviewed fathers commented on the importance of their presence, their children were more inclined to complain about their fathers' absence. This was a prevalent theme in the accounts of children with working fathers as well as for children whose fathers were not living with them. Some children claimed that they did 'nothing' with their father because of his work.

What sort of stuff do you do with your dad?
He just really works so I don't really do anything... (Rubina)

This was a common perception among children whose fathers worked shifts. Amir complained: 'I've only been to the park with him once. Because he goes in the night mostly, so I don't see him'. Where fathers were engaged in fulfilling their 'traditional' role as breadwinner, their children tended to interpret this negatively, in terms of paternal absence, and a number said they wished their father worked less.

6.2.5 Caregiving fathers

The idea of the caregiving father, taking a share in domestic work and childcare (what Palkovitz 1997, has referred to as child maintenance), was important in some families. The relative input of fathers into caregiving work appeared to depend to some extent on family circumstances. For example, Adam's parents both worked, which was the apparent reason for Adam's father sharing some of the childcare (taking children to school, cooking, cleaning). Najma's father did the majority of the cooking, an arrangement which had seemingly begun when his wife had a long-term illness, and continued because he was a good cook. Bashira's mother said that when her husband was home from work he would help her in various ways:

> When he's around he can look after them and he will read them a story and, you know, he takes over my jobs when he is here. (Bashira's mother)

It was clear, however, that in the majority of these families such work was still mainly the mother's responsibility. Fathers were more likely to be seen as 'helping' than as taking over the caring role (see Coltrane 2004), and indeed Habiba referred to her father as 'helping mum' rather than as seeing any of these tasks as his.

In most cases, then, fathers adopted certain specific caring tasks: most commonly maintaining discipline (discussed above), and helping with transportation (usually by taking children to school or mosque). Children often viewed the latter role as integral to fathering: for example Rubina said, 'mostly what my dad does, he fetches people', while Khalid gave a similar account of a father's tasks:

> Go to a job and do work... come back and tell the children off if they are bad.... and drive a car. You can drop people off. (Khalid)

Fathers might also be allocated certain types of housework. Hasan's father, for instance, described himself as being in charge of 'sort of manual sort of DIY work', while his wife took care of internal housework. These models of father involvement in caregiving appear to be closely allied to Dowd's description of 'men fathering as a secondary parent' (Dowd 2000, cited in Morgan 2003:381).

However, the mothers in the sample – with the exception of Bashira's mother (quoted above) – did not mention these aspects of father involvement in caregiving. Rather, they tended to tell a somewhat different story, recounting a lack of significant involvement in caregiving on the part of their husbands reminiscent of Dowd's category of 'fathers who are limited or disengaged nurturers' (2000:4 cited in Morgan 2003:381). As Aisha's mother remarked, 'he pretty much leaves me to it'. Similarly, Zabar's mother felt she did 'everything at home'.

> *Would you see that you've got a particular role with the children that's similar or different from their father's role?*
> Totally different.
> *So how is it different?*
> Cos ... he comes home, he doesn't do anything, on a weekend sometimes if he (...) then he'll bath them... straighten their hair or something ... he takes them out, but it's nothing like in the house that he'd do with them as much as like reading or something, helping them with their work, take them to school, bring them back, take them to mosque, I do all that, I do... at weekends he'll tend to (...) take them to the park (...) But everything at home I'll do for them. (Zabar's mother)

In some families, this lack of paternal involvement was discussed in religious terms. For instance, Jamila's mother described how, to her dissatisfaction, her husband made recourse to Islam to justify his lack of involvement in work at home:

> ... in the mornings he goes to work and in the evenings he comes 7 o'clock, eats his dinner and goes to bed... (...) I take them to school, home, make the dinner, eat, everything I'll do it. My husband says 'Islam say like that, the mother looks after everything', I say 'no, should be both together'. He says 'I don't have time'. (Jamila's mother)

Other mothers, such as Hasan's, drew upon the idea that 'men can't do both' to argue that their husbands were lacking in the skills or knowledge for daily childcare.

> We think that husband brings the money and he's the breadwinner of the ... family but I think women can do both but men can't do both. Men can't bring children up like how a mother can, so being a dad and being a mum is quite different. (...) Like my husband, he

doesn't know what kind of things they like to eat, what their habits are, nothing. (Hasan's mother)

Hasan's mother may have been acting as a gatekeeper to limit her husband's involvement, highlighting the importance of mothers' influence in mediating father-child relationships (Allen and Hawkins 1999; Parke 2004). In most cases, however, mothers came across as dissatisfied with their husband's level of involvement with caring 'work', in contrast with the fathers' self-presentations. Other studies have similarly found fathers' reports of their own involvement to be more favourable than mothers' (see e.g. Coley and Morris 2002).

6.2.6 Fun fathers

Fathers as sources of fun comprised an aspect of paternal engagement that was salient in both children's and mothers' accounts. A significant number of children, when asked 'what do you do with your dad?' gave answers along the lines of 'mess around', 'play' or 'joke around'. Fathers were frequent partners in computer games, sports and trips to the park. This supported findings from the wider survey, that children were likely to play sport or games more often with their fathers (50 per cent) than with their mothers (36 per cent). In the survey, boys were more likely than girls to play sport or games often with their father (60 per cent compared with 40 per cent). These findings accord with the conclusions of other research on fathers (e.g. Parke 1996; Parke 2004). In the interview study, boys were more likely than girls to mention playing sport with their fathers, but father-child 'horseplay' seemed to occur with both boys and girls, as Najma's account demonstrates:

What sort of things do you usually do with your dad?
My dad? Um, errr... we go out together, and sometimes we play together.
What sort of play?
Like my dad pretends to fight me. (Najma)

In contrast, not many children in the interview study referred to 'fun' activities with mothers: those who did often cited less energetic pursuits such as crafts, board games or story telling.

As Frosh and colleagues also found in their study of boys' lives (Frosh, Phoenix et al. 2002), the idea of a 'fun' and laid-back father-child relationship was sometimes contrasted with the more serious or practical relationship children had with their mothers.

> My dad always jokes around with us and everything. My mum takes it seriously. (Hasan)

Mothers talked about the 'fun' aspects of fathering in similar terms. Hasan's mother echoed her son's comments, presenting herself as the responsible parent, obliged to stop the fun in order to serve food and send the children to bed:

> ... as soon as [husband] comes in he's like shouting and tickling with them and you know, having fun, so sometimes I have to stop them and usually he just carries on for about half an hour, forty five minutes, as soon as he comes home. They play for a bit and then I have to shout that it's time to eat, so they eat, even after that, sometimes they watch telly. Sometimes they are doing something with my husband and then I have to tell them it's time to go bed. (Hasan's mother)

Aisha's mother similarly perceived her own role as more important than the 'good time' aspects of her daughters' relationship with their father.

> With their dad it is all the social side, it's all about having a good time, 'can we go here', 'can we go there', but with me it is things that are important they will come to me. (Aisha's mother)

Thus while for children, 'fun' interactions with their fathers were viewed positively and enthusiastically, for mothers they were imbued with a different meaning and were in some cases interpreted as a lack of support in the more serious aspects of parenting.

6.2.7   Indulgent fathers

Fathers as loving or indulgent figures constituted a further theme in the representations of fathers that permeated the interview accounts. The positive affect associated with being a male parent was often raised by fathers themselves. Jamila's father described it as 'precious':

> Families are very precious things. When I come from my work and I see the children and I talk with them and sit together, it's a very happy feeling. (Jamila's father)

He went on to say that he loved his daughters best, explaining that

> In our religion if you have two daughters, yeah, and you give them proper education and food and clothes (...) the father has a big room in heaven. (Jamila's father)

Rubina's father was also reported as favouring his daughters over his sons, and being more indulgent with them:

> My mum's very strict. My dad, she's my dad's favourite so my dad's very, very soft on her. (Rubina's elder sister)

This stronger daughter-father feeling may relate to the fact that in South Asian Islam girls are traditionally seen as repositories of the family 'honour' and as needing protection (Chattoo, Atkin et al. 2004).

For their part, mothers often presented fatherly indulgence as an indication that fathers took their role less seriously:

> ... my younger one he doesn't like to eat carrots and things, not much, much vegetables. So if I have to force them and my husband is here, he would say 'Ok, just leave it if he doesn't want to eat' but I won't leave it (Hasan's mother)

This divergence of views often arose in the context of spending money. Several mothers said their husbands were too quick to pay for things the children wanted:

> He's very polite. Children if they want anything, I'm a bit, 'oh, how can I' (laughs), [my husband], money-wise, he's spending it immediately. I'm thinking, and my budget and this and that, he just.. when he's finished his money then... (laughs) I watch my budget and maybe he's not. He spends a lot of money

on the children. He's a good father, he's very good. (Adam's mother)

Children were adept at capitalizing on their father's lenience – a number described situations in which, if their mother would say no to something, they would go and ask their father, knowing he would agree.

6.2.8   Good fathers

An analysis of the ideologies of fathering expressed by the fathers, mothers and children in the study gives rise to a range of themes. The more traditional representations of fathers, as providers and authority figures, were clearly present across all families, reflecting received cultural and religious expectations of fatherhood. As others have suggested, in poorer families (such as many in this sample), where financial stability is hard to achieve, men who have lower levels of involvement with their children may still be seen as 'good fathers' if they work hard to provide financially for their families (see Coltrane 2004).

In addition, themes identified in wider fathering research, including presence, coaching, help with caregiving, fun, indulgence and other forms of father involvement, were also apparent. As in the case of mothering, religious expectations were often cited as justification for fathering roles.

The comparisons between different informants' perspectives on fathering were also noteworthy. There were various aspects of convergence, particularly relating to traditional norms of breadwinning and to the father as 'head of household'. However, fathers seemed relatively contented with their current contributions to caregiving, fun and affective ties (though the fathers who refused interviews may not have been so committed), while mothers appeared less satisfied with their husbands' levels of domestic support. Children were aware of and subscribed to models of fathering that involved breadwinning and authority, but also valued spending time with their fathers, and in some cases expressed a wish that their fathers would work less and play more.

6.3   Co-parenting and the role of others

While both mothers' and fathers' roles were multifaceted and varied, there were important differences between the two which reflected the broad male-outside/female-inside dichotomy that has been associated with gender representations in Islam (Bhatti 1999; Sherif-Trask 2004). Mothers were primarily connected with domestic and childcare work, with loving, nurturing and day-to-day teaching. Fathers' main responsibilities were concerned with breadwinning, and being a paternal 'authority', brought in to discipline and motivate their children and to ensure their success in the outside world. Children themselves perceived these gendered obligations, viewing mothers as serious and loving, fathers as both authoritative and fun but often absent.

Of course, this broad picture belies the variety present in parents' daily interactions with their children, based on pragmatic negotiation. In practice, a number of fathers were involved with caring work in the home, and there were several working mothers. However, the traditional division of labour was still recognized as a cultural and religious norm and (in some families especially) was a factor in individual identities and practices. This recalls Parke's (2004) suggestion that mothers and fathers might be differentially involved in the various domains of their children's lives.

6.3.1 Patterns of co-parenting

Co-parenting is a psychological construct that refers to

'the ways that parents and/or parental figures relate to each other in the role of parent. Co-parenting occurs when individuals have overlapping or shared responsibility for rearing particular children, and consists of the support and coordination (or lack of it) that parental figures exhibit in childrearing' (Feinberg 2003:96).

Co-parenting, according to Feinberg's analysis, consists of four components: agreement over childrearing values, division of labour, support (or undermining) of the other parent, and joint family management.

Among the families participating in the study, a number of alternative patterns of co-parenting were evident. An examination of divisions of parenting labour elicits four broad patterns:

Delineated roles with mutual support – this model, in which parents recognized delineated but complementary spheres of responsibility, and supported one another's different contributions, was the most prevalent. Hasan's father summarized this type of arrangement:

... generally tends to be sort of divide round sort of work where I tend to do the sort of manual sort of DIY work and my wife generally takes care of the sort of internal housework, care of the children, stuff like that. Yeah, so, but it's nice to have some divide in that respect, yeah. (...) if they've got plays or school activities, or something, we normally go together. It's normally a joint operation, joint collaboration you know. (Hasan's father)

Within this pattern, one parent was often the main decision-maker. This was commonly the father (but not always: in mixed-generation families the tendency was for the second-generation parents, whether mother or father, to have greater authority in decisions because of their superior familiarity with the education or health systems in the UK).

Shared parenting roles – a collaboration in which both parents took on relatively similar roles, negotiated according to pragmatic factors such as availability and work pressures, was relatively unusual in this group of families, but most closely approximated by Adam's parents, who tended to divide childcare around the timing of Adam's father's shifts, rather than on any conceptual basis. Family decision-making involved negotiation and discussion between both parents, or between parents and children.

Unsupportive/uninvolved fathers – this model, in which mothers took the main responsibility for the children and did all domestic and caring work, while fathers remained less involved, was predictable in single parent families (though some fell into the next category). It could also be applied to Jamila's (and possibly Bashira's) families, where the fathers ran their own businesses, worked very long hours and offered relatively little support or input at home, even when they were present:

... my dad's like, he's just silence. Whatever my mum says my dad is just being quiet. (Jamila)

Extended co-parenting – particularly in the newly-extended households (such as Yasmin's and Rubina's), and also where there were late-teenage siblings – particularly daughters – at home (as in Khalid's and Munir's families), the division of parenting labour extended beyond the mother and father. In these families teenage and adult siblings had a significant role in younger children's upbringing, domestic labour, and the transmission of religious and cultural values. In some instances this sharing of domestic duties extended outside the household to involve of local family members (see Chapter 8). These families frequently involved extended family members in family decisions – adult siblings and their spouses were, for example, key decision-makers in

Yasmin's family, while in Amina's and Rubina's families maternal aunts, uncles and grandparents played a central role.

An interesting implication of the latter co-parenting pattern is that, in many families, parenting roles were not in practice confined to mothers and fathers, but shared with others in the household – notably older siblings – with extended family members (aunts, uncles and grandparents) also playing a significant role (a pattern also reported by Chamberlain 1999, in the context of Caribbean kinship in the UK). In some contexts, moreover, parents imported resources from the wider South Asian community to help achieve their parenting goals. This pattern had interesting implications for the transmission of cultural and religious values. The generational transmission of religion exemplifies how this worked in practice.

6.3.2 Co-parenting religious transmission

As described in sections 6.1 and 6.2, the generational transmission of religion was seen as a key parenting responsibility for both mothers and fathers. It was noted that religious nurturance was achieved in a number of ways: through talking, teaching and encouraging, and through a deliberate strategy of modelling or observation. Both parents were held to be important in this process: although I was told that the 'mother is the child's first teacher', fathers also saw their reinforcement of religious practice as significant.

In practice, the actual divisions of religious parenting labour were negotiated depending on a number of factors. One was parental interest: Adam's mother was more concerned than his father about religious transmission, and was thus the parent who told religious stories and organized Islamic classes. Second was parental knowledge; first-generation parents had often received superior religious education and accordingly took on a major part of this role in mixed-generation couples. For example, Hasan's mother knew how to pronounce Arabic correctly so she was the one who helped the children with their homework and prayers (although her husband still maintained that he had a distinctive role in reinforcing his children's religious practice). Thirdly, parental availability affected who would spend more time helping the children: Bashira's mother (like Hasan's) was at home more and in consequence listened to the children's homework practice.

Additionally, in some families aunts, uncles or other relatives provided some of the religious nurture. For example, if Aisha needed help with her homework after Islamic classes she turned to the most religiously observant person in the family, her maternal aunt, who lived next door. Yasmin had learned most of her religious knowledge from her adult sisters. Zabar's mother often asked her own father to explain difficult issues to the children, because he was more know-ledgeable than she was.

However, all these families also routinely drew upon community resources to enhance this process, by sending their children to Islamic classes where they could learn to read the Qur'an. This was seen as an important element in their religious education; as Hasan's father com-mented, it provided a 'lot of reinforcement for our back-up' – that is, it went hand-in-hand with religious nurture in the home.

> One of the key things about being a Muslim parent is that you bring your children up to be a good Muslim and that's possibly, probably why we all send our children to Arabic classes so they get to learn and understand what Islam teaches them and what is expected of them. (Aisha's mother)

This inclusion of community resources as a central aspect of parenting illustrates the way in which children's socialization was, in practice, seen to be a responsibility not just for mothers and fathers but shared across other family members and the wider community.

6.4   Conclusion

This chapter has explored parenting roles and relationships as an aspect of family practices, and in particular has put forward representations (including both the being and doing) of motherhood and fatherhood, as conveyed in interview accounts. It was shown that each role was associ-ated with a range of sometimes contradictory responsibilities and obliga-tions – for example, authoritative fathers versus loving fathers. Throughout, the presence of gendered imagery has demonstrated how gender is enacted through family practices (West and Zimmerman 1987).

The findings draw many parallels with wider representations of fathers and mothers and other research findings from both sides of the Atlantic. Not least, the study echoes others in finding that mothers were expected to take more responsibility for planning, emotional work, housework and child maintenance (Hochschild 1989; Deutsch 1999), while fathers' interaction with, availability to and responsibility for their children was at a lower level than mothers' (Parke 1996; Marsiglio, Amato et al. 2000).

The continuing importance of religious and cultural value systems was also apparent, for example in the religiously-derived nature of the emphasis on fathers' breadwinning and authority, and mothers' domestic roles. Most importantly, the transmission of religious values was constructed as a key parenting goal. It was notable that both mothers and fathers were perceived to have complementary roles in this process: mothers as the 'child's first teacher', with a particular role in instructing children on how to pray, while fathers also had a position as the child's 'coach' and role model, encouraging religious observance. These perceived roles were sometimes tempered in practice by pragmatic factors, with daily activities being allocated according to parental availability, knowledge or interest.

As well as being defined as a central duty for both mothers and fathers, the role of other individuals – siblings, but also extended family and the wider community – was also vital, highlighting the extent to which 'co-parenting' was achieved beyond the immediate mother-father-child triad.

7
Children's Roles and Relationships

The meanings of parenthood and childhood are deeply intertwined (Valentine 1997) since beliefs about the duties of mothers and fathers towards children invariably implicate ideas about the nature of children and their needs. Chapter 6 pointed to a number of ways in which children affected parenting practices in these families, a phenomenon that has only recently received substantial attention in sociology (see Ambert 1992). This perspective on children as active social agents within families (James and Prout 1997; Mayall and Zeiher 2003) developed largely through the recent sociology of childhood and entails an emphasis on attending to children's own insights on family life (Brannen and O'Brien 1996). The attendant view of children as social actors worthy of study in their own right (Qvortrup 1994), alongside the notion that childhood is a socially constructed phenomenon (La Fontaine 1979), leads on to a consideration of the meanings of childhood and children as the focus of the current chapter.

As with mothering and fathering, the associations relating to childhood in the South Asian Muslim families in this study were multifaceted. Representations held by both children and parents embodied notions of 'good' children (responsible, helpful, obedient and clever) on the one hand, and 'just children' (naughty, incompetent and needing supervision) on the other. In daily family practices, children trod a fine line between growing autonomy, and continued surveillance and control, the balance being negotiated through ongoing day-to-day interactions. Children's awareness of the continuing transition in their own roles illuminated the more general dynamism of family relationships. Alongside wider societal notions of childhood, religiously-informed constructions of children as innocent (Husain and O'Brien 1999) and entitled to *hadana* or the fulfilment of physical and emotional needs including care, protection, socialization, education, love, attention and devotion (Sherif-Trask 2004) were also present.

7.1   'Good' children

As has been reported elsewhere (Brannen, Dodd et al. 1994; Husain and O'Brien 1999), images of the 'good child' were closely related to the moral dictates of Islam, with a particular emphasis on children's duty to respect and obey their parents. It was striking that, when asked how a child should behave, most children mentioned these requirements.

> ... you have to obey your parents and care about them and all that stuff and parents have to take care of you, I am not exactly sure of that, but you have to obey your parents. (...) You have got to respect each other as well, as well as our elders, like if someone if younger than me they have got to respect me, even if I am not related. (...)You have to listen to what they say and not swear or do not commit any violence with them. You have got to be nice to them. (Amina)

Obedience and respect were often explicitly placed in a religious context, as when Khalid's mother said 'respect your parents, (...) that's what Islam teaches you'. Respect of parents' wishes was particularly important, as illustrated by Amir's description of how he would 'let his mum win':

> I want to watch The Simpsons and she says 'no I want to watch Coronation Street and Emmerdale'.
> *Who usually wins that?*
> My mum, because if I put it on The Simpsons they would call me a rude boy cos I don't listen, so I just let my mum win because my mum is older. (Amir)

Similarly, Farid's father talked about how children must respect the roles of other family members as dictated by traditional hierarchical and patriarchal values.

> [Children] should always look at the father figure as their hero, as the master of, you know, the house. You should always take lessons from, advices from the male person. (Farid's father)

As argued in Chapter 3, respect also involved behaving in such a way as to uphold one's family reputation, as Hasan was aware:

> ... *what should you be like if you are a child?*
> Not to behave badly because if you do then everyone will talk about you. (Hasan)

In addition to showing obedience and respect, other characteristics of 'good' children included 'being clever' – something that many children considered essential:

> ... *what should a child do?*
> Try to be good, try to be clever, try to be clean. (Khalid)
> ... they should help their parents if they need it, do all their home-work, learn things and do well at school. (Farid)
> Listen to the mum and go and learn and concentrate on your work, and get homework and that. (Jamila)

This theme is related to the fathers' position as an educational coach and motivator, and also reflects the value placed by parents on educational success (see Chapter 3).

'Good' children were also helpful children. The obligation to help one's parents (and especially one's mother) was emphasized by several children:

> Sometimes help the parents if they are sick and make them tea and everything. (Habiba)

Helpfulness was also considered by parents to be a particularly desirable trait. Ali's mother said of him:

> He's very polite, a very polite child, and if I tell him to help me he helps me. (Ali's mother)

In addition to help with household tasks such as washing up, cooking and cleaning, children would sometimes help in other ways; as Munir commented 'I help my mum to learn how to use the computer. I do a lot'.

It was clear that in these families the most help was given by the oldest children, who were often assigned extra responsibilities. Adam's special job was to ensure that his younger brother and sister were awake in the morning. Bashira described her morning in similar terms:

> The first thing is the alarm goes off and then I get up and I have to wake my sisters up and sometimes they don't wake up and then I have to get my uniform from upstairs and come downstairs and go to the toilet and brush my teeth and wash my face and then I make my sisters' and my packed lunch..(...)... and then I set the plates and spoons and the cereal and the trays... (Bashira)

Bashira's morning routine was in some respects comparable to that of some of the mothers in the sample, since her obligations towards other family members were central. Talking more generally about her position in the family she said it was 'fun and not fun', and went on to explain:

> It's fun because I can be, I can help my mum and I know lots of things and I do them right and sometimes when my sister does them she doesn't get them right. (...) Like cooking and washing the dishes.
> *So what are the not fun bits?*
> I have to be responsible and sometimes when I'm not I don't like it. (...) It makes me feel sad and happy. Sad is because I have to look after everybody and you are busy and afterwards you get 'why didn't you look after somebody' and then you get told off as well, and it's happy because then I get lots of kisses and hugs from my mum. (Bashira)

Amina, another oldest daughter, who also helped her mother with the housework and the care of her younger siblings, experienced similar emotions. One of the first comments in her interview was 'I really like helping my mum'; her mother described her as 'very sensible'. The help with domestic work given by these eldest girls (also reported by Brannen 1996), although it was often taken for granted and sometimes demanded hard work, was nevertheless appreciated because it served as a means of acquiring respect within the family (see also Mayall 2002). Amina and Bashira were both able to demonstrate their increasing maturity and competence through their responsible behaviour, which earned them more autonomy (see Leach 2003). These examples of children contributing regularly to household labour serve to call into question the common characterization of children as 'priceless but useless'

(Scott 2003:114), a construction which has historically served to render children's labour invisible within sociology (Morrow 1994).

7.1.1   Children growing up

Throughout most children's accounts, there was an underlying awareness of change and growth, manifested in their constant looking forward to the future and back to the past. This sense of being on the brink of maturity was clearly important to children. The prospect of their development into adulthood prompted the recognition that childhood was experienced as a process of slow but ongoing transition. Zabar's comment was typical:

> ... now I am going to sleep in the loft on my own, because I am getting a young, like a teenager and I am growing so fast, I don't know myself if I am growing, but the people outside they can see me but I can't see myself. (Zabar)

The excitement of getting older was tinged with a sense of ambivalence, as Bashira's remark shows.

> I don't want to be nine, I want to be ten. (...) My mum said as you get older your life gets shorter and shorter so I want to be older but I don't want to be older. (Bashira)

In a similar vein, Habiba said 'I don't like growing up, I like being small', a reminder that maturity was not viewed positively by all children.

One of the ways in which their sense of growing maturity was experienced by these 9–11 year olds was in the awareness of their superiority over younger children. As Ahmed said, being ten was fun:

> ... because you are Year 6 you can boss around the lower ones in Year 5, Year 4 and Year 3 thinking that they are all cool. (Ahmed)

Amina's experience of being the oldest in her family gave her a similar sense of satisfaction.

> You just feel more mature, knowing that you can handle more than your younger siblings. (Amina)

As this comment indicates, getting older also meant that children were allowed to do more. Several talked about the positive aspects of being 9, 10 or 11 in these terms.

> It's fun being ten because when you are younger than ten you can't do certain things, like, but as you get older you can do more things. (...) if I am going swimming I don't need an adult with me, like I can go with my friends swimming and we can all go and play about there and we have fun. But when I was younger I wouldn't really be allowed it because I am too young, so I like being ten. (Aisha)

Alongside new privileges came a rejection of things that were seen as 'childish', and a newly serious attention to one's behaviour. Amina had much to say about this.

> ... we don't play hide and seek or anything because we are too old for that (...) [Being aged 10], you think more about your life than you used to.
> *Like in what ways?*
> I don't know, how you should live it really, I'm not exactly sure. About your habits. Because when you are little you don't have very good habits do you, but when you grow up you have to have very good habits.(...) You can't be laid everywhere, you can't be huddled up you have to stay relaxed, you can't have your arms up and everywhere like you used to do when you were little you have to sit comfortably and maturely. (Amina)

Parents, too, indicated their awareness of their children's increasing maturity. Zabar's mother described how 'he's coming to that age':

> ... because he's ten now he's coming to that age, he's becoming a teenager so he's becoming a bit rebellious, so it will be over even the smallest things, you know, like I'll say to him, 'give the remote to them' and he'll start shouting and he'll just throw the remote or something (Zabar's mother)

The teenage years were viewed as a kind of 'dangerous age' during which children were at risk of 'going the wrong way', as Mehmood's mother explained.

> ... age twelve to twenty, you know the mind is so unbalanced. (...) the children don't know what's the right or wrong. It's parents' duty

to explain them, they have to keep an eye on them. (Mehmood's mother)

Many parents – and particularly those with daughters – were accordingly anticipating the onset of their children's teenage years with some anxiety. As Najma's mother put it:

Especially with a girl. I feel more... responsible. Because she had her first bra. Bra, not period. I don't think I could handle a period, a bra was hard enough for me. (...) I was trying to delay it. It's going to be very hard for me to come to terms with that. And I think the period's going to be even harder for me. (...) I don't know what it is, I'm very scared. Not scared that she's going to do something wrong or whatever like that, but just scared that she'll grow up. (Najma's mother)

However, parents also saw their children's transition towards maturity as a positive enhancement in terms of religious growth. Hasan's father described how he had responded to his son's increasing years by encouraging him to begin praying 'properly'.

His prayer time, we're saying for example that he should start praying by the time he's eight, yeah. Eight to nine yeah. Try and encourage him to do so. And I say to him 'You've got to start doing the, you've got to start getting your prayers in order, because if you don't, you're just gonna just sway.' (Hasan's father)

As was noted in Chapter 5, fasting at *Ramadan* provided another barometer of children's growing maturity that was greeted with pride and excitement by both children and parents.

7.2   Children's power and agency

Children's agency, or 'their capacity to act positively in matters that concern them' (Robinson, Butler et al. 2003:76) has received increasing attention due to the emphasis in childhood research on children as social actors (Mayall 2002; Jensen and McKee 2003). In the current study, children's slowly growing maturity was accompanied by an emphasis on greater agency, as manifested by the extent of control they had over family decisions, especially those directly affecting their lives. There was a general recognition that parents needed both to protect their children, and simultaneously to enable them to develop through allowing them to participate in decisions (see Leach 2003). Children's agency was open to negotiation as they gained in maturity.

> ... he's obviously a young man now. He wants to do things his way. Yeah, and it's obviously you know making sure that we open it up slowly for him, that he knows that he can't do too much like that. But yeah, I mean you know depending on his ability and what I think his maturity level is, I'll give him that flexibility, yeah. (...) it's important that he discovers his way and you know I'd go along, you know, with letting him have that opportunity, have that flexibility and the freedom where I think he deserves it. (Hasan's father)

Hasan's agency was something his parents had power to 'open up' for him, in response to his proving that he 'deserved' it. Children's power within the family setting, while increasing, was nevertheless ultimately controlled by their parents.

Some topics, such as clothes and food, were agreed by parents to be more open to debate than others. Within them children were able to negotiate increased autonomy. A majority of children maintained that they were able to decide what to wear, though in reality their choice was limited to the range of garments provided for them, usually by their mothers (see Chapter 4 for a discussion of dress as symbolic of cultural expression).

> Mostly I wear, most, most days I wear the same clothes, and, sometimes my mother suggests, but she doesn't tell me what to wear, she suggests. (Ali)

A number of children participated in more significant decisions. For example, Tariq and Jamila both had decided which senior school they would go to (possibly because both sets of parents were first-generation immigrants and therefore had only a limited knowledge of local schools). Similarly, if the teacher was too strict, Hasan was allowed to veto his father's suggestions of which mosque he should attend.

> ... if he tells me I say 'no because he is strict', but if I don't know [the teacher] then I try that place out and then if I like it I will stay, but if I don't then I will leave. (Hasan)

His mother confirmed that it was his decision.

> His decision, yeah. We left it up to him that if he wanted to do the Qur'an by heart, whichever teacher he wanted to go to, we would send him, so he chose that. So that's where he's going. (Hasan's mother)

As this comment suggests, some mothers embarked on a discourse of 'the child's choice' in justifying decisions which concerned their children. Hasan's mother went on to say 'we don't want to force the child, if the child wants to do it then [he will]'. Similarly, Aisha's mother explained that Aisha went to Islamic classes through her own choice:

> ... it's all because she wants to do it, as opposed to because we're forcing her to do it, I always think if a child wants to learn they will. (Aisha's mother)

Aisha herself was also aware of this discourse, and argued that children should be able to 'have their say' in decisions adults made about them.

> ... they should have their say in things that adults say.
> *What sort of things should they have their say in?*
> Like if you wanted to go to [local secondary school] but then your mum is choosing where you want to go but your dad wants somewhere else, the child is going to go there, so the child should choose. (Aisha)

These comments imply that children's agency was seen in positive terms, reflecting a wider societal recognition of their rights to participation in decision-making (see e.g. Beck 1997; Thomas 2000).

7.2.1 Children's autonomy

Images of children's growing maturity and agency also led to increases in their day-to-day independence. Children's autonomy at this age was limited to certain areas, particularly those concerned with personal care, and was labelled (for example by Hasan's father) in terms of their being 'grown up enough to start looking after themselves'. Again, Tariq's mother considered it important for her children to be independent after a certain age:

... he's old enough now. I don't hang around with them too much, I like them to be independent (...) it's good for them, and if they depend on me it is too much for me. (Tariq's mother)

Similarly, Zabar's mother viewed her son's increasing independence in positive terms.

... he does everything for himself, he'll wash his face, gets changed, everything himself, have breakfast, sometimes goes to school himself if he has to go early. (Zabar's mother)

In some cases children's autonomy was enhanced as a result of practical circumstances: Yasmin recollected that, when her mother was ill, she was able to prepare her own snacks, having been told to 'do it yourself, you are a big girl now'. Aisha and her sister had been granted more independence than other children because both their mother and their father worked full-time.

They are independent, they have accepted that, mum is going out to work and they help along and do things for themselves. (Aisha's mother)

As children gained in maturity and were able to fulfil the requirements of being 'good' Muslim children (responsible, obedient and helpful as described in section 7.1.1), they were awarded greater freedom. This freedom was partly expressed in the home, in terms of an ownership of time. Children were allocated their 'own time' in response to completed tasks such as homework or housework.

They come home, eat something. Whatever they want to do. And Sunday, try to do their homework, reading, writing, and after that free day, they are free. (Mehmood's mother)

Increasing autonomy was also reflected in permission to leave the house alone. Bashira, who as the oldest daughter acted responsibly in helping her mother at home, was considered independent enough to visit the sweet shop without supervision.

She is quite independent for her age...(..) She can do anything I don't have to supervise her most of the time but mostly... she does go out but most of the time I go out with her, if she says 'mummy can we go to the sweet shop' I'll say she can go, and if it is not dark, if it's a nice day. (Bashira's mother)

Hasan was exploring his boundaries; his father saw him as gradually becoming capable of venturing out alone.

... he's coming to the age now where he's just started stepping out right yeah. He's going out, he's just going out with one or two of his friends to the town and stuff. And I mean a year or so ago, we weren't even allowing him to go down the road, yeah. But he's coming up to secondary school in a few months now. You gotta, you gotta let go like, over time yeah, we've started doing that with him, you know, with bikes and stuff over the summertime last year, he was allowed to go round the block for the first time you know. So you know, it's that slow departure to obviously step with moderation. (Hasan's father)

Children were thus attaining increased autonomy by degrees. As their parents' remarks show, factors such as the time of day, the weather, and the presence of trusted friends were used to moderate the levels of freedom that were negotiated. Together, the perceived increase in children's maturity leading to greater autonomy served to enhance their self-realization (Prout 2000), within the context of religiously-informed definitions of responsibility and maturity.

7.2.2 Children as agents of religious transmission

Section 6.3 described how families in this study routinely imported community resources to assist with the goal to transmit religious knowledge and beliefs across generations, in the form of Islamic classes (*madrasahs*) which children attended after school. This use of outside provision opened up another area of agency for children within families: the possibility to participate in religious transmission themselves.

In many contexts the community provision of religious education was relatively recent and therefore some parents (especially second-generation parents) had not themselves been to Islamic classes as children. Their own parents had been recent immigrants, working hard to survive and struggling to adapt to the UK, and so had little opportunity to teach them much about religion. Accordingly, quite a few mothers told me they were learning more about religion from the new knowledge their children had acquired through Islamic classes:

... she will come back and teach me things... she knows a lot more than I do, she is really fantastic in that. (Aisha's mother)

Aisha would listen to her mother praying and correct her pronunciation, in a striking reversal of the situation in, say, Hasan's family.

The development of Islamic classes is an element of the wider shift in the Muslim community in Britain described by Smalley (2002). As communities have become more organized, the nature of religious participation among the second- and third-generations has moved towards the provision more formalized religious nurture outside the home (but percolating back into the family sphere). The newly developed formal religious participation for children had important implications in that, because of this outside influence, religious transmission was not always downwards: children were bringing new knowledge and teaching to their parents. Such a finding constitutes a challenge to the accepted concept of 'downwards transmission'. In these families religious transmission was an interactive and fluid process with children actively shaping family practices and values. The emphasis here differs from that in Miri Song's work (Song 1996; Song 1997) on how the children of Chinese immigrants are the modernizers. In the present study the children were acting as re-instaters of tradition. In this sense generational transmission was also occurring 'upwards'.

In a few families, older siblings were the most knowledgeable (having attended Islamic classes themselves) and accordingly able to teach their younger siblings about religion – one might label this as 'sideways transmission'. For example, there were adult brothers or sisters who had learnt about Islam at college and were passing on these ideas to their younger siblings. The nature of Yasmin's religious education was transformed as a result of this process.

It's strange because [religion] wasn't really a guidance for us [older sibs] but with them [younger sibs] it is a guidance and they can see, understand it more and even to come up to us and ask questions about it. It was strange for us because when we grew up we didn't know enough about Islam or anything so it wasn't guidance to us at all until I went to college and went to a few talks going on, and then I started realising I should be doing this. (Yasmin's elder sister)

This reflects the process other authors (e.g. Bauer 1997; Jacobson 1997) have termed high-Islamization, in which a growing number of young Muslims have begun to distinguish between cultural traditions and religious traditions, and have opted to follow religion while not necessarily subscribing to the culture of their parents. The result is a more conscious reflection on and renegotiation of religious beliefs and values, signalled by such practices as reading English translations of the Qur'an in order to understand and evaluate what it says about rules for behaviour. Yasmin's and Rubina's older sisters both used this new knowledge to challenge the necessity of accepted cultural practices such as marrying first cousins.

7.3   They're 'just children'

The preceding discussion has concentrated on religiously-informed images of respectful and responsible children, and the negotiated increases in agency and autonomy that rewarded them, especially in the context of growing maturity. Children's agency within the family was also evident within a religious context, in that children were shown to be acquiring new knowledge outside the home which allowed them to act as transmitters of religious tradition in their own right.

However, a somewhat contradictory set of representations also emerged, conveying children as vulnerable, incompetent and in need of protection. It could be argued that such notions are linked to the Islamic construction of children as innocent (Husain and O'Brien 1999) and entitled to the fulfilment of physical and emotional needs (Sherif-Trask 2004). This view of childhood can also be identified in wider society (Valentine 1997). Such considerations were advanced mainly by parents. To take a case in point, Adam's mother, who argued that her children deserved leniency, refused to take them to Islamic classes for five days a week, as was the norm in her community.

> Five days is too much for my children. Because they need more things, for example I take them swimming.... mosque three days a week only, and just one hour. Some mosques they have two hours. It's too much for the children now. Because they need to play as well. Because they are at school the whole day, you know, the whole day. ... play, study, watch TV (...) they need these things to enjoy their life. (Adam's mother)

In this example the children were portrayed as needing free time to play and relax. Similarly, Rubina's parents were lenient over prayers and fasting since they took the view that their children were too young to participate in these religious practices. In doing so, they flouted the formal Islamic requirement for children to pray when they reached the age of 7.

> ... you are supposed to start your prayers and your fasting at the age of seven. That is the age where they say it is compulsory for them to do it. But cos...my mum and my parents, they like, the way they think is like, you know, 'There'll still small. They go to school'. (Rubina's sister)

The corollary was that parents should not expect too much of children. For example Mehmood's mother viewed her sons as unable to concentrate.

> You know, the children don't know how to concentrate on one thing. They feel a little pressure, 'oh we don't want to do it, it's so hard', this and that. (...) (Mehmood's mother)

Hasan's father portrayed his son as being 'naughty', but commented that this was normal for his age.

> I don't want to monitor him all the time frankly, but he's more active and boisterous than the other two, yeah he is a bit more, I think a bit more naughty than the other two. Not that there's anything wrong with that at his age. (Hasan's father)

This view of children as 'just children', deserving leniency and time to play, emerged in children's interviews as well as those of parents. For her part, Amina argued that children could not help being 'silly', but that as adults they would need to meet Islamic requirements for good behaviour.

> ... sometimes they can't help but be silly because everyone is silly once in a while when they are young. But when you grow up it is important to respect your elders, it is a sin if you don't. (Amina)

For most children, the notion of being 'just children' was interpreted in terms of their rights to be treated indulgently – as Najma, Mehmood and Aisha maintained:

> ... *what if you're a child in a family, what should you do?*
> Get spoilt. Get, every, um, toy. (Najma)

Um, ok. Let's see. Play, watch cartoons, play station,... (Mehmood) [children should be] the most loved. Whatever they need they should get it, say they need it for school and stuff. They should be quite cheeky, because they wouldn't be like a child [if they weren't]. (Aisha)

7.3.1 Supervised children

Parents were prone to link the image of children as immature or incompetent with the belief that they needed protection and control. The continuing salience of this representation of childhood has been argued by other authors too (e.g. Mayall 1994). In the families in this study, parental control and supervision were made manifest through a range of activities in the form of monitoring, shepherding and sheltering children.

Monitoring involved constant surveillance, based on the assumption that children needed unbroken attention to ensure their wellbeing.

I'm always keeping an eye on what they're doing, who they're with (...) ... if I give them money and they go to the shop I... in the beginning I used to go with them, now I let them go themselves but I still want to know what they've bought, what they've done and everything (...) I let them do what they want but so long as I know what they're doing and who they're with then it's, you know, okay. (Zabar's mother)

From a different perspective, Mehmood's mother was afraid that his health might suffer if she did not monitor him constantly.

... if he's with the mother, if something happens she will know straight away. (...) it's a bit scary you know, to leave the children alone. Mehmood slept with me till he was seven (...) But I think sometimes there are some problems, I don't let him sleep alone, he can't breathe. (Mehmood's mother)

Shepherding children was a related strategy, based on the notion that they were not competent and thus needed constant guidance.

[I] make him breakfast and iron his clothes. And give him, because he can't eat properly himself, I... make sure he eats. And I take him out to school. (Munir's mother)

A number of parents shared the view that they needed to make most decisions for their children because they knew what was best for them.

Adam, Zabar, Mehmood and Munir all acknowledged that their parents decided what they wore, ate and did, and where they went to school.

Sheltering children from perceived risk was another concern of parents, and was related to the conception of children as vulnerable and needing protection. This included, for example, sheltering children from certain television programmes, but arose most often in the context of parents letting their children go outside alone (see Valentine 1997). Tariq's mother kept him inside because she felt he was 'too young'.

Until I can control him I will keep him I the house, he is very young, not nice for walking the streets. (Tariq's mother)

Adam's father would not let him go to the local park without supervision.

On his own I don't allow, I think it's too young at ten, even though he's sensible, I don't normally allow him to play out on his own. (Adam's father)

Zabar's parents made similar prohibitions. While the exercise of this practice was not rigid but rather depended on circumstance, it nevertheless contrasted with the increasing autonomy granted to children such as Bashira, Yasmin and Hasan, who were beginning to be allowed out alone.

Contrary to the conclusions reached in other studies, that boys are allowed to go further from home without supervision – a tendency that has been noted both in British-based South Asian families (Bhatti 1999) and in the UK more generally (e.g. Matthews 1987, cited in Valentine 1997) – it was the boys' parents in this sample who talked most about monitoring, shepherding or sheltering their children. The more extensive attention to surveillance of boys in this study may relate to the fact that in the particular age range covered in this study (9–11) girls are often viewed as more responsible, rational and competent than boys – a finding that Valentine also reported in her study of 8–11 year olds and their parents in North-west England (1997). Valentine notes that these attitudes are in tune with psychological research suggesting that boys' emotional and physical development is slower, and that they are more disobedient than girls (Downey, Braboy Jackson et al. 1994, cited in Valentine 1997).

7.4 Conclusion

Children's daily experiences in their families approximated to what O'Brien (1995) has termed negotiation-in-context. That is to say parents and children were engaged in negotiating, informally and through daily interactions, the tension between children's needs for increasing autonomy, and parental inclinations towards continuing surveillance. These negotiations took place in the context of religiously- and culturally-informed beliefs about children. On the one hand, 'good' children were respectful and obedient children. A parallel narrative portrayed them as 'just children', incompetent and needing protection.

Within the constraints and opportunities offered in this normative context, children and parents were able to negotiate increases in autonomy and agency, particularly through the argument of increasing maturity. This echoes other authors who have argued that children's participation in family decisions is characterized by a tension between control and self-realization (Prout 2000). Thus it can be argued that constructions of childhood held by the families in this study represented some convergence with wider societal models – for example, in the perceived tension between rights for autonomy or participation, and need for care and protection, images of children that have been noted in other research (Mayall 1994; Valentine 1997; Leach 2003). However, these wider models were understood and negotiated in the context of specifically Islamic notions of 'good Muslim children' as respectful, obedient, helpful and hardworking. Thus there may be some specificity in South Asian Muslim children's family experiences, particularly in terms of their aspiration to a religiously-inspired rhetoric of desirable behaviour.

Other research has pointed to the importance of gender in structuring children's family experiences (see Mayall 1996; Bhatti 1999). In the families in this study, too, understandings of gender were related to discernible differences in the way children were parented. Most saliently, the degree of responsibility as against that of immaturity differed for boys and girls, with boys more commonly portrayed as needing parental protection or control. Alongside this gender effect, the children's place within the family structure also influenced their family experiences. The eldest children (particularly girls) were expected to help with domestic work, but were correspondingly perceived as more responsible and competent than those who occupied the position of youngest child, and enjoyed relatively greater autonomy.

8
Connections: Resources and Stressors

This chapter extends beyond the immediate family group to explore the wider structures outside the household, examining their nature and significance in family practices. Extended kin outside the home, neighbourhood and community, work and school, as well as wider political and media influences, were mentioned frequently by parents and children. These outside connections functioned at some points as positive resources, and at others as pressures, threats or constraints on family practices.

This chapter analyses the nature and sources of formal and informal support available to parents – such as the role of extended kin or of religious institutions or wider community in providing support – and more generally, the multitude of connections that family members created, sustained or deemed important. These connections, or social networks, can be seen as constituting forms of social capital[30] which offer a positive resource to families, in the form of both 'bonding' within groups, and 'bridging' between groups (Putnam 2000). In contrast, the negative connections that families experienced, in the form of threats or constraints, can be viewed as 'risk factors' (Ghate and Hazel 2002), frustrating access to resources (Phillipson, Allan et al. 2004), and hindering parents and children in their family practices. Previous research has suggested that, although South Asian families may need such support as much as any other group (Qureshi, Berridge et al. 2000), few services are specifically targeted at minority ethnic families (Henricson, Katz et al. 2001) and most are perceived as inaccessible or inappropriate (Butt and Box 1998).

The chapter begins by presenting quantitative survey data comparing Muslim parents' use of different sources of support with that of parents from other groups. Qualitative interview data is then used to explore the nature and importance of links with local, national and trans-national extended kin, and examine formal and informal connections with the religious community. The focus then shifts to the connections established in the secular or mixed settings of neighbourhood, school and work. The final section delineates the ways in which family members situated themselves in relation to the wider world, especially in the context of post-9/11 views of Muslims in Britain.

8.1   Uses of formal and informal support

The quantitative survey data offer a contextual insight into the kinds of connections that Muslim parents found important, as compared with other groups. Some indications of the sources of support used by parents can be gained from the questionnaire. Respondents were given a list of people and places and asked whether they, as parents, had ever gone to them for help, advice or support in bringing up their children. Across all ethno-religious groups, family (74 per cent) and friends (64 per cent) were most likely to have been used for support – although mothers were significantly more likely than fathers to report that they had approached either family (81 per cent of mothers versus 62 per cent of fathers) or friends (74 per cent versus 44 per cent) for support.

Chart 8.1   Sources of help, advice or support for parenting

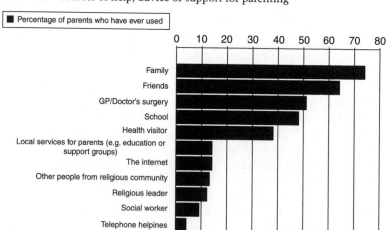

Base: all parents (n=149)

About half the parents also mentioned the GP or child's school as a source of help, advice or support. As Chart 8.1 shows, social workers, local parenting services, the internet and telephone help lines had been used by only a minority of parents, perhaps because parents tend not to seek or experience contact with them unless things go 'wrong'.

Parents' use of support from these different sources varied by religious group. Muslim parents were more likely than others to have received support through their religious community. Around a quarter (23 per cent) said they had received help from a religious leader, while a similar proportion (25 per cent) had received help from someone else in their religious community (the equivalent figures for Christian parents were much lower at 4 per cent and 6 per cent). However, for Muslim parents as for others, the most common sources of support were still family (used by more than 7 in 10) and friends (used by 6 in 10).

The greater reliance on religious sources by Muslim parents may reflect a relatively higher level of engagement with their religious community, as was suggested in Chapter 3. In this sense, their religious membership, and the networks and resources that accompany it, could be seen as a potential source of social capital for many Muslim families. The qualitative interview data (see section 8.3 below) also indicated that families for the most part viewed their links with the religious community as important. However, the interview data also indicate that other connections – particularly with the extended family, but with school and work as well – may be as salient, especially for some family members.

8.2   The extended family

For most families in the interview study, the presence (whether physical or symbolic) of extended family members[31] was significant in their family practices. In line with previous research findings on British South Asians, many of the families in the study were both locally embedded (Shaw 2000) and highly transnational (Mason 2004). Most children had aunts, uncles, cousins and grandparents scattered locally and nationally in the UK, as well as active links with relatives 'back home' in Pakistan or India (and sometimes elsewhere in Europe or North America). As will be seen below, contact with relatives varied in nature and frequency, partly depending on proximity, but was usually described as important by parents and mentioned spontaneously by children. These extended family links can be viewed as a positive form of social capital in the classic sense since they entail reciprocal exchanges of practical, emotional and financial support (Edwards, Franklin et al. 2003). More subtly, as has been argued by Reynolds (2004) in the context of Caribbean families, extended kinship ties also constitute a social capital resource in that they assist families in creating and enacting (ethno-religious) values and identities. Reynolds labels this as 'bonding' social capital, after Putnam's (2000) analysis, since it entails social cohesion and within-group solidarity. Family dynamics supporting the maintenance of kinship are discussed in the work of previous authors such as Finch and Mason (1993) who point to the particular role of female family members in building and sustaining kinship ties. For the families in this study their extended kin played an important role in helping to activate the value narratives explored in Chapter 3, especially the transmission of cultural and religious traditions and the forging of distinctive identities ('us as different').

8.2.1 Local kin

A significant group of families in this sample had relatives living in the same local area, particularly where second-generation parents had themselves grown up locally and had parents and siblings nearby. This pattern also occurred, though less extensively, where first-generation parents had other relatives who had also moved to the UK (sometimes to marry into the same family). Traditionally South Asian families were patrilocal, newly married couples being expected to live with the husband's parents (Ballard 1982; Ballard 1990; Becher and Husain 2003). However in this sample the pattern was more mixed, partly because there were several examples of second-generation women who had 'brought over' a husband from Pakistan or India to the UK. In these cases it was the woman's relatives with whom the couple made a local base – an example of the way in which practical needs lead to the adaptation of traditions. In some families, both maternal and paternal kin lived locally – especially where the mother and father were first or second cousins, since there would often be other similarly interrelated marriages within the same family group – a child could, for example, have a maternal aunt married to a paternal uncle. Such intermeshed relationships were often quite difficult to untangle, and reflected the value placed on sustaining a strong and interlinked *biraderi* or kinship network in which people might be related in multiple ways (Shaw, 2000).

Close daily contact

For a significant group of families, extended kin formed a strong local network entailing frequent contact and support (see also Beishon,

Modood et al. 1998): this was most often the case with maternal kin. Rubina's family provided a typical example. As her older sister remarked of her mother's relatives:

> I've got my grandmother's house over there, where my uncle lives and his children. I've got an auntie round the corner. I'm moving to next door to her. I've got an auntie round this corner. I've got one down the market and I've got two in [Essex]. They're the furthest. (Rubina's elder sister)

Such families effectively maintained a sense of extended communal living. Indeed, three had recently expanded to house the spouses and offspring of grown up children (see Chapter 2). Other families had organized their living arrangements to enable two related families to occupy houses on the same street; others again had relatives only a short walk away. As was indicated in Chapter 2, these close local links meant that households were to some extent permeable in that they spread across a number of locations and encompassed more members than the immediate nuclear family. Thus Zabar's mother said of herself and her sisters, because they lived locally and saw one another often, 'we're still in a family'.

Such families were close in terms of both physical and emotional proximity. Extended family members were closely involved in one another's lives and in what went on. Rubina's sister explained that they saw their extended family

> ... every day. Yeah, we, we all, round everywhere. [My aunt] come back from holiday on Saturday. So did my dad. So they were all round here and yesterday we all went round there to see her. So it's like, you know, everyone goes there. Like, you know, something happens, everyone knows it, so they're round here straightaway. That's what it's like. (Rubina's elder sister)

Extended kin played a central role in daily routines; for example, one mother visited her parents daily to help with housework and to care for her sick mother.

> I'll go round every day and see [my Mother] and the kids will go round on the weekend and see them, so I'm a lot in contact with my parents and my brothers and sisters. (Zabar's mother)

Local extended kin were often particularly salient in children's lives. Several were routinely cared for by grandparents, aunts or uncles: Amina's maternal grandfather took the children to school every day. In some families this informal childcare was invaluable in allowing the parents to work: in Aisha's family, where both parents worked full time, the maternal grandmother came round at 7am every day to wake the children up, give them breakfast and take them to school.

For both children and parents, contact with extended local kin did not simply provide practical support but was also significant socially and emotionally. Rubina described her typical weekend day as follows:

> I go to my cousins who just live opposite me and I go to her and play and then we go to my other cousin's house and we play then for long, and then we come back and all my cousins are round and they live far away from us and they come round our house and then we play with them, and then it goes dark and then my dad drops them home. (Rubina)

She played with her cousins every day, walked with them to school and mosque, and called them her 'small gang'. In these households, the extended family was a real and constant factor in daily life, with family members exchanging much-needed practical support in providing childcare and housework as well as emotional guidance and companionship.

Many of these families, then, were living in what Smalley (2002:96) has described as 'nuclear family households, extended family lives'. Such an arrangement was viewed by most as highly desirable. Even where families had not attained this state, it was often presented as an ideal, as with Hasan's father whose parents lived in Lancashire:

> It would ideally be better to have a sort of close extended family here... family's family at the end of the day. (Hasan's father)

In the majority of cases these local ties appeared to be strongest with maternal kin. As one child commented:

> The most often I see is my mum's side. (Munir)

Zabar's mother quoted above as emphasizing frequent links with her own relatives commented that '[the children] don't see much of my husband's family at all'. This pattern does not reflect the patrilocality often associated with traditional South Asian families (see Ballard 1982; Ballard 1990), but it does support suggestions that women tend to take on more 'kin keeping' tasks within families (Finch and Mason 1993; McGlone, Park et al. 1999), and also recalls earlier community studies of working class English families (Young and Willmott 1957).

Looser links

The group of families described above enjoyed regular and routine contact with extended family members, serving both practical and social purposes. In other cases, local kin were seen less often, but contact was nevertheless viewed as important. Often such contact was mainly social, and took place on special occasions. Relatives might share meals together at weekends, and, most importantly, celebrated religious holidays together:

> The festival *Eid*, when we have a big feast and end of fasting, we all get together with the family, you know. Sometimes it will be in this house, sometimes in my brother's house, my sister's house. (Farid's father)

These types of contact helped to define the salience and 'specialness' of religious festivals, in that a 'proper' celebration of a festival such as *Eid* (especially in children's eyes) necessarily involved getting together with the rest of family. This pattern appeared relatively more common for local paternal kin, even where maternal kin were seen more frequently. For example, in Khalid's family maternal relatives were seen several times a week, but his mother said of her husband's relatives 'only occasionally we go there, you know, like celebration days and stuff'.

Further along the spectrum of contact was a small group of families who either did not have local kin, or did not have frequent contact with them. This group is important because it contradicts often-repeated assumptions that South Asian communities in Britain invariably enjoy strong family ties, will 'look after their own' and thus do not require other kinds of support (see Becher and Husain 2003). Conflict often arose when in-laws put pressure on parents (for example, by making unwelcome suggestions about the children's upbringing), as was revealed by one mother. The resulting reduction in contact escalated the problem:

> You know the mother in law there put the fire on it. You know, says I don't contact them. Anyway. Leave me alone, I have other worries

as well. (...) it's quite difficult, better to stay out of their way, you can breathe easily. It's the main thing for everybody. (Mehmood's mother)

Relationships could be strained if a member of the family behaved in a way that was counter to expectations. An example is provided by Yasmin's sister, who had rejected an arranged marriage and instead married someone from a Bangladeshi background, leading to semi-estrangement with local extended family:

When you marry outside the family then you're not part of the family, well I don't want to be part of it! We have got some other family here but since I got married to my husband I don't talk to them, they don't really like me talking to their daughters or whatever. Better off without them anyway. (Yasmin's elder sister)

In particular, it seemed that in-laws were not always viewed positively, especially by women. Najma's mother, whose only local relatives were from her husband's side of the family, wistfully commented that she was sometimes lonely because 'I don't have any real family here to visit anyway'. Her feeling that her in-laws were not 'real family' seemed partly to relate to the fact that they had not provided the support she and her husband hoped for when she was ill.

That strain made me and my husband realize, my family wasn't here to help. His sister didn't have time. His other brother's too busy working, his wife worked as well. You can't rely on family when you've got... they couldn't really offer me what I needed. (Najma's mother)

These accounts modify the perception of a universally close and positive extended family. Although that certainly served as an ideal, in some cases family dynamics were a source of strain in extended family relationships, or at least failed to provide adequate support. This finding is supported by other research: Sonuga-Barke and Mistry (2000) found that extended family ties could sometimes break down or prove stressful to individual family members, and particularly to women, who were at risk of experiencing anxiety and depression associated with the demanding roles of mother, wife and daughter-in-law.

8.2.2   National kin

A number of families had national links with extended family members in other parts of the UK. This was often the case where one parent had grown up elsewhere in Britain and moved to London on marriage. These national links in some ways represented a kind of halfway house between the types of connection experienced with local and transnational kin. Although the majority of contact took place over the telephone, travel was easier and cheaper and visits more frequent than for overseas relatives. Families would make contact with their relatives on special occasions such as religious holidays, but would also spend longer periods visiting them, particularly during the school holidays. Contact with nationally-based cousins was salient and often mentioned by children. Hasan's family were typical. Hasan referred early in the interview to his cousins, and his father had a good deal to say about the importance of these connections:

> We generally go up every couple of months, yeah, occasions and certain stuff. Kids love going up there cos all their cousins are up there. (...) It's been really, I mean it's like, almost like, whenever you go up, you catch up, you know. (...) What we try and do is during their holiday periods, normally take them up to Lancashire, yeah. They then spend a few days up there with their cousins, of course, and so forth, then they're seeing, they're not so isolated here, they're seeing them and meeting them, growing up with them as well at the same time (Hasan's father)

This father's comments echo Mason's findings on transnational visits concerning the importance of both being together on special occasions and of prolonged face to face contact with kin in order to know them better, rather than just to know of them or know about them (Mason 2004). As reported in Mason's research, such visits were important in allowing children to acquire mutual knowledge that could be sustained over time and built into 'shared kinship biographies' (Mason 2004:425), here shown in the father's use of the phrase 'growing up together'.

8.2.3   Transnational kin

Much has been written on the significance of transnational family relationships for minority ethnic families in the UK (see for example Goulbourne 1999; Ballard 2002; Gardner and Grillo 2002; Mason 2004). Family relationships in the present sample were broadly consistent with this previous research. Family members spoke of kin in multiple locations (including 'back home' in India or Pakistan as well as in Europe and North America), with whom they engaged and sustained active relationships. Such relationships involved mutual obligations of support as well as being part of family narratives around closeness and 'passing on' cultural traditions.

Families made an effort to visit their relatives abroad at least every few years. These visits were, as Mason (2004) found, mainly based on the contention that face to face contact was important in sustaining kinship ties. Amongst other things, they were seen to be important in allowing young children to meet their relatives, as well as allowing family members to be present during key moments:

> I took them to Pakistan about three years ago because my father died (...) and they hadn't met their grandfather and their uncles so we took them out there. (Aisha's mother)

This mother went on to comment that 'I'd like to have somewhere they can go back to, I wouldn't want the children to lose that link': an indication that she saw visits to transnational kin as a means for her daughters to build an affinity with Pakistan.

In contrast to Mason's research, which found more of an emphasis on visits to the country of origin rather than vice versa, many of these families felt visits in both directions to be important. I was given several examples of grandparents coming over for extended stays.

> [My wife] brought her mother and father over here in the summer, and that was really good to have the grandparents in the house. Because it means that you know you've got an extra layer and it helps her, it helps the children, having a wider understanding, having older people around, yeah. Because everybody needs that experience. (Hasan's father)

As this quote suggests (and in line with Mason's analysis), transnational visits were seen as important because they allowed children to benefit from spending time with family members, enhancing the transmission of cultural and religious values through the provision of an extra layer of family generation, and helping the children to understand their family identity.

The importance of visits and of contact with family members was also underlined in the cases where families could not afford to make

regular trips. For them, other means of contact, such as the telephone[32]
became particularly important.

> I miss them very much.
> *What kind of contact do you have with them?*
> Only phones. We phone them up. We just phone them, that's it, go
> after a few years to see them cos we can't afford it, going there with
> kids. It's so difficult. Really expensive. I went in 2001 was the last
> time I went. (Bashira's mother)

This mother added that, given the relative distance of her parents and
siblings, she often felt lonely, with 'no social life, that's hard'. Long
distances were perceived as particularly serious by, and for, female relatives. As another mother explained

> If for one day I don't speak to my mum she gets worried. Because
> I'm, I'm the only daughter so and because I'm far as well, that's why
> she needs to speak to me every day. (Hasan's mother)

Telephone contact, while not a substitute for visits, was nevertheless
an important means of sharing news as well as for seeking and giving
advice.

It is important to note that, while the pattern described above was
the norm in this sample, a small number of families did not refer to
such close contact with national or transnational extended kin. The
most extreme case was Adam's family (who also did not have a local
extended family). The father, whose brother and father lived elsewhere
in the UK, said that he 'rarely' saw them;

> Once a year perhaps but usually about once a month on the phone,
> that's about it; he's just usually too busy. (Adam's father)

He later commented that he didn't 'particularly get on with' his father.
Similarly, when referring to his wife's family (all of whom lived
abroad), he implied that a rift had occurred:

> [My wife's] got a family and the only one she talks to is her sister
> who lives in [America]. (Adam's father)

This may relate to the fact that Adam's family was low both on religiosity
and on South Asian cultural affiliation and saw the maintenance of

cultural-religious traditions as less of a priority than some of the other families in the sample. Such exceptions to general practice are a reminder of the diversity within South Asian Muslim groups that has not always been appreciated by policy makers.

8.2.4 Extended kin: resources and stresses

For the majority of families, connection with extended kin was seen as a priority, and an important source of emotional and practical support. Local extended families were a particularly strong resource, creating for many families a sense of extended family living, and for others providing a key component of religious celebrations and special days. Contact with national and transnational kin was also central to the maintenance of family, with a particular emphasis on visits as serving to achieve contact and familiarity between family members and to develop shared family identities.

Extended kin (particularly the maternal grandmother) supplied practical help in childrearing. Such support also went in the opposite direction, often in terms of helping elderly parents financially and with their housework, drawing attention to the reciprocal nature of kin relationships. Less tangible support consisted of advice delivered both personally and from afar: many parents commented that they would always ask their own parents if they needed advice; several claimed that they had never gone 'outside the family', partly because in a large extended family there would always be someone who could help. This assistance related particularly to physical and social childrearing, but also to religious nurture. As Zabar's mother said of religious rituals and holidays, 'if we don't remember every time I'll ring up my mum and ask her'. Relatives were therefore an important component in the transmission of cultural and religious traditions, and in shaping family practices.

In less positive terms, stress and conflict also existed in the milieu of extended kin relationships. In some cases this was short-lived and due to practical pressures:

> When my family's coming here, oh my god, so many, the children, all together is 15 people, sometimes all coming together, oh god, don't believe it, I am so tired because I am cooking and washing. (Jamila's mother)

However, in some more serious cases supportive kin relationships had broken down. Even where contact was maintained, not all parents felt able to share problems with their extended family. For example, one single mother said that although she was given considerable support by her family, if something untoward happened she would only tell her mother, because there would otherwise be 'negative talk'. And while most children spoke about their extended kin in wholly positive terms, there were a few who disliked their cousins and did not enjoy being made to spend time with them. Such examples serve as a warning against the assumption that all South Asian families enjoy close and supportive relationships (Qureshi, Berridge et al. 2000).

8.3 Religious community links

We now look at the ways in which families situated themselves within their wider religious community.[33] Family members' accounts contained several, overlapping notions of community, including their local neighbourhood (a theme discussed in section 8.4); their local 'religious community' in the form of other South Asian Muslims in the area; and the more formal religious community symbolized by the mosque (which ultimately represented the global Islamic community or *ummah*). Formal and informal religious networks played an important part in the enacting of family practices for most families in the study. As with extended family links, they provide further examples of bonding social capital in that they involve building cohesion and trust within communities.

8.3.1 Local religious communities

Patterns of 'chain migration' to Britain from South Asia, whereby early migrants helped other friends and relatives to find housing and jobs in the same geographical area, has resulted in a tendency towards close-knit local British South Asian communities (Shaw 2000). The families in this study were no exception: they lived in areas in which a high proportion of the population was South Asian. It was not unusual for several South Asian families to live in the same street, with children who attended the same schools and Islamic classes, forming social networks that were important to both parents and children. Where extended family members had a local presence, these social networks also overlapped with kin connections.

It was clear that such religious community networks could constitute a positive resource for parents. As noted in section 8.1, the questionnaire survey revealed that Muslim parents were more likely than parents from other groups to report having received help, advice or support from other people in their religious community – around one in four Muslim parents had done so, compared with around one in twenty Christian parents. Further, 60 per cent of Muslim parents stated that they had received help or support from 'friends': it is likely that this category also encompasses local religious networks. In the interview sample, there were many instances of close bonds between families and their local South Asian friends, involving the exchange of mutual support and friendship. Informal socializing enabled families to, as Hasan's father put it, 'keep in touch with... what's happening outside'. Local families would be invited to share in family celebrations, as Zabar described:

> I had to go to my auntie's because she's had a little baby girl and we had a celebration at this hall. All the Asians were invited. (Zabar)

In addition to their social benefits, such networks were helpful in practical terms. Aisha's mother explained how the local families had got together to pay for the hire of a local hall to which they could send their children for Islamic classes, enabling her daughters to walk there with neighbouring children while she was still at work. Local friends could even become sources of financial support for parents, as Khalid's mother explained:

> ... if somebody is buying property or they need money, everybody puts around. All the community does, all the Muslim community do that. (...) All the community is good about that, all the Muslims, even friends and you know, they, they trustworthy, they help each other out, if they got money. (Khalid's mother)

For children, too, the presence of other South Asian Muslims influenced their experience of the neighbourhood. For Aisha, it helped to shape her identity as Muslim, but also 'just like anyone else' (see Chapter 3). When asked what it was like to grow up in a Muslim family, she replied

> It is the same as if you were growing up in a Jewish family, because there are other Jewish people around you so you don't feel left out, you are not the only person; because on this side there are lots of Muslims and they are really close to us [lists the names of all her neighbours]. (Aisha)

As well as helping to construct their ethno-religious identities, the presence of local Muslims also shaped children's social lives, in that they spent a lot of time playing with other South Asian Muslim friends. Although an observer might assume that such local play between children could occur regardless of religious or ethnic affiliation, for Rubina's elder sister it happened specifically because of the South Asian nature of the area:

> ... a lot of Asian children in this road. We do have, like, other races down here but they hardly come out, so very less... but our road is like you know, it's very hard to tell them to do something. They go, 'No, no, but we're playing', especially when they've got holidays, that's like summer holidays, they spent just the whole of summer outside, they never came in. (Rubina's elder sister)

In the context of the local community, the approval of other local families was very important: a family's reputation depended on the behaviour of its members and on its socio-economic success. As was described in Chapter 3, parents felt under pressure to 'keep up with the neighbours', particularly in terms of material possessions and language use (Urdu being more 'respected' than Punjabi). Children were sometimes involved in this process, as when Najma wanted a birthday outing that was as good as the neighbours', leading her mother to remark, 'she wants to take ten children bowling with her on Tuesday... she doesn't think about money!'. The emphasis on respectability could result in gossip and diminished reputation if family members acted in ways that conflicted with accepted cultural norms. This was the case for Adam's family, who acknowledged that they did not fit in with the local Muslim community:

> ...she don't wear her sari and all that, you know, she can do on a special occasion but normally a skirt or a track suit bottoms ... and she goes to the school sometimes to drop the kids off and you've got all these women there wearing their... they sort of look down on her because she's not wearing nothing, but I just tell her to ignore it. (...) my missus don't particularly get on with the Asian community in this area.... (Adam's father)

The separated mothers in the study were also acutely conscious of negative gossip. Amina's mother, for example, was aware of the community opinion that a 'Muslim girl like me won't be able to cope on my own'. This put pressure on her and also on her daughters, since if they 'went bad' it would be blamed on the fact that their father was not present.

Thus alongside the social and practical benefits that derived from a socially cohesive local South Asian Muslim community, there were sometimes elements of stress. One strategy was to disassociate oneself to some extent – an option that was chosen by Adam's father, as mentioned above, and also by Aisha's mother:

> I wouldn't go to anyone else, the community or everything. To be honest we have never really been involved too much with the community, not with what goes on and that. (Aisha's mother)

These defecting families were both relatively low on religiosity and high on the dimension of 'becoming British' (see Chapter 2), so their strategy might be seen as part of a wider family narrative of moving away from South Asian traditional affiliations. These latter examples, involving perceptions of 'the community' as controlling, homogenous or not allowing change, help to illustrate that 'community' can mean different things depending on personal and family positions within it.

8.3.2 Formal religious communities: the mosque

In addition to the informal social networks between local South Asian Muslim families, religious membership had a more formal side, represented by families' interactions with their local mosque. Again, there was some overlap between mosque affiliation and the more informal local network. Hasan's mother explained,

> Because it's quite near us and all our neighbours' children and whoever we know, they all go to the same mosque. (Hasan's mother)

Husain and O'Brien argue that the local mosque has been a 'fundamental aspect in the creation of a cohesive Pakistani community' (2001:19), providing not only a place of worship but also a focal point for socializing and a key element in children's religious education (a function that Bartels 2000 refers to as the 'social responsibility' of mosques).

For many of the families in this study their local mosque did indeed offer this range of resources, of which children's education was the most universally used. It was reported earlier in this chapter that a

Chart 8.2   Help or support received from religious community, by religion

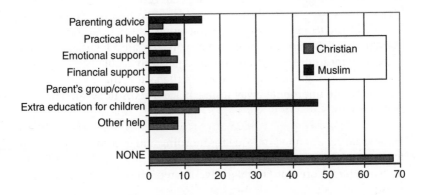

% Who have received each type of support

Base: Christian parents (n=52) Muslim parents (n=56)

quarter of Muslim parents responding to the questionnaire had received help, advice or support from a religious leader. In a separate question, parents were asked in more detail about the types of help or support they may have been given by their religious community. As shown in Chart 8.2, it is clear that Muslim parents in general received more help than Christian parents from their religious community, a large proportion of which comprised of extra education for children (i.e. Islamic classes or Sunday school). This type of help was reported by 47 per cent of Muslim parents (compared with 14 per cent of Christian parents); so around half of all Muslim families in this area were sending their children for extra educational support.[34]

These findings underline the distinctive experiences of Muslim families in accessing and using sources of support and advice for parenting. It appears from the quantitative data that their membership of the formal religious community is accompanied by networks and resources on which they can draw to achieve their parenting goals – particularly in terms of enhancing their children's religious nurture. The qualitative data reinforced the contention that children's religious education received through mosques provides an important benefit of religious community membership. The majority of children in the interview study attended a local mosque for their Islamic classes, and as described in Chapter 6, this played a key part in fulfilling the generational transmission of religion.

In addition to children's regular attendance at Islamic classes, more general connections with a local mosque appeared to be particularly valued by some fathers, as this comment suggests:

> One of the things that sort of attracted us to this area was the fact that there's a mosque nearby, yeah. It was an advantage in that sense. I mean I like to attend the mosque fairly regularly, and do my prayers in congregation. It was one of the factors that I wanted to be somewhere not too far away from a place of worship, yeah. (Hasan's father)

Hasan's father attended mosque for morning and evening prayers (and went to a mosque near his work for prayer during the day). At weekends, he had more time to take advantage of the social resources the mosque offered.

> I would normally go and see a few people like yeah, outside the mosque and just talk to them, and so forth and try have them see, it's rather a social time. (Hasan's father)

For many fathers, then, the mosque was an important space both for worship and for social interaction, in a way that it was not for their wives. In fact, only one mother in this study (Khalid's mother) regularly attended the ladies' section of a local mosque for worship, although Farid's mother sometimes attended the weekly 'ladies' gathering' at her family's mosque which offered lectures on family issues. Aside from children's Islamic classes, very few parents when questioned appeared to consider the mosque or Imam a suitable source of advice on family issues. For most, it was a place to help further their child's education, and for the men to pray and to reinforce and extend community social networks.

This analysis suggests that an individual's formal links with the mosque depended on his or her position within the family with regard to age and gender. For children it was usually the venue for Islamic classes, for many fathers (but not for most mothers) it was a place of socialization as well as worship. The less formal links with other South Asian Muslims in the area were, moreover, important socially and practically to all family members, and provided a means to build their reputation and construct their identity as members of a Muslim community.

8.4 Secular lives outside the home

The family connections with extended kin and the religious community discussed so far in this chapter were South Asian and Muslim in nature. We have seen that, in addition to being common sources of practical, emotional and social support, such connections were important in allowing families to build and transmit their cultural and religious values and identities. Such connections might usefully be thought of as forms of bonding social capital in Putnam's sense, in that they relate to within-group trust and reciprocity and are thus inward-looking (Putnam 2000).

Families also made connections that were not specifically South Asian Muslim (although they were not exclusively non-Islamic either), in the context of wider secular or mixed settings such as local neighbourhood, community services, school and work. Again following Putnam (2000), these can be viewed as forms of 'bridging' social capital since they are outward-looking, involving relationships of trust and reciprocity between different communities. As we shall see, they are also key channels through which families articulated and enacted values concerned with 'sameness' and 'difference', cultural change, and aspirations for social mobility. They could also entail elements of stress, however, particularly when the outside world was felt to be at odds with family values and belief systems.

8.4.1 School

School was a central feature in daily life, especially for children. Educational attainment was an important aspiration in a majority of families (see Chapter 3), and in consequence links with school were taken seriously. Amir said

.... my brother is Year 11, taking his GCSE's and my other brother is nearly on Year 9 SAT's and my brother is in Year 6 with me, so it is a very busy and hard year for all of us. (Amir)

At the time of interview these children were in year 5 or 6 and thus anticipating their SAT exams and entry to secondary school, both of which were serious preoccupations. Parents (or sometimes older siblings) would contact teachers at the first sign of concern about their child's progress. According to the questionnaire survey 46 per cent of

Muslim parents had sought help from their child's school, the third most popular source of support after family and friends.

School is nice, it makes me feel warm and comfortable. (Habiba)

As Habiba's comment illustrates, children were generally positive about school, and particularly about the friendships they made there. One of the salient aspects of school relationships concerned the construction of children's identities in terms of 'sameness': of being just like anyone else. This sense of sameness arose largely because school was a mixed setting in which friends could come from all backgrounds (in contrast to the largely South Asian Muslim social circles that predominated outside), and indeed Aisha, Yasmin and Hasan had best friends from other religious backgrounds.

'they have all, not only Muslim friends, all... you know, all kind of friends' (Hasan's mother)

The sense of being 'just like anyone else' also arose because of the beliefs that were encouraged at school concerning anti-bullying, tolerance and respect for other people's values.

... in school if someone bullies us or says something about our religion we do tell, and they do get into trouble. (Rubina)

Similarly, Bashira told me 'my teacher believes every religion'. Children displayed knowledge of other religious beliefs and often drew parallels with being Christian or Jewish. However, Rubina's comment betrays the fact that bullying still occurred. This could take different forms – for example Ali, who was Ahmadiyya, was bullied by 'different type of Muslims to me', indicating that children were aware of difference at many levels.

School exposure to other belief systems meant that children sometimes came home with ideas that ran counter to their parents' values. A case in point was Mehmood, who shared a bed with his mother until the age of seven (a common practice in South Asia) but subsequently wanted to sleep alone when he discovered at school that this was what other children did. Najma's mother, in her turn, was horrified when she discovered that Najma had learnt in the playground about the meaning of the words sex and rape. Leading on from this awareness, some parents worried that, as children got older, they would be negatively affected by peer pressure (from all children, but particularly non-Muslim) and would behave in ways that would damage the family's reputation. Tariq's mother and father were apprehensive about him joining secondary school in the following year:

> It is really important when they go to school the friendships they get into. In High School the ages they don't know what they are doing, like drugs and things it is really hard. It's really worrying. (Tariq's mother)

These fears reflect a wider concern about the threats inherent in Western society to the maintenance of South Asian cultural traditions (see Chapter 3).

8.4.2   Work

As described in Chapter 2, seven families in the interview study were workless; the remaining families were made up of one group in which only the father worked and another in which both parents were working. In general working parents viewed their employment as contributing positively to family life, helping to provide extra resources for their children. This point appeared to be taken-for-granted by working fathers but was commented on specifically by some working mothers:

> I am working for them so they can have what they want and they have got used to that lifestyle. They understand if mum goes out to work then we can have this ... (Aisha's mother)

By contrast, in workless families (such as Najma's) the lack of income from employment was experienced as stressful, particularly when they were not able to buy things their children wanted.

A further benefit of work was seen in the personal development or fulfilment that increased parents' quality of life in general:

> ... I wanted a career for myself (...) I don't want just to be a mum. It is fantastic that I am a mum and I wouldn't be without the girls, but I need a life for me as well, and I have actually achieved something with my life... (Aisha's mother)

Paid work was an important means of securing the social mobility desired by parents (see Chapter 3). In addition, it was constructed, especially by some mothers, as having social benefits in terms of providing networks and preventing loneliness.

> It just gets me out of the house; the children are in full time school, especially I've got no family here, I'm on my own. So I try to, it just gets me out of the house. So, and I like to socialize, does me good. (Hasan's mother)

Again, it was interesting to note that most of the comments along these lines were made by mothers – possibly because in the light of the traditional assumptions that deterred women from working (Beishon, Modood et al. 1998; Ahmad, Modood et al. 2003), they felt it necessary to offer some rationalization for their behaviour.

However, the predominant theme which emerged in conjunction with work-family linkages concerned time. Working families, and dual-earner ones in particular, closely reflected the experience of 'work-rich, time-poor' families described in other studies (Gregg and Wadsworth 2000). In such families work was often experienced as impinging on home life. Working parents described the pressures as stressful and tiring, with a constant process of juggling to fit everything in, and a sense of guilt about the limited amount of time they spent at home. Children, too, complained that they did not see their working parents as much as they wanted to.

> My dad comes in at 7 or 6 o'clock and I don't have time to see him, he goes to the shop and when he comes back he goes to sleep because he has to wake up in the morning at 6 o'clock. (...) I don't even talk to him that much he is so busy we just watch TV and that's it. (Jamila)

The view of work as a negative constraint on family life was especially clear where fathers were doing shift or night work. As Adam's father said, 'you can't really do a lot when you're on nights because you're tired all the time generally'. Shift work interfered with family routines:

> Shift work, which breaks up in my family, it's not proper with my family, shift work. (...) I have to go early. Sometimes I have to stay overnight at work as well. Half my mind is sometimes here because there is something worries about the family of course when you're out there. (Farid's father)

Children whose fathers worked on night shifts universally commented that they did not see their fathers much, and enjoyed few shared activities with them:

> *What do you do with your dad?*
> I've only been to the park with him once. Because he goes in the night mostly, so I don't see him mostly (Amir)

The experience of work as generating 'time crunch' or 'time scarcity' in families has been extensively discussed elsewhere (see for example Daly 2001b, and Chapter 5 of this book).

Some children were clearly concerned about what they perceived as the mentally or physically stressful aspects of their parents' work. For example, Ahmed and Amir both wanted their father to stop driving a minicab because it was dangerous. Similarly Zabar worried about the effect of manual work on his father:

> I want my dad to get a real job like a manager and work at an office and stuff, but he can't do that because he has just come here and he didn't learn that in his own country and now he is doing building work and getting more money but he gets very tired and his arms hurt and we have to make him relax. Tomorrow he's going to relax properly. (Zabar)

For these children work was viewed not only as impinging on family time but more seriously as limiting their father's ability to fulfil his role within the family. This view of work as dangerous runs counter to the construction of school as a warm and safe place (and is not a common theme in research on UK children's views of parental work).

8.4.3 Neighbourhood and community

The links between families and their local neighbourhoods had both positive and negative aspects. The borough is a socially and culturally diverse area: parents sometimes commented on this as being a 'good thing'.

> Community-wise as well, cos you can see it's a mixed area, so it's nice in that sense. You've got a lot of different people from different aspects, different walks of life, yeah, different ethnic minorities. Lot

of local people here as well. I like this area quite a lot... (Hasan's father)

The previous section described how children were meeting and mixing socially with non-South Asian Muslim children at school. Parents had similar experiences with non-Muslim neighbours, friends and social contacts.

I just done a course, adult education course (...) And I really enjoy that, you know, mixing up with other people and you know, so nice when, you know, go out... (Khalid's mother)

In some cases, especially with neighbours, these friends had provided reciprocal exchanges of support similar to those sustained with local South Asian friends. This non-Muslim social contact offered an example of the narrative of being 'just like anyone else' in action.

Parents also made use of community resources and services, and of their GP's in particular. Nearly half the Muslim parents in the questionnaire study stated that they had gone to their doctor for support, and in the interview sample the doctor was similarly cited, especially by mothers, as a trusted source of advice and help. For some it was a positive consideration if the doctor was not a member of the local South Asian Muslim community. Aisha's family had changed doctors because their previous doctor was South Asian and consequently, in their view, failed to understand Aisha's anxiety problems.

We had an Asian doctor and every time we went to her she was 'oh no, don't worry about it' and I thought, because she is Asian, she doesn't possibly understand that maybe there is something a bit more deeper... (Aisha's mother)

For another group of families, however, the local neighbourhood was a source of anxiety because of the high levels of crime or disorder. The resulting fears were captured by Tariq's mother, who remarked:

I don't know where my son goes and what he does, because you see some children and they are under age and they are smoking, they go to the shops with their friends and steal the sweets and everything and they run and I see in front of my eyes. (...) I don't want that to happen to my child. (Tariq's mother)

Parents accordingly felt that they had to keep their children under surveillance. As Adam's father commented, 'East London seems to have got really violent... it's a lot more dangerous for the kids, that's my reason for not letting them play outside'. Amir and Ahmed's mother made the same point: in view of her worries about bullying, muggings and racism she would not let them play outside alone.

In some families the sense of fear was extreme. Mehmood's family lived on the 14th floor of a block of flats in which there was a high level of crime – the lifts were often vandalized, necessitating climbs up many flights of stairs; cars were stolen, and the family had recently been mugged.

It's so difficult for them and me. Have to go up, down, up, down. I have to say 'don't do anything', this and that, lifts aren't working (...). Every day we're dealing with this. They get depressed as well. It's a fact you know. We're not living the normal life. (Mehmood's mother)

Although Mehmood's mother had shared her fears with Social Services, she concluded that 'nobody's helping'. Her lack of satisfaction with Social Services was not unique: Habiba's mother complained that the council did not respond to her concerns about overcrowding (Habiba's elder brother had to sleep in the sitting room as there were not enough bedrooms). Munir's mother, too, had wanted advice about her children but had not known where to get it. She was especially worried that because her English was not fluent, nobody would be able to help her. For some families, then, the mixed local area was experienced as supportive and positive in its diversity, while for others fear of crime and a sense of isolation gave rise to considerable stress.

8.4.4 The wider world: Islamophobia

The final part of this chapter explores the ways in which family members situated themselves with reference to the wider world, in terms of their experiences of discrimination and their beliefs about society's perceptions of Muslims. These issues are particularly salient in the context of observed post-9/11 changes in public and policy views of Muslims in Britain, which have led to what the Muslim Council of Britain has described as 'a relentless increase in hostility towards Islam and British Muslims'.[35] This has involved increasing Islamophobic sentiment in the media (Ansari 2002) and also a growing perception of British South Asians as a policy 'problem' (Reynolds 2004; Van der Veer 2004), which has further intensified following the London terrorist attacks in 2005. The connections with wider world views are related to the ways in which families enacted narratives of 'sameness' and 'difference' in the context of minority-majority relationships.

Encountering Islamophobia

In line with the beliefs of commentators such as Ansari (2002), there was a general perception among parents that the levels of prejudice they encountered had increased since the events of September 2001. In particular, parents worried about their children being bullied or harassed (although this concern was not mentioned by children).

> ... there is still a lot in schools where you are seen just as an Asian and you're still Muslim (...) and when they go to mosque, 'people', Aisha will say, 'really stare when we are walking up the road because I've got the headscarf on', and it really upsets her and I said to her, 'don't worry about it and if someone speaks to you about it come home and let me know, don't let that upset you', but it is difficult. (Aisha's mother)

There was also a belief that Muslims were being discriminated against in the job market.

> ... when they look for jobs and for an interview and they look at names, you see my name there, (...) immediately must say 'Oh he's a Muslim you know, he might be one of them, you know, who knows you know.' So it makes it a very difficult thing for a normal Muslim I think. (Farid's father)

'One of them', referred to Islamic extremists or terrorists who at the time were being frequently featured in the media. It was clear from the interviews that recent world events had strongly affected the way in which family members were able to relate to wider society. As Farid's father went on to say,

> ... what's going on at the moment, it makes us sort of, you know, cornered up, because you are sort of in Islam, or because you got a, sort of my, talking about myself because I've got a beard and I'm

looking more sort of Islamic, it doesn't mean that I am, you know, one of those bad people, something like that, people would look at me. (Farid's father)

Responding to negative perceptions of Islam

Family members responded to these experiences of discrimination with a variety of strategies. A common tactic was actively to situate themselves as unrelated to Islamic extremism and terrorism. It was evident that parents, and especially fathers, felt a need to explain recent Islamic terrorism and distance themselves from it. As Adam's father put it, 'Muslims are getting a bad press... it's like the guys you see on telly are like our version of the National Front'. Parents often made comments designed to counter what they suspected I, as a white non-Muslim, might be assuming. For example, Ali's father talked at length about the outside world and its false perceptions of Islam, and admitted at the end of the interview that when I had first contacted him, he suspected that I had been sent by the government to find out whether he constituted a terrorist threat.

A number of parents described experiences in which they had felt obliged to defend themselves against associations with terrorism.

It happens when you got friends, like you got friends at work you know, who's not into religion like Islam, and then they talk 'How come this is happening? How come your brothers are doing this?' You know, 'Doing jihad and doing this, saying this and doing that. And how come you just going on normally you know, you not worried about it?' And you try to make him understand. (Farid's father)

They were finding themselves having to give a justification of this kind more and more often, to non-Muslim acquaintances, but also to their own children. Parents dealt with this by making a clear distinction between 'normal Muslims', and 'bad Muslims' (meaning extremists or terrorists). For example, Adam's father tried to reassure his son that 'this guy, you know, he's not a proper Muslim, proper Islam is about peace'. It was frequently explained to me that terrorism went counter to Islamic teaching.

Aisha will come home and the children have made comments, like terrorists, and they are upset by that... with everything they're hearing, parents speak about and on the TV at the moment there is a lot of uncertainty and tension and that kind of upsets me because there are things happening at the moment but that is not what we would teach our children and that's not what Islam teaches children. Islam does not teach Muslims to go out and be terrorists but that is how people see it (Aisha's mother)

In a similar vein, a number of mothers were at pains to assure me that women were not oppressed in Islam, an assumption that they assumed I would share. It was clear that negative public views of Islam were a cause of concern to family members, particularly on parents.

8.5 Conclusion

This chapter has traced the wealth of connections that South Asian Muslim family members built and sustained outside the immediate household, exploring the ways in which these links were experienced as both resources for and constraints on family practices. In terms of resources, it has been useful to distinguish connections between bonding networks that enhance within-group cohesion (family, cultural and religious), and bridging networks that enhance trust between groups (Putnam 2000; Reynolds 2004).

We began by presenting quantitative survey data comparing Muslim parents' use of different sources of support with that of parents from other groups. Muslim parents were more likely than Christian parents to receive help or support from their religious community, suggesting that their religious membership, and the networks and resources that accompanied it, could be seen as providing extra social capital for many Muslim families. Some possible policy and practice implications of this will be explored in the following chapter.

The nature and importance of links with local, national and transnational extended kin were also explored. The accounts presented here reinforced the findings of earlier research underlining the continued importance for most families of extended kin ties, which persisted even at transnational distances, entailed the mutual exchange of practical and emotional support, and sustained the transmission of cultural and religious values. Women were seen to have a particular role in building and sustaining kin networks.

Connections with the religious community were also important – both the informal social networks linking with other local Muslims, and the formal relationship with the mosque (which ultimately represented the global Islamic community). For a majority of families (though not for all), connections with the local Muslim community provided social benefits as well as practical help, while the mosque was an important element in children's religious nurture, and a social sphere, especially for fathers.

Both extended kin and religious community networks can be seen as examples of bonding social capital (Putnam 2000), and as interlinked with the family values of religious centrality, cultural transmission and distinctiveness outlined in Chapter 3. However, not all such connections were positive. In a small number of families, relationships with extended kin were experienced as stressful, while some also found that the 'gaze' of the close-knit and socially cohesive local community put them under pressure.

The latter part of the chapter explored the bridging connections established in the secular or mixed settings of neighbourhood, school and work. School was valued as a setting which fostered tolerant mixing between friends of different cultural backgrounds, although some parents were concerned about possible peer pressure on children to act in ways counter to their own cultural and religious beliefs. Work was a positive source of financial capital, but imposed time stresses on families. Neighbourhoods were viewed by some families as threatening, especially in terms of fear of crime or vandalism. Finally, the chapter reviewed ways in which family members (and in particular parents) situated themselves with reference to the wider world, taking into account post-9/11 views of Muslims in Britain. Prejudice and discrimination were considered to have increased since September 2001 and were a recognizable source of stress. It was in these wider connections that family aspirations were played out, and families enacted narratives of 'sameness' and 'difference'.

9
Conclusion

The research described in this book aimed to illuminate family practices among South Asian Muslim families in contemporary Britain through the collection of interview accounts from mothers, fathers and children, and a survey in primary schools. The intentions of the study were to explore maternal, paternal and child perspectives on family practices in South Asian Muslim families, particularly as relating to religious and cultural practices. A secondary aim was to examine the nature and sources of support currently available to South Asian Muslim parents, and ultimately to generate knowledge that would help develop more culturally sensitive family support services.

Despite increasing empirical knowledge about the correlational links between Christian religions and family life, it has been widely argued that 'the absence of social science research about religion and families from other major religions of the world represents a major gap in empirical knowledge' (Mahoney et al. 2001:560). In investigating South Asian Muslim families in the UK, this book responds to wider calls for more detailed qualitative research with non-Christian, non-US populations, that can uncover the processes and meanings behind religion-family linkages. In a consideration of religious family practices, especially through a qualitative lens, the book illuminates the 'being' and 'doing' of religion in a family context. The analysis also incorporates the inter-related themes of cultural practices and cultural group membership (or, ethnic practices) as closely associated with how people 'do' family, thus demonstrating the cross-cutting boundaries between family, religion and culture.

These findings can be situated within a number of broader debates within social science: from wider questions about the nature of the relationship between individual agency and social structure (Giddens 1979; Giddens 1984; Thompson 1989; Bourdieu 1990; Berger and Luckmann 1991), to current trends within sociological enquiry, including increased attention to the everyday (Bennett and Silva 2004), time (Hägerstrand 1975; Daly 1996; Adam 2000) and space (Giddens 1984; Soja 1989; Lefebvre 1991; Massey 1994); the growing sociology of consumption and questions of cultural capital as an expression of social distinctions (Bourdieu 1984; Edgell, Hetherington et al. 1996; Gronow and Warde 2001); and discussions of social networks and capital as family resources (Edwards, Franklin et al. 2003; Phillipson, Allan et al. 2004). The research is also situated within an historical context of increasing diversity in family forms alongside democratization of the family (including an emphasis on children's rights, feminism, individualization and secularization), and a rising awareness of the existence of alternative and contrasting value systems. Most pertinently, the growing acknowledgement of Britain as a multifaith and multi-ethnic society has been underscored by public debates on what it means to be Muslim and British.[36] As Britain diversifies, an understanding of family practices among different ethno-religious populations becomes more important than ever.

This chapter concludes by summarizing the key findings arising from the research and discussing some implications for policy.

9.1 Key findings

A small but growing body of research illuminates the lives of British Muslims, through both quantitative demographic evidence (much enhanced by 2001 Census data) and qualitative insights into experiences and processes. This evidence (for a detailed review, see Becher 2005) conveys a number of themes, including the general structural disadvantage faced by many South Asian Muslims in the UK, although there are significant levels of diversity within communities. Existing research also underlines the dynamic processes of negotiating tradition and change that are central to family and community life, with the active maintenance of cultural and religious traditions occurring alongside transformation in response to new opportunities and challenges. This book contributes to that knowledge, particularly by drawing together the perspectives of individual family members on the following key findings.

9.1.1 Religious family practices

This study explored the notion of 'religious family practices' (those relationships and activities that are constructed as being to do with both religion and family), a concept that was wider than the 'religious nurture' explored by previous authors, and thus allowed a consideration of the active roles played by all family members (including children) in jointly shaping religious involvement. The inclusive nature of religious family practices also enabled recognition of the multiple dimensions within the concept of religion, including ritual, knowledge, morality, experience and community membership in addition to the narrower measures of belief and attendance.

Of the range of belief and value narratives that 'mattered' to people in their family practices, explored in Chapter 3, religion was the most central. Islam was seen as providing a framework for living: guiding moral choices, shaping family expectations and framing daily activities. This aligns to the wider idea that religion provides a 'worldview' (Geertz 1973; Larson 2000; Lau 2000). It also indicates that what Mahoney and colleagues refer to as the substantive (or content-based) element of religion-family linkage (Mahoney, Pargament et al. 2001) was important for South Asian Muslim families. Alongside the notion of the centrality of religion, however, there also existed a theme of religious moderation, with parents valuing the idea of being 'not strict' in their religious family practices: this highlights the possibility that new norms might be emerging for parents in this ethno-religious group, in response to societal perceptions of 'strict Muslims' as representing a threat to modern liberal society.

By exploring family members' accounts of religious family practices in the context of their daily lives, this research has shown the 'doing' of religion to be interrelated with the 'doing' of family practices in a whole range of ways. For example, through their patterns of consumption and material choices, families were eating, wearing, speaking religious family practices and so establishing and sustaining their religious and cultural identities. Thus in eating *halal* food (whether English or South Asian cuisine), through telling religious stories in their language of origin, or by wearing South Asian clothes to an extended family gathering, family members could 'place' themselves as South Asian and Muslim. Indeed it was through such actions that family beliefs and values were constituted and understood. Similarly, everyday family time-space was permeated by the extra dimension of sacred time-space, with the two dimensions having a fluid relationship so that prayer times could be altered in the light of domestic demands (and similarly, family space could be transformed into a temporary sacred space with the use of a prayer mat). Longer-term cyclical sacred times (particularly the holy month of *Ramadan*) also punctuated secular life, serving to reconnect families with kin, community and tradition.

In terms of family roles, too, Islam was of central importance. Religiously-informed expectations of motherhood, fatherhood and childhood were salient. For example, there was a belief that the generational transmission of religion should be a central project of parenting, supporting US research on Christianity which suggests that religion may frame the parental role as a 'sacred calling' central to a parent's life, and more generally impart 'spiritual meaning' to family roles and relationships (Mahoney, Pargament, Murray-Swank and Murray-Swank 2003). Both mothers and fathers were seen to have vital roles in this: the mother as the 'child's first teacher', and the father as a coach, motivator and role model. Similarly, constructions of 'good' children, as obedient, helpful, respectful and clever, represented distinctively Islamic views of childhood. Other, wider societal constructions of family roles were also evident, but these were often understood in the context of the religious versions. So for example children were seen to tread a balance between a right to autonomy and a need for surveillance (both themes discussed in the sociology of childhood literature), but in this context responsibility could be demonstrated and autonomy 'earned' through meeting the distinctively Islamic expectations of 'good' children.

All these examples point to the usefulness of the concept of religious family practices when attempting to illuminate family practices. For these contemporary South Asian Muslim families, the extent to which religious family practices permeated family practices resonates with Dollahite and Marks' recent suggestion that highly religious families may work to 'sanctify the family' by living religion at home, and confirms their contention that 'much of religion's power lies in sacred familial processes that take place out of public view' (2004:537).

9.1.2 Lived negotiations of tradition and change

This study confirmed the emphasis given by other researchers (e.g. Husain and O'Brien, 1999) to the negotiation of cultural tradition and change as central to South Asian Muslim family life. Alongside religion, family members' orientations towards the importance of maintaining South Asian traditions, on the one hand, and the desirability (or inevitability) of the adoption of new cultural practices in response to the British context, on the other, represented key sets of values that 'mattered' in their family practices.

The focus on family practices, and the collection of multiple accounts, revealed that the negotiation of tradition and change was lived out through daily activities and interactions as well as through family relationships and the connections that families forged outside the household. 'Keeping tradition' was especially emphasized in certain areas: notably the enduring importance of 'respect', both in showing it (for one's elders and for the family hierarchy), and in eliciting it (to maintain the family's reputation). This was demonstrated in aspects of cultural consumption – one could ensure respect by wearing South Asian dress and demonstrate it by addressing community members in the language of origin – and also in the supportive social networks forged with extended kin and the local South Asian Muslim community. On the other hand, cultural transformation was associated with notions of 'fitting in', and enacted in the adoption and adaptation of British cultural practices – wearing British clothes, eating English food, embracing changes in role expectations (particularly the acceptability of women working), and forging 'bonding' connections in mixed or secular settings of school and work.

Importantly, rather than tradition straightforwardly representing 'structure' and change entailing 'agency', both the maintenance and the transformation of tradition involved active negotiation between family members, in an interplay between structural and agentic factors. A variety of strategies and orientations could exist within one family, depending on context and family dynamics. Religion remained an important underlying theme: the maintenance of tradition, including the emphasis on respect and the disapproval of marrying outside the ethno-religious group, often derived legitimacy from religious beliefs. Similarly, cultural adaptation was commonly practised selectively in order to preserve religious acceptability: the eating of English food 'so long as it's *halal*' was one example.

This primacy of religion in both tradition and transformation underlines the fact that affiliation with South Asian cultural traditions was not necessarily concomitant with affiliation to Islam. Rather, the study has shown that it was possible for these two dimensions to overlap, and even to co-exist, in a range of ways. There were individuals and families (notably Rubina's and Habiba's) who were highly affiliated to South Asian culture, but for whom religion was relatively less salient. Conversely, other families (like Yasmin's, Hasan's and Khalid's) were maintaining or even strengthening their affiliation with Islam, while simultaneously embracing cultural change, thus remaking the link between religious and cultural practices.

9.1.3   The role of siblings and 'sideways transmission'

In eliciting children's perspectives on family practices, the importance of siblings emerged as a salient theme. Not least, birth order was significant shaper of the experiences of the 9–11 year olds in this study, with eldest children being expected to take on more responsibility and earning increased autonomy as a result, while youngest children were often seen as relatively less competent and more in need of protection.

The importance of siblings was especially apparent where children had older teenage or adult siblings, who tended to feature as significant figures in their family experiences. Some of these families had created what were described in Chapter 2 as 'newly extended' households. This pattern, in which older siblings continued to live in the family home after marriage, bringing in their own spouses and offspring, demonstrates the dynamic nature of families across time. It also illustrates the permeability of South Asian Muslim households as identified by other authors (Smalley 2002; Shaw 2000), and more generally highlights the open nature of some families in modern Britain where domestic (often nuclear) units may be embedded in wider extended networks (what Morgan 1975, referred to as 'modified extended families').

Where teenage and adult siblings were resident in the household, the model of extended co-parenting tended to assign to older children a share in the parenting responsibilities, a pattern identified by other writers in the context of minority ethic families in the UK (e.g. Chamberlain 1999). These siblings frequently played a considerable part in younger children's upbringing, encouraged their educational and career aspirations, and were active in the transmission of religious and cultural values.

In Chapter 7 the example was given of older siblings acquiring more religious knowledge than their parents, and accordingly making distinctive contributions to their younger siblings' religious education. This was labelled as an example of the 'sideways transmission' of religious values which could exist alongside the more commonly recognized 'downwards transmission' through generations. Sideways transmission was linked to the phenomenon of high-Islamization identified by others (e.g. Bauer 1997), which entails an increasing interest in engaging with religious teachings, and a privileging of religious over cultural identity, among a younger generation of Muslims in a migration context. This high-Islamization was especially evident in some families in the current study, where it was often 'driven' by younger, second-generation family members such as adult or teenage siblings, and had a profound impact on the religious knowledge and experience of the 9–11 year-old reference children. High-Islamization thus appears to be an important theme for understanding South Asian Muslim family practices in contemporary Britain, where 'being Muslim' is a component of identity and a marker of minority group membership. Moreover, the agency of younger family members in its production was apparent in this study.

9.1.4 Community religious nurture and 'upwards transmission'

Chapter 6 described how parents routinely imported community resources from outside the household to assist them in their parenting practices. Most particularly, Islamic classes (*madrasah*) at a mosque or local teacher's house were a central element in parents' achievement of the generational transmission of religion. Many parents had not themselves had the opportunity to attend such classes as children, however. The newly developing community provision for religious education was seen to reflect a shift towards more organized religious participation as Muslim communities have become more settled in Britain (Smalley 2002).

This newly formalized religious nurture outside the home was, in many cases, creating a role for children as agents of religious transmission within the family, as they were bringing home newly-acquired knowledge that they imparted to other family members, including their parents. The result was that, in addition to the 'sideways transmission' discussed above, there was also an element of 'upwards transmission' of religious values through the generations. Such a finding constitutes a challenge to the accepted concept of 'downwards transmission', and highlights the possibility of intergenerational transmission being a rather more fluid and interactive process.

In this aspect of religious family practices, then, children were acting as re-instaters of tradition. This emphasis is in contrast to other work (e.g. Song 1996, 1997) which has painted children of immigrants as cultural modernizers – although the study identified other areas of family practices in which children did indeed act as drivers for change (such as persuading their mothers to cook English food). It is also in contrast to Jackson and Nesbitt's (1993) conclusion that for Hindu children in Britain the increasingly formalized and structured nature of religious nurture meant that religion was becoming more a discrete area of influence rather than a whole way of life. In the case of these South Asian Muslim families, formal nurture received in structured settings outside the home was clearly being fed back into the family sphere, rather than remaining separate.

9.1.5 Outside stressors

Chapter 8 drew upon notions of social capital to conceptualize family connections outside the household. As in previous research, the current findings highlighted the general importance of extended family networks, with links being maintained not only locally, but also nationally and transnationally. These kin networks were salient for children as well as parents. A majority of families also enjoyed positive supportive links with their local South Asian Muslim communities – both informal (through friendships and social networks) and formal (through their mosque) – which served as sources of practical, emotional and social support. These instances of 'bonding' capital can be seen as representing the functional aspect of religion-family linkage (Mahoney et al. 2001), offering sources of solidarity and assisting in family religious and cultural transmission.

However, it was noted that a small group of families did not have local extended kin, or at least did not enjoy frequent or positive contact with them. There were also instances in which families did not have relationships with national or transnational extended kin. Similarly some families were not particularly embedded in local community or did not see it as a source of support: instead it could be stressful, a source of negative gossip or pressure. These examples are significant because they contradict often-repeated assumptions that South Asian communities in Britain invariably enjoy close and supportive family relationships, will 'look after their own' and thus do not require other kinds of support (see Becher and Husain 2003; Qureshi et al. 2000).

Also assessed in Chapter 8 were 'bridging' connections with neighbourhood, school, work and the wider world, through which families could build links of reciprocity. Again, it was important to note that such links were not always experienced as positive. They could entail elements of stress or constraint, particularly when the outside world was felt to be at odds with family values and belief systems: for example where work imposed time stresses, or where neighbourhoods were threatening. Most strikingly, it was clear that the post-9/11 shifts in public discourse about Muslims had had a profound effect on these families' interactions with the wider world. Parents in particular spoke of increased Islamophobia at work and at school, and were acutely aware of negative views of Islam as a result of the perceived 'terror threat'. As 'normal Muslims' they were concerned to distance themselves from 'fundamentalists', and this necessity influenced their interactions with non-Muslims, as well as with their children.

9.1.6   Gendered religious family practices

Previous research has suggested a gendered element to religious practices. One study found that the meaning of family religious rituals was more important to husbands' marital satisfaction, while the routines associated with rituals (the ritualistic behaviour per se) were more important for wives (Fiese and Tomcho 2001). In children, too, the religious behaviour of boys may be more affected by parental religious behaviour than that of girls (Flor and Knapp 2001). The current study found a number of gendered aspects that contribute to the impression that 'his faith' and 'her faith' might be different (Snarey and Dollahite 2001). The collection of multiple perspectives lent themselves well to an exploration of the complexities of gendered religious practices, especially as crosscutting with generational factors.

There was some evidence that mothers were doing the most work in maintaining religious and cultural traditions. As Chapter 5 reported, while it was men and children who most commonly attended mosque, women were frequently doing 'behind the scenes' religion work in ensuring that husbands and children attended. Similarly, Chapter 8 echoed other research (notably Finch and Mason 1993) in highlighting numerous examples of mothers working to build and sustain kin networks: for instance, a sense of close extended family living was most frequently maintained with local maternal kin, while links with paternal family were often looser. In addition, Chapter 6 identified Muslim mothers as having a key role in religious transmission, with the notions that 'your mother holds the key of heaven', or that 'heaven is under your mother's foot'.

It is also arguable, though, that in some senses mothers were acting as drivers for change. Chapter 3 raised examples of mothers 'working on' their husbands to persuade them gradually of the desirability of change and assimilation, or acting as mediators between their husbands and children. In Chapter 8 I described how mothers were more likely to actively defend their decisions to go out to work, often on the grounds of personal satisfaction. It is possible that in the light of the traditional assumptions that deterred women from working, these mothers felt it necessary to offer some rationalization for their behaviour. Thus alongside working to maintain family traditions and connections, mothers may also be pushing for cultural transformation in certain areas of family practices.

Fathers, for their part, also appeared to have distinctive experiences of family practices. As shown in Chapter 5, they demonstrated less 'behind the scenes' religion work than mothers, but more public involvement in religious family practices. As a result of their religious participation at mosque, they experienced more demarcation than women between sacred and family time/space. They needed to attend mosque at designated prayer times, unlike women who tended to pray at home wherever (and to some extent whenever) was convenient. Fathers were likely to see themselves as having an important and distinctive role in explicitly encouraging and motivating their children's religious observance, in a religious version of the wider father involvement discourse.

In some respects, children were able to experience both mothers' and fathers' perspectives. For example, they attended Islamic classes at mosque (and some boys additionally attended mosque with their fathers) but also prayed at home with their mothers. In contrast to conclusions reached in some other research studies (e.g. Bauer 1997) boys were not necessarily more religiously observant than girls. Indeed some of the children with the highest levels of religious interest and awareness were girls (such as Amina and Bashira) who were able to articulate their personal religious interest through wearing a headscarf (sometimes despite their mothers' wishes). This latter point links more generally to children's religious agency, in which they were able to use the knowledge they gained in Islamic classes to demonstrate their commitment through fasting during *Ramadan*, following guidelines for Islamic dress or educating their parents or younger siblings about the 'right' way to pray. Additionally in the context of children's gendered experiences, it was interesting that, in contrast to other research (Bhatti 1999; Chattoo et al. 2004) which has focused on slightly older children, in this study boys were more associated with a need for sheltering and monitoring, while girls were often viewed as more 'responsible' and deserving of autonomy. This was possibly due to the Islamically-informed criteria for responsibility (being helpful and obedient) being more likely to be met by girls than boys in this group of 9–11 year olds. It is possible that a reversal may occur at the point of adolescence, when girls' autonomy may be seen as more in need of containment due to the particular association between family respect and young women's behaviour (Chattoo, Atkin et al. 2004).

9.1.7 Religion-culture-family linkages

In a broader sense, the study has addressed some theoretical questions around the complex interrelations between family practices and the cross-cutting concepts of culture, religion, ethnicity, gender and generation. It has been suggested that these factors interact in multi-dimensional ways. For example, as discussed above, the ways in which people 'do' religion may depend on their simultaneous positioning on other dimensions, such as their gender and generational status. Similarly family, cultural and religious practices can be seen as permeable and indeed mutually constituted, so that, for example, cultural norms derive legitimacy from religious beliefs. Further, the exploration of 'practices' highlighted the interlinking between the domains of belief and action. Actions do not simply reflect beliefs, but are also the means through which people understand and experience their beliefs, an argument that was illustrated through the examples of eating, wearing, speaking and watching family practices in Chapter 4.

This research has demonstrated the range of competing and alternative narratives underlying South Asian Muslim family practices. So alongside religion as a central value system there existed a number of other themes that also mattered: the negotiation of cultural tradition and change; boundary construction and maintenance (narratives of 'us' and 'them'); and aspirations for educational, religious and social mobility. Furthermore, within each of these themes there was a variety of possibilities, some contradictory ('us as different' alongside 'us as just like anyone else', or the centrality of religion versus being 'not strict').

This multiplicity of choices was used flexibly by family members, depending on situation and context. Different combinations of values could coincide (as already stated, the contrasting ways in which cultural and religious affiliations were combined is an important example of this) and individual family members frequently held different orientations. This resonates with Swidler's (1986) conception of cultural 'tool-kits' or repertoires on which individual actors draw selectively to create strategies of action, and underlines the fact that, for the South Asian Muslim families in this study, family practices were not straightforwardly determined or homogenous but were negotiated through a diverse range of value systems. This perspective is a useful addition to previous research that concentrates on the effect of one set of values alone – for example, Dollahite and colleagues' focus on 'highly religious families' (Dollahite and Marks 2004; Marks 2004) which takes little account of other factors such as culture or gender. It also draws attention to the importance for researchers of accounting for differing affiliations of individual family members, when seeking a nuanced understanding of family religiosity.

9.2   Policy implications

One objective for this study was to add to knowledge about normative
parenting practices across diverse communities. Existing research
(Henricson, Katz et al. 2001) had suggested that current family support
services were being under-utilized by minority ethnic families, and
that few targeted services existed. It was hoped that by improving
knowledge, more culturally sensitive and accessible services could be
developed. Similarly, researchers in the field of religion have called for
more investigation of the relationship between the family and religious
institutions, especially in providing social support (Parke 2001; Holden
2001). It is hoped that this research has contributed through chal-
lenging myths and stereotypes (for example, the assumption that
South Asian families are universally able to rely on extended family for
support), encouraging reflexivity in practice and policy. Additionally,
the study raises some more concrete recommendations for practice
(Becher and Husain 2003).

Evidence from the qualitative and quantitative elements of the
research indicates that for Muslim parents, their religious group membership is likely to influence family life in a number of ways: many
(especially fathers) attend mosque often, and a significant proportion
send their children for extra education there; their religious views are
perceived as important in bringing up their children, as are the views
of their religious 'leaders'. Not least, they may be more likely to look to
their religious community for formal and informal support. These patterns are in contrast to those for parents from other groups (such as
some Christians), suggesting relatively higher levels of involvement
with the religious community for many Muslim families, a conclusion
that is particularly powerful given that the sample was not accessed
through such communities, but through the secular setting of mainstream education.

These findings have important implications for the delivery of
parenting support that is both appropriate and culturally sensitive.
It would appear that religious communities, and perhaps Muslim communities in particular, present relatively undeveloped opportunities for
the delivery of tailored support to parents. Many Muslim parents are
already engaged with and open to supplementing their parenting with
resources drawn from religious settings such as Mosques and Islamic
schools. There is also an apparent level of trust and engagement within
religious community networks and with religious leaders, which could
mean that support offered through these channels would be readily

accepted. Equipping such existing channels to widen the scope of support they offer to families, and increasing their resources to do so, may be an effective way of providing support to parents that is both religiously sensitive and easily accessible. This would require non-Muslim professionals to work sensitively in partnership with Muslim colleagues in the voluntary sector and religious leaders in order to deliver such services.

However, more research would be required to fully explicate this area. The emphasis of the study on daily normative practices meant that seeking help for problems was only explored incidentally, since few parents had actually gone beyond the immediate family for help with parenting. Thus although the evidence demonstrates the possibility of accessing parents through faith community settings, it does not conclusively establish whether, and what sorts of support would actually be required. A related research study has interviewed practitioners and discussed possible models of support for South Asian Muslim parents (Becher and Husain 2003).

9.3 Conclusion

The research described in this book yielded rich information on family practices in a specific ethno-religious milieu, that of South Asian Muslims in urban Britain. The focus on one group and location was valuable in allowing a deeper analysis of the dimensions of religiosity and cultural affiliation in a family context, and allowed attention to the multiple contrasting perspectives of individual family members. Similarly, the use of multiple methods helped to build a contextualized picture, interpreting the qualitative data within the context of a wider set of patterns.

Given the general resonance with themes in the existing literature, the issues raised in this study are likely to have relevance across other contexts too. The findings particularly contribute to theoretical knowledge of family practices in minority faith and ethnic contexts in Britain. More such research with other religious groups – especially Muslims of other national backgrounds, and families of other religious groups – would confirm and deepen the findings, and help to further untangle the relationships between culture, ethnicity and religion. It is hoped that future research will add to these insights.

Appendices

A. Research methodology

This section gives an outline of the research methods, including the initial aims, research questions, sampling and access strategies, design of research instruments, fieldwork and data analysis.

a. Research aims and questions

The study was intended to provide normative data on parenting values and practices amongst South Asian Muslim families in Britain. The first working aim of the research was to *map family practices from the perspectives of South Asian Muslim mothers, fathers and children, focusing particularly on the role of religion.* Associated research questions were:

- What are the main issues facing South Asian Muslim parents raising children within a faith community?
- What are the distinctive roles and experiences of mothers, fathers and children in South Asian Muslim families?
- How do families negotiate tradition and change within a contemporary British context?
- What are the belief systems held by South Asian Muslim families concerning family practices? How do these relate to, for example:

  - Daily routines, in particular those focused on food, dress, leisure, space and time?
  - The obligations and responsibilities of parents?
  - The contemporary emphasis on children's rights and agency?
  - The negotiation of discipline, child autonomy and parental control?

A second working aim was to *examine the nature and sources of help and support for parenting in South Asian Muslim families*, in order to contribute to the National Family and Parenting Institute's aim to develop more culturally sensitive parenting education and support, and to discover:

- How do parents go about seeking help for family problems?
- What are the main formal and informal support systems available? To what extent are they provided by the faith community? What is the role of extended family members (including transnational kin networks) in providing support?
- What is the nature of the support? What are the values it promotes and to what extent does it contain a faith message?
- Are these support systems adequate for all family members?

b.   The research population

It was decided to focus on interviews with one ethno-religious group, in order to achieve in-depth insight into the research questions. This was particularly important because of the overlapping but distinct categories of religion and ethnicity/culture, which would make comparisons between two or three ethno-religious groups very difficult to untangle in a small-scale study. The use of an initial questionnaire survey with a wider range of families than in the interview sample would add to this in-depth understanding by placing the group in question in the context of broader patterns.

Muslim families were selected as Britain's largest minority religious group, and as a population that has come under increased scrutiny from policy makers, politicians and the media in recent years. More information was needed on the parenting preferences and needs of Muslim parents, especially in the light of anecdotal evidence from practitioners who argued that current parenting support services were viewed as culturally inappropriate, and were thus under-used by Muslim families (see Becher and Husain 2003).

However, Muslims in the UK form a large and fragmented population, with a large variety of national/ethnic allegiances and a range of denominational ties. It was therefore decided to sample from the largest group of British Muslims, those of South Asian origin, and more specifically those of Pakistani and/or Indian origin. The selection of a specific ethno-religious group meant that within-group comparisons were easier to unravel. By limiting the focus, it was also easier to incorporate a range of levels of religious affiliation, from those 'believing without belonging' to more religiously observant Muslim families.

c.   Research methodology and design

The research was interpretive and exploratory in approach – the aim was a careful piecing together and filling in of a picture, in an approach that was inductive and hypothesis-generating (Hammersley 1992).

The approach involved the collection of information from multiple informants. Handel (1996) has argued that, traditionally, family research has been deficient in focusing exclusively on one relationship (e.g. the mother-child or marital relationship) and often using data from only one informant. Handel emphasizes that 'no member of any family is a sufficient source of information for that family' (1996:346). Consequently, there has been a growing awareness within family research of the importance of collecting accounts from multiple family members (Marsiglio, Amato et al. 2000).

Multiple methods were also used, in order to capitalize on the varying strengths of different approaches (Patton 1990:13), and to offer a comprehensive and contextualized picture (Sandelowski 2002). Qualitative and quantitative methods were integrated in the research design, but were used for different purposes according to their strengths – what Mason and May (2004) have described as 'meshing' methods. More specifically, a quantitative survey was used as groundwork for the qualitative study, in a facilitative and complementary combination (Hammersley 1996).

Ethical issues, particularly in relation to informed consent, confidentiality and anonymity, were salient throughout the planning and conduct of the study.

d. Research settings: location and access

After an examination of 2001 Census data, an outer London borough situated to the North East of London, was selected as an area that represented a sufficient range of ethnic, religious and social diversity, including a relatively high density of South Asian Muslims. Hood (2004) reported that among children aged 0–15 in the borough, only 45 per cent were White British – a relatively low figure when compared with the average for Great Britain as a whole, which was around 86 per cent. The next largest groups of children in Waltham Forest were Pakistani (12 per cent), Black Caribbean (9 per cent) and Black African (8 per cent). Figures for religious diversity are not available for children, but the 2001 Census offered some information on overall religious diversity in the borough. The proportion of Christians (of all ages) was lower than the national average (57 per cent compared with 72 per cent in England and Wales as a whole), while there was a relatively high proportion of Muslims (15 per cent, compared with 3 per cent nationally). Figures for other religious groups were similar to the national average. In line with patterns for London as a whole, children in the borough experience relatively high levels of poverty (Hood 2004).

Families were approached through state primary schools, in order to obtain a range and diversity in the types of families studied. Going through schools also made it readily possible to focus on one age-group, since the initial research took place within class groups.

e. The questionnaire study

i. Aims and purpose

Quantitative methods were used at the outset, in the form of a school-based questionnaire survey. The questionnaire survey was designed to give a cross-sectional overview of the research issues, in order to facilitate comparisons between faith and ethnic groups. In addition, the questionnaire study provided the means of identifying a sub-sample of South Asian Muslim families who could be followed up for in-depth interviews.

ii. Questionnaire development

Separate short questionnaires were developed for children and parents. Where possible, questions from existing surveys were used or adapted.

The questionnaires were then subjected to intensive qualitative piloting using cognitive interviewing methods[37] in order to ensure that questions were meaningful, unambiguously worded and user-friendly.

The final questionnaire content was as follows:

A four-page questionnaire for children, covering:

- age;
- gender;
- household composition;
- frequency of activities with mother and father;
- self-defined religion;

- frequency of attendance at religious services;
- attitudes towards religious services (favourite and least favourite things);
- country of birth;
- self-defined ethnicity (categories offered: 'Asian or Asian British'; 'Black or Black British'; 'Chinese'; 'Mixed'; 'White British'; 'Other (please write in)').

A separate, eight-page questionnaire aimed at parents, covering:

- relation to child;
- perceived influences on parenting;
- past and future sources of help, advice or support for parenting;
- perceived best and worst things about parenting;
- gender;
- age;
- self-defined ethnicity (self and partner);
- household composition;
- self-defined religion (self and partner);
- religious attendance (self and partner);
- family support from religious community;
- an optional section asking permission to re-contact, with space for parents to write in contact details if they wished to do so.

The inclusion of demographic measures of household composition, ethnicity, and religion were useful in identifying the families which met the criteria for the follow-up interviews.

iii. Sampling and recruitment

A simple random sample of 10 schools was selected from a list of all primary and junior schools in the borough (a total of nearly 50 schools), to help ensure that a suitable range (in terms of proportions from minority faith/ethnic groups, or levels of deprivation) would have the opportunity to participate. The Head Teachers of these 10 schools were invited to participate in the study. Five schools were unable to take part because of staff workload, high staff turnover or problems with buildings, all of which meant they did not have the resources to facilitate the research process. This left 5 schools, spread across the borough, where the Head Teachers agreed to participate.

In each participating school, all year 5 classes (age 9–10) were included in the study. Thus every year 5 pupil present in each school on the day of fieldwork was given an opportunity to participate.

iv. Fieldwork procedures

Before fieldwork began in the borough, the relevant documents and procedures were piloted in a large primary school situated in another outer London borough with comparable ethnic and religious diversity. As a result of this pilot, the research methodology was refined in several respects.

Fieldwork took place on 1 day in each participating school. For the first 3 schools, fieldwork was carried out in June–July 2003. A further two schools were visited in September–October 2003.

The parents of the year 5 children at each school received a letter a few days before the fieldwork was due to begin, informing them that the study was to take place and giving them the opportunity to 'opt out' if they did not want their child to take part.

Fieldwork was carried out in a half-hour session in each year 5 class. The research study was introduced and the questionnaire carefully explained to pupils, with considerable emphasis on ensuring free and informed consent in the classroom setting. The anonymity of the study was stressed, as was the fact that there were no right or wrong answers, and that participation was voluntary. Pupils were then given approximately 15 minutes to complete the questionnaire.

After all the children had finished, they were asked to take a questionnaire home for their parents to fill in (an Urdu version was also offered), and to bring it back to school in time for collection a week later. In each school a small prize was offered to the class with the highest rate of parents' questionnaires returned. In order to increase the parental response rate, there was a 'prize draw' of a £20 voucher for one parent at each school, details of which were given on the front page of the parents' questionnaire. Child and parent questionnaires were anonymously linked via serial numbers.

v. Response rates

Response rates within the classroom were very high, at around 90–95 per cent across all schools. Non-participation was largely due to absence; only one child did not take part because her mother had contacted the school to 'opt out' of the study.

In contrast, despite the incentive of a £20 'prize draw', and frequent return visits to schools, the return rate of parental questionnaires was lower at 46 per cent – a figure which is however acceptably high for a self-completion survey (Burgess 2003).

The information given in the children's questionnaires allowed some examination of the differences between parental responders and non-responders. It appeared that there were no discernable differences between children whose parents did and did not complete the questionnaire, in terms of gender, age, household size, frequency of activities with parents, or religion. Some small ethnic group differences were apparent, however: children whose parents completed the questionnaire were slightly more likely to be white British than children whose parents did not respond (33 per cent compared with 22 per cent). Children of non-responders were correspondingly slightly more likely to describe themselves as 'Black or Black British' (19 per cent of children whose parents did not respond, versus 10 per cent of those whose parents did), or as being of 'Other' ethnicity (18 per cent versus 13 per cent).

vi. The final survey sample

Age and gender

A total of 327 children completed the questionnaire, a very large majority of whom were aged either 9 (49 per cent) or 10 (50 per cent), although 1 child was aged 8 and 4 children were aged 11. Pupils were evenly split between boys (51 per cent) and girls (49 per cent).

Responding parents, of whom there were 149, were mostly in the 30 to 44 age group (77 per cent), although 10 per cent were under 30 and 13 per cent were over

45. These parents were 71 per cent female and 29 per cent male. When asked to indicate their relationship to the child, two thirds affirmed that they were the child's mother and 24 per cent the child's father. The remaining 8 per cent identified themselves as other people, usually relatives such as aunts, uncles or siblings.

Among Muslim families, a slightly higher than average proportion of fathers (28 per cent) and others (13 per cent) filled in the questionnaire, while among Christian[38] families, mothers were more likely (78 per cent) and fathers less likely (14 per cent) to have completed the questionnaire. This may reflect a differing distribution of household responsibilities for engaging with school matters (see Table A.1).

The vast majority (96 per cent) of children reported that they lived with their mother. Some three-quarters (76 per cent) listed their father, and another 5 per cent mentioned their stepfather or mother's boyfriend, indicating that around 8 in 10 lived in two-parent households.

Religion and ethnicity
The children who completed the questionnaire belonged to a wide range of ethnic and religious groups. The largest religious groups were Muslim, 37 per cent, Christian, 37 per cent and 'no religion', 19 per cent. In terms of ethnicity, 31 per cent of children described themselves as 'Asian or Asian British', 27 per cent 'White British', 15 per cent 'Black or Black British', 16 per cent 'Other' and 9 per cent 'Mixed'.

The majority of the children completing this survey were born in the UK (86 per cent). The rest were born in a wide variety of countries; the next most common was Pakistan (8 children). Most of the children of minority ethnic origin in this sample were accordingly second- or even third-generation immigrants.

vii.   Analysis
Data from the questionnaires was entered into SPSS, a statistical computer package, and analysed for a variety of factors to highlight any patterns of difference, particularly between the two largest faith groups (Muslim and Christian). Where parents had also completed a questionnaire, these were linked to the child's answers, to broaden the analysis. An initial report on the survey findings was sent to all participating schools.

Table A.1   **Which parent filled in the questionnaire, by parent's religion**

	Responding parent's religion		All parents
	Christian	Muslim	
Responding parent's relationship to the child			
Mother	78 %	56%	66%
Father	14%	28%	24%
Other person	6%	13%	8%
Base	*51*	*54*	*143*

Because of the differential response rates, the results from the children's questionnaires are more reliable than those of the parents and thus form the bulk of the analysis, although findings from the parents' questionnaires are also used. The report therefore presents statistical data from the perspectives of children, using children as a unit of analysis – a practice that is relatively unusual in quantitative research (Qvortrup 1990), despite recent trends in this direction (Madge 2001; Collingwood Bakeo and Clarke 2004; Hood 2004).

Where quantitative data are reported in this book, differences between groups are significant to the 5 per cent level, unless otherwise stated.[39]

f.   The qualitative interviews

i.   *Aims and theoretical approach*

The collection of qualitative accounts of family practices from South Asian Muslim mothers, fathers and children were the primary source of data in this study. In-depth interviews, with the resulting 'thick description' (Geertz 1973:6), were a particularly appropriate method for illuminating family practices, since the concept is based on the notion of beliefs, values and actions constructed through interaction. The qualitative approach was subtle enough to capture the richness of family experience, and enhanced sensitivity to context and meaning (Lee 1993). Qualitative semi-structured interviews also allowed a more even balance of control over their form and content than structured approaches (Brannen 1988) helping to open up a space in which participants could introduce issues which they saw as important – a vital possibility in an exploratory study.

ii.   *Sampling and access*

The interview sample was selected strategically (Mason 2002) from the questionnaires that were returned by parents during the survey. The families in the sample varied across the following dimensions (which according to existing literature might lead to meaningful variation in family practices):

- First- versus second-generation parents
- Extent of cultural assimilation/cultural reconstitution and change
- Extent of religious affiliation/observance (e.g. 'believing without belonging' versus families high in religious affiliation/membership of faith community)
- Socio-economic context
- Family area of origin
- Gender of child
- Whether the family had sought help for family problems or accessed family support services

The factors held constant in order to increase depth and comparability were:

- Whether or not the family was part of a visible minority ethnic group (all were South Asian)
- Geographical location (all were in an outer London borough living in neighbourhoods with a relatively high proportion of families from the same background)

- Whether or not parents were from different faith groups (there were no 'mixed marriages')
- Age of child (all were 9–11 at time of interview).

In order to be part of the potential follow-up group, then, the child and the responding parent needed to have identified themselves as both Muslim and South Asian Indian or Pakistani ('Asian or Asian British' for children). In addition they needed to have returned a parent questionnaire in which they had responded positively to the follow-up question and provided contact details. Of the 327 children who completed a questionnaire at school, 78 (24 per cent) were both 'Asian or Asian British' and Muslim; 35 (45 per cent) of these returned parental questionnaires. Of these 35 parents, 20 (57 per cent) had given permission for me to re-contact them, and provided address details. All 20 were followed up by letter addressed to the contact parent, and then telephone call or visit, inviting them to participate in the qualitative study. Of the 20 families contacted, one refused (explaining that they were going through a 'difficult time' and did not want to participate), and one was impossible to contact despite repeated telephone calls and personal visits. The remaining 18 families participated in the study.

In the interests of securing informed consent, the nature of the research, their role within it, confidentiality and anonymity arrangements, and the intended use of the findings was fully (and age-appropriately) explained to participants. This was treated as an ongoing yet informal process, and consent was negotiated at a number of stages and with individual family members separately. In each family parental consent was secured before discussing the interview process with children, and each child's consent was sought before conducting the interviews.

Each individual participant was given a £10 voucher (postal orders for parents and a choice of shopping vouchers for children) as a 'token of thanks' for their time.

After the interviews, tapes and transcripts were labelled just with serial numbers rather than names, and were kept securely.

In the interests of anonymity, pseudonyms are used, and any particular identifying details omitted, in the interview extracts contained in this book.

iii.   Planning and conducting the interviews

The research interviews took place in the participants' family homes, at a time specified by them, and were spread over a period of seven months, from September 2003 to April 2004.

Interviews were conducted in whichever area of the house the interviewees preferred. As a result, some interviews were more formal than others – usually I was in the smart front room reserved for visitors (see Shaw 2000), but in a few cases the interviews took place at the back of the house, in the kitchen or communal area.

As other researchers have discovered, it was sometimes difficult to find a private space for interviews. Other family members expected to sit in, and sometimes the children themselves expressed a wish for a parent or a sibling to stay. Although I explained my preference for privacy and a quiet environment for recording, I always respected family members' wishes and in several interviews other people remained in the room.

Each interview began with some warm-up questions and general chat, in order to build rapport. During the interview itself a topic guide was used (of which there were separate versions for mothers, fathers and children) to steer the interview through a number of themes, but this was used organically and flexibly rather than rigidly. Pilot interviews with two families had given invaluable assistance in refining topic guides. The interviews covered the following general areas:

- Warm-up
- Family composition and background
- Talking through 'typical' day in their household (and differences for weekend day; holiday)
- Family roles: their own role and the roles of others; who does what
- Religion in family life: importance of Islam
- Help and support needed and obtained (parents only)

Interviews with parents lasted between 45 minutes and 2 hours, with an average of about an hour and a quarter. Interviews with children were shorter at some 45 minutes to an hour, and sometimes included a break if children were tired. During the interviews with children, I was aware of the preference to talk about specific, concrete situations rather than abstract topics (Armstrong, Hill et al. 1998) and was careful to take guidance from their own language (Weber, Miracle et al. 1994). I was concerned to give children a sense of control over the interview process (Grover 2004), through letting the interview proceed at their chosen pace and in their preferred mode (sitting on the floor; moving around and looking at things they showed me, and so on).

I was aware of the fact that I was a white British researcher working with South Asian Muslims, and thus fundamentally in the position of an outsider (and a member of the majority group in the wider sense). It was an issue that I needed to consider carefully, not least in order to assess my own impact on the research process. I recognized that being an outsider brought both advantages and disadvantages. The disadvantages were mainly in terms of access (it may have been harder to 'get in') and language difficulties (by not speaking Urdu or Punjabi I probably lost some interviews). Additionally there was the possibility of inadequate levels of rapport or understanding, something I tried to solve by being a sensitive and empathetic interviewer. In other respects I found it an advantage to be able to present myself as a naïve outsider. With limited initial knowledge, it was also easier not to make assumptions. It was a further benefit that people were able to confide in me, as a non-member of the local South Asian community, without being concerned about their family's reputation.

Field notes were made immediately after each interview, providing records of my own observations and impressions during the interview visit.

Language issues

A few first-generation mothers (Habiba's and Munir's), who had not grown up in Britain, were not confident in their English ability. As I did not speak Urdu or Punjabi and did not have the resources to employ a professional translator,[40] the usual outcome was that these mothers asked a daughter (Habiba's mother asked Habiba herself) to sit in on the interview and to help interpret (usually replies came from mothers first, in basic English, and were then expanded upon through the interpreter). It was important to consider role of the interpreter as active in producing the interview accounts, especially when deciding how to translate the cultural meaning of concepts (Temple and Edwards 2002) a dynamic to which I tried to be sensitive during the analysis. In particular I was cautious about using the translated parts of interviews as stand-alone evidence, and relied instead on the mothers' own words, using the translations to check meaning.

Many parents did not have English as their mother tongue, but spoke it with varying degrees of fluency and were happy to be interviewed in English. I looked out for possible translation issues where people were not being interviewed in their first language, using the tactic of asking the same question in different ways, and checking back with the respondents, to be sure that I had understood their intentions. In the chapters that follow, I have reproduced the grammar and syntax used by respondents, to indicate the fluency with which their answers were given.

iv.   *Interviews achieved*

As described above, I achieved interviews with 18 families in the sample (of 20 approached), with a total of 44 interviews. The child identified in the school survey phase was interviewed in all 18 families – in fact, as one family contained twins, I interviewed 19 children in all.

I interviewed the child's mother in 16 families. In the two remaining families I interviewed a 'mother figure', the grown-up sister of the reference child. In both cases this was suggested by the family, when I asked who would be the best person to talk to about bringing up the child in question. These adult sisters both lived in the family home with their own husbands and children and played a central and significant role in the reference child's upbringing.

Fathers were the group to whom it proved the most difficult to gain access, as other researchers have also reported (Costigan and Cox 2001). I interviewed fathers from 7 of the families. Five fathers were not present in the home. The remaining 6 fathers all refused interviews despite strenuous efforts on my part. This was for a variety of reasons – 2 did not speak any English at all; 2 refused due to heavy work commitments (despite my offer to interview them at the workplace) and to the remaining 2 I had no access (not even to request an interview) as a result of maternal gate-keeping. The 7 full family 'sets' which included interviews with fathers were rich sources of data on fatherhood. In the remaining 11 families I also collected a substantial body of secondary data on fathers and their roles by talking to mothers and children.

v.   *Analysis*

The interviews (excluding the two in which the interviewees had preferred not to be recorded, and two in which the equipment failed) were all transcribed in line with the conventions of social research interviewing[41] and analysed with the help of Nvivo software.

A grounded theory approach theory (Glaser and Strauss 1967; Glaser 1978; Strauss and Corbin 1998) was adopted as a starting point, based on the assumption that careful analysis of what people say can illuminate their lifeworlds, and help towards achieving a closely grounded understanding of the ways in which they make sense of their experiences. The topic of family practices in South Asian Muslim families is still open to exploration and discovery, and by using a data-driven method, a theoretical understanding could be achieved which would have been impossible with hypothesis-testing. However, reflecting the proposition that preconceptions cannot be totally avoided in analysis (Bulmer 1979; Charmaz 1995), the analytical approach here was closer to 'constructivist grounded theory' (Charmaz 2000:522), accounting for an interplay between theory and data. Accordingly, the literature was consulted in tandem with the development of an analytical framework, with attention paid to the researcher's role both in jointly constructing the interviews, and in selecting and building the themes into an analytic framework.

Open coding was initially carried out with 5 transcripts, and involved careful line-by-line familiarization, identification of concepts from the data (including comparison with previous uses in the transcripts of the same concept) and writing of memos to record emerging impressions. I then moved to axial coding and mind-mapping, which involved drawing linkages and connections between themes, thus creating loose groupings of broad concepts and their sub-categories. At this point I sorted the codes I had created into a framework, with clusters of concepts around 5 broad areas of family practices: family stories; family beliefs and values; family time and space; family roles and processes; family resources and connections.

The analytic framework was used flexibly as a means of organizing the detailed line-by-line coding and analysis of all transcripts. This was an iterative process in that the storyline continued to develop during coding, and I continued selectively to code certain categories in further detail. In beginning to write up the data I developed the framework further into a 'storyline'. Data analysis was thus an active process of 'making meaning' (Esterberg 2002:152) rather than simply uncovering conclusions inherent in the data.

Following the tenets of grounded theory, the analysis remained close to the data and I depended on constant checking to verify and refine emerging ideas (Charmaz 1995), particularly seeking 'negative instances' within the data when developing the analysis (Mason 2002). I also checked with insider informants (South Asian Muslim friends and colleagues) and against the existing literature, to ensure that my interpretations rang true. To further enhance analytic rigour, I triangulated findings within the data by making comparisons between multiple informants within each family, and externally against the questionnaire findings. This is a key strategy by which reliability, validity and trustworthiness can be maximized in qualitative research (Golafshani 2003).

vi.   The final interview sample

The 18 families who were interviewed for the second stage of the study represented a range in terms of gender of child, ethnic background, parental work status, father presence, level of religious observance (estimated from the questionnaire and interviews), and generation (in terms of whether parents were born here or elsewhere). The characteristics of these families are summarized in Table A.2, and further background data given in Table A.3.

The socio-economic and demographic characteristics of the interviewed families are described in detail, and their correspondence with wider demographic patterns considered, in Chapter 2.

Table A.2   Characteristics of interviewed families

Gender of child	11	boys (including 1 set of male twins)
	8	girls
Ethnic background	15	Pakistani
	3	Indian
Religious observance	1	low
	5	low-medium
	4	medium
	4	medium-high
	4	high
Fathers' work status	11	working full-time
	2	not working
	5	father not present
Mothers' work status	2	working full-time
	3	working part-time
	13	not working
Parents' generational status	8	both parents first-generation immigrants born outside UK
	10	One parent first-generation, the other parent born and/or brought up in UK

g.   Representativeness and generalizability

i.   *Scope and limitations of the survey and interview samples*

As noted earlier the study focused on a specific outer London borough. Many of the issues and experiences raised by families in this setting are likely to be relevant across other urban locations in Britain. Nevertheless, it is important to remember that the specific context of this borough – an urban area with a relatively high proportion of Muslim families (and thus a fairly well-developed community provision, including many local mosques and Islamic classes) – may give rise to family experiences which differ from those living in rural situations or areas with a low minority ethnic population.

Within the borough itself, the families interviewed were identified through a random sample of mainstream state primary schools. The use of state schools means that a wide range of Muslim families is likely to be reflected in terms of levels of religious observance – those who are 'culturally' Muslim or 'believe without belonging' as well as those with strong observance levels. There are no private religious schools in the borough for children of the target age group, so even highly observant families are likely to use state provision – although the most motivated may move to live in an area near such a school.

In this book, the survey responses of Muslim children or parents are in some cases contrasted with those of Christian children or parents. This particular comparison is used because those two were the largest religious groups in the survey sample (each constituting just over a third of the total). Other groups

Table A.3 Background data on interview sample

Family no.	Gender of child	Child's place	Interviews done[1]	Household size	Resident parents	Resident children	Resident adult children	Resident grand-children	Other resident adults	Religious observance[2]
1	2 boys (twins)	youngest	M C C	6	2	4	0			Low-medium
2	boy	middle	M C	6	2	4	0			High
3	girl	oldest	M C	4	1	3	0			Medium
4	boy	oldest	M C F	5	2	3	0			Low
5	boy	youngest	M C	5	1	3	1			High
6	boy	middle	F M C	6	2	4	0			High
7	girl	only	C M F	3	2	1	0			Medium-high
8	boy	oldest	C M F	5	2	3	0			Medium-high
9	boy	middle	M C F	6	2	3	1			Medium-high
10	girl	youngest	S C	10	2	4	1	1	2	Low-medium
11	boy	oldest	M C	5	2	3	0			Low-medium
12	boy	oldest	M C	3	1	2	0			Medium
13	girl	youngest	M C	5	2	2	1			Medium-high
14	girl	youngest	S C	11	1	3	4	1		High
15	girl	youngest	F M C	9	2	2	2	3	2	Medium
16	boy	youngest	M C	5	1	1	3			Low-medium
17	girl	oldest	M C	6	2	4	0			Medium
18	girl	oldest	M C F	4	2	2	0			Low-medium

Table A.3 Background data on interview sample – *continued*

Family no.	Ethnic origin	Generation[3]	Father's work status	Mother's work status	NS-sec[4]	% Muslims in Ward[5]	% Asians in Ward
1	Pakistan	mixed	FT (nights)	PT	3	17	20
2	India	first	FT (shifts)	No	5	25	22
3	Pakistan	mixed	Not present	No	0	23	20
4	Pakistan/India	mixed	FT (shifts)	PT	4	21	22
5	Pakistan	mixed	Not present	No	0	19	18
6	Pakistan	first	FT	No	1	19	18
7	India	mixed	No	No	0	25	25
8	India	mixed	FT	PT	1	25	25
9	Pakistan	first	FT	FT	2	21	22
10	Pakistan	first	FT	No	5	14	15
11	Pakistan	mixed	FT	No	5	19	19
12	Pakistan	mixed	Not present	No	0	23	20
13	Pakistan	first	No	No	0	19	19
14	Pakistan	first	Not present	No	0	14	15
15	Pakistan	first	FT	No	3	23	20
16	Pakistan	first	Not present	No	0	19	18
17	Pakistan	mixed	FT	No	3	19	19
18	Pakistan	mixed	FT	FT	5	14	15

[1] M = mother; C = target child; F = father; S = adult sister (mother-figure)

[2] Religious observance was a snapshot measure based on questionnaire completion and field notes. The measure is based on the researcher's impression of a combination of factors including observance of prayers; attendance at mosque; children's attendance at Madrasah; expressed importance of religion in family practices. See Chapter 8 for more discussion.

[3] first = both parents first-generation immigrants having arrived in UK as adults; mixed = family contains one first-generation parent and one second-generation parent (born and/or brought up in the UK). See Chapter 2.

[4] Based on National Statistics Standard Economic Classification self-coded version: 1 = Managerial and professional occupations; 2 = Intermediate occupations; 3 = Small employers and own account workers; 4 = Lower supervisory and technical; 5 = Semi-routine and routine; 0 = never worked and long-term unemployed.

[5] Ward data is based on 2001 Census neighbourhood statistics (ONS 2001), http://neighbourhood.statistics.gov.uk/dissemination

were too small to be eligible for statistical analysis. However, these two groupings were themselves ethnically very diverse. For example some 37 per cent of
Christian children were white British, while the rest were from a variety of
ethnic groups. The Muslim children were only 71 per cent Asian: the second
largest group of Muslims were of 'other' ethnicity (17 per cent), with a few
mixed (5 per cent), white British (4 per cent) and Black or Black British (3 per
cent). These comparisons therefore need to be viewed as somewhat simplistic,
and are provided in order to show the general contrast between Muslims and
other groups, rather than to indicate any firm population characteristics (particularly for Christians). Ideally the sample would have been large enough to allow
for more disaggregation between subgroups than is possible here.

Similarly, since the study focused on children aged 9–11, the findings represent the specific issues for children at this developmental stage. However, the
open nature of the interviews, as well as the fact that most parents had children
of other ages and often referred to past and future considerations during interviews, mean that many of the key themes relating to family life in general are
also illustrated in the qualitative data.

ii.   How representative is the interview sample?

The objective of qualitative sampling is usually to capture and represent the
range and diversity that exists in the population under scrutiny (Mason 2002).
In the case of the present enquiry, the overall aim was to study families of South
Asian Muslim origin. Within qualitative research, one would not seek to reflect
the exact proportions within the wider population being studied (for example,
it is not necessary to reflect directly the actual ratio of families of Indian or
Pakistani origin). One would however attempt to encapsulate a sufficient range
of characteristics to make worthwhile comparisons. As shown in chapter 2, the
sampled families arguably reflected the current demographic profile of South
Asian Muslims in Britain: they lived in an urban location with a relatively high
proportion of neighbours from the same ethno-religious background; they were
mostly not well-off (40 per cent were workless) and there was a relatively high
incidence of poor mental and physical health. The 9–11 year-olds in these families had their own distinctive trajectories: most were born in the UK and had
lived in the same area all their lives and thus had much more 'settled' life stories
than their parents. All children spoke fluent English. They had busy schedules,
attending Islamic classes after school or at the weekends. Most were in large
families with a number of siblings who featured strongly in their daily lives.
These features together indicate that the experiences of the sampled families are
likely to be more widely relevant to other South Asian Muslim children and
parents in Britain.

The most significant limitation of the interviewed sample is likely to have
been language ability. The importance of this factor is difficult to assess.
Although parents' questionnaires were offered in Urdu, no completed Urdu
questionnaires were returned. All the families returning questionnaires therefore
had at least one member able to read and complete the version in English. It is
likely that there were some Muslim families in which the parents' level of
English was insufficient to allow participation. As already noted, some fathers
did not participate at the interview stage because of poor English skills. The

implication is that those Muslim families with limited English – probably more recent arrivals to the UK – are under-represented in the study.

Secondly, while the sample included both first- and mixed-generation families, there were no families in which both parents were second-generation immigrants. As discussed in Chapter 2, such families are currently comparatively rare, which probably explains why none were present in the sample. However, it is possible that such families would hold different orientations towards negotiating tradition and change in a British context, and so at least some of the issues and challenges they face might be different.

In a similar vein were the difficulties in recruiting fathers for the study, which meant that fewer participated in interviews than I had hoped – out of the 11 families with a resident father, only 7 took part in interviews. This is a notoriously hard-to-reach group, though it is possible that a male researcher (particularly from a South Asian background) might have had more success. I was lucky in being able to gain substantial data on fathers from mothers and children in every family. However, the implications of fathers' lower participation are that the sample of participating fathers may be skewed towards those who are particularly motivated and involved with their children. This was apparent in some of the interview data – for example, as discussed in Chapter 6, virtually all the interviewed fathers stressed their active role in encouraging their children's educational achievement. Research would be needed with a wider range of fathers before concluding that this was a trend common to all South Asian Muslim experiences of fatherhood.

In conclusion, more research would be needed before attributing the findings to Muslim families from national or ethnic groups other than Indian or Pakistani, or to non-Muslim South Asian families. The London-based nature of the data should also be borne in mind. Most importantly, the reliance on English at both the questionnaire and the interview stage suggests that there may be issues not captured in this sample for families recently arrived in the UK.

All in all, however, the interviewed families would appear to represent Indian and Pakistani families with children in the mid-childhood years in outer London relatively well. It can also be reasonably argued that the issues raised will have resonance across other geographical contexts, and will contribute more generally to theoretical knowledge of family practices in minority faith and ethnic contexts.

Notes

Chapter 1 Introduction

1 The 2001 Census found that people from ethnic minority groups made up 9 per cent of the population in England, an increase of around 50 per cent in the ten years since 1991, when the figure was 6 per cent.

2 Speech made at Labour Party conference, 2001: online at http://www.bristol. ac.uk/Depts/GRC/FP/new_page_177.htm. More recently, the focus has had negative overtones as concern about immigration has increased. Labour MP Karen Buck pointed out on 22nd June 2004 that 'Islam, asylum, immigration and terror have become conflated in the public mind'. This ambiguity is captured in the title of the Home Office White Paper *Secure Borders, Save Haven: Integration with Diversity in Modern Britain* (February 2002).

3 See Hansard Written Answers 30th June 2003.

4 Being brought forward by the Serious Organised Crime and Police Bill: see www.homeoffice.gov.uk/comrace/faith/crime/index.html.

Chapter 2 Family and Demographic Contexts

5 Shaw (2003) indicates that brides and grooms are 'brought over' in roughly equal proportions.

6 Data from www.statistics.gov.uk/neighbourhood.

7 The two main branches of Islam are Sunni and Shi'a. The split occurred after the death of Muhammed in 632 AD as a result of different beliefs about who was Muhammed's legitimate heir. Sunnis constitute the majority in Islam (some suggest 90 per cent).

8 The Ahmadiyya, who are persecuted in Pakistan, base their beliefs on the teachings of Mirza Ghulam Ahmad, who controversially claimed to be a latter-day prophet.

9 Equivalent figures for parents are 53 per cent of Muslim parents (n=51) and 18 per cent of Christian parents (n=50). Base sizes are too small to break down reliably by gender of parent but it appeared that Muslim fathers were slightly more likely to attend at least once a week (23 out of 39) than Muslim mothers (20 out of 43).

10 This does not directly reflect previous notions of acculturation, or of tradition versus modernity, since both ends of the spectrum involved active negotiation and cultural reconstruction.

Chapter 3 Family Beliefs and Values

11 The analysis here follows the agenda set by the ESRC Research Group on Care, Values and the Future of Welfare (CAVA) based at the University of Leeds between 1999 and 2004 (see e.g. Deacon and Williams 2004).

12 Following other researchers (Finch and Mason 2000; Ribbens-McCarthy, Edwards et al. 2001), the term 'narrative' is used in this analysis to refer to evaluative moral 'stories' respondents told to make sense of their experiences. This is informed by the recent emphasis in qualitative research on interviews as narratives (Josselson and Leiblich 1993; Riessman 1993; Coffey and Atkinson 1996; Crossley 2000), although the current research did not adhere to narrative methodology per se.

13 The base sizes for other religious groups were too small to allow meaningful conclusions (Hindu=7, 'Other'=5), so only Christian (N=52) and Muslim parents (N=56) are included in the comparison. Twenty-seven parents had 'no religion'. Sub-group sizes were also too small to allow comparison of mothers and fathers within particular religious groups.

14 By referring to themselves as 'not strict', participants may have been referencing wider societal portrayals of Muslim involvement in potential terrorist activity – see Chapter 8 for further exploration.

15 The idea of wives 'working on' husbands also recalls other work on couple relationships: for example, Janet Finch (1983) has written of wives' personal projects as involving investment in, and facilitation of, their husbands' work.

16 The terms 'social nurturance' and 'spiritual nurturance' are adapted from Smalley's (2002) use of the concept of 'religious nurturance', to demonstrate a more nuanced conception of parenting as involving not just physical care giving but also emotional and social care.

17 That it was usually mothers who talked in this way was partly because in the interview sample, the mixed-generation families more often contained a second-generation mother and a first-generation father. However, it was probably also related to a pattern commonly discussed in the literature, namely that women are more likely to be the ones doing family/emotional 'work' (see for example Finch and Mason 1993).

Chapter 4   Cultural Consumption, Cultural Expression

18 See also Bauman (1988), Giddens (1991) and Beck (1992) who argue that the creation of self-identity is largely achieved through symbolic consumption. The growing sociology of consumption has increasingly represented consumption as identity-forming, and thus as having symbolic and communicative significance (see Gronow and Warde 2001).

19 A parallel may be drawn here with more general British discourses contending that 'home cooked food' is preferable to processed food or ready meals. However, in the present context the value given to home cooked food has an additional dimension in that it marks cultural belonging to a minority group.

20 Douglas (1996), using the example of shopping, argues that in looking at cultural tastes to understand group membership, it is important to attend to aversions as well as to preferences (i.e. what people will *not* eat, as well as what they will eat).

21 General Household Survey, Living in Britain, 2002 (ONS), http://www. statistics.gov.uk/

22 UK Time Use Survey, 2000 (ONS), http://www.statistics.gov.uk/

Chapter 5   Time and Everyday Family Practices

23   No discussion of time can occur without also implicating notions of space (Massey 1994), although Morgan points out that although in practice time and space are inseparable, it can be useful to distinguish the two theoretically (1996:137). The relationship between domestic and sacred space in this research is reported elsewhere (Becher 2005).

24   In this chapter, 'family time' is used to mean the aspects of routine, ritual or daily timetable that family members talked about in the context of their family lives. This often equates to 'domestic time' since it takes place in the within the household setting, although of course it is not confined to the home.

25   Later theologians have however suggested that rather than being distinct from the ordinary or profane, sacredness may be immanent or always present.

26   This 'stepping out' process could be seen as involving a temporary shift from *linear time* into *cyclical time*; see McKenzie Leiper (2001) for a summary of traditional and feminist perspectives on these different notions of time. Other authors have similarly portrayed women's experiences of cyclical time as an 'oasis in a busy life' (see Jerrome 1992:57 on older women's Christian fellowships).

27   A similar but less pronounced pattern existed for Christian children: 25 per cent of boys compared with 15 per cent of girls attended church 'often' with their father.

28   This is contrary to Eliade's notion of the sacred being totally distinct from the profane. See Silva (2004) for a discussion of a similar issue of family time being shaped by technology.

Chapter 6   Parenting Roles and Relationships

29   These images recall similar connections between motherhood and the sacred that exist in other religious traditions: for example, Catholic representations of mothers, symbolized by the Virgin Mary, as blessed and divine (Warner 1976).

Chapter 8   Connections: Resources and Stressors

30   The conception of social capital used in this chapter draws on the work of the Families & Social Capital ESRC Research Group, who identify social capital as 'the ways that people create social networks and social relationships, and to the trust and norms of engagement that ease these interactions. As forms of social capital, networks and trust are seen to generate social solidarity and inclusion' (Franklin 2004:2).

31   The terms 'extended family' and 'extended kin' are used in this Chapter to refer to family members outside the strictly-defined nuclear family (i.e. two generations of parents and children). As noted in Chapter 2, three families had extended households, with an adult child's spouse and offspring living

in the household with them, but for the majority their extended kin lived elsewhere.

32   It was interesting to note that newer means of communication, such as email or text messaging, were not mentioned. Other researchers (e.g. Reynolds 2004) have suggested that the growth of these technologies should change patterns of transnational communication between kin. Their lack of salience in these data may reflect the fact that mothers – the main family members who talked about telephone calls – may be less likely to use such technology. Children and fathers tended to restrict their descriptions of kin contact to visits per se.

33   The use of this term is not intended to suggest that there is a homogenous South Asian Muslim 'community', but refers to the notion of 'community' as used by the interviewees themselves. Family members belonged to a range of different groups (based among other things on national, regional, linguistic, religious, kin and gender identities) which could be more or less salient depending on context (see Shaw 2000:10).

34   Given that all the interviewed families were sending their children to Islamic classes, either at a mosque or a local house, it is possible that there was some under-reporting in the questionnaire. Some parents may not have classed their children's Islamic lessons as 'help, advice or support in bringing up their children'.

35   MCB press release, 'The Rise of Institutionalised Islamophobia', 1st June 2004. See www.mcb.org.uk.

Chapter 9   Conclusion

36   See Guardian special report *Young, British and Muslim,* 30th November 2004.

Appendices

37   This method, increasingly used by social research institutes in the UK, is based on insights from cognitive psychology about the processes which survey respondents go through when answering a question. Respondents are asked to fill in the questionnaire in the normal way, then probed for their understanding of key terms, the strategies used to recall information, the sensitivity and acceptability of questions, comprehensibility of layout and ease of completion. See Willis (2004) for details.

38   As well as those who ticked the 'Christian' box on the questionnaire, this category also includes those who ticked 'other' and wrote in answers such as 'Roman Catholic', 'Catholic' or 'Church of England' (6 children, 8 parents). These answers were re-coded as Christian.

39   Data were tested for significance by comparing confidence intervals using Z-scores.

40   There is in any case mixed evidence about the effect of bringing in a third-party translator (see Temple and Edwards' discussion of translator effects, 2002).

41   See Economic and Social Data Service advice on transcriptions at http://www. esds.ac.uk/qualidata/create/transcription.asp and also O'Connell and Kowal (1995).

References

Adam, B. (2000). 'The temporal gaze: The challenge for social theory in the context of GM food.' *British Journal of Sociology* 51(1): 125–142.

Ahmad, F., T. Modood, et al. (2003). *South Asian Women and Employment in Britain: The Interaction of Gender and Ethnicity*. London: Policy Studies Institute.

Ahmed, S. (1981). Asian girls and culture conflict. *Social and Community Work in a Multi-Racial Society*. J. Cheetham. London: Harper and Row.

Alanen, L. (1990). Rethinking socialization, the family and childhood. *Sociological Studies of Child Development*. P. Adler, P. Adler, N. Mandell and C. Spencer. Connecticut: JAI Press. 3.

Allen, J. M. and A. J. Hawkins (1999). 'Maternal gatekeeping: Mothers' beliefs and behaviors that inhibit greater father involvement in family work.' *Journal of Marriage & Family* 61: 199–212.

Ambert, M. (1992). *The Effect of Children on Parents*. New York: The Haworth Press.

Ansari, H. (2002). *Muslims in Britain*, Minority Rights Group International.

Anwar, M. (1981). *Between Two Cultures: A Story of Relationships Between Generations in the Asian Community in Britain*. London: CRE.

Anwar, M. (1986). Young Asians between two cultures. *Race and Social Work: A Guide to Training*. V. Coombe and A. Little. London: Tavistock.

Anwar, M. (1998). *Between Cultures: Continuity and Change in the Lives of Young Asians*. London: Routledge.

Arendell, T. (2000). 'Conceiving and investigating motherhood: The decade's scholarship.' *Journal of Marriage & Family* 62(4): 1192–1207.

Armstrong, C., M. Hill, et al. (1998). *Listening to Children*. Glasgow, Centre for the Child and Society, University of Glasgow.

Ballard, C. (1979). Conflict, continuity and change: Second generation South Asians. *Support and Stress: Minority Families in Britain*. V. S. Khan. London: Tavistock.

Ballard, R. (1982). South Asian families. *Families in Britain*. Rapoport, Fogarty and Rapoport. London: Routledge.

Ballard, R. (1990). Migration and kinship: The differential effect of marriage rules on the processes of Punjabi migrations to Britain. *South Asians Overseas*. C. Clarke, C. Peach and S. Vertovec. Cambridge: Cambridge University Press.

Ballard, R. (1994). The emergence of Desh Pardesh. *Desh Pardesh: The South Asian Presence in Britain*. R. Ballard. London: Hurst.

Ballard, R. (2002). The South Asian presence in Britain and its transnational connections. *Culture and Economy in the Indian Diaspora*. H. Singh and S. Vertovec. London: Routledge.

Bartels, E. (2000). 'Dutch Islam: Young people, learning and integration.' *Current Sociology* 48(4): 59–73.

Bartkowski, J. P. and X. Xu (2000). 'Distant patriarchs or expressive dads? The discourse and practice of fathering in conservative Protestant families.' *The Sociological Quarterly* 41: 465–485.

Bauer, J. (1997). Muslim children in Birmingham: Interviews with Muslim children. *WRERU Occasional Papers.* Coventry: WRERU. 1.

Bauman, Z. (1988). *Freedom.* Milton Keynes: Open University Press.

Becher, H. (2005). Family practices in South Asian Muslim families: Parenting in a multi-faith Britain (unpublished PhD thesis). *Department of Social Work and Psycho-Social Studies.* Norwich: University of East Anglia.

Becher, H. and F. Husain (2003). *Supporting Minority Ethnic Families: South Asian Hindus and Muslims in Britain: Developments in Family Support.* London: National Family & Parenting Institute.

Beck, U. (1992). *Risk Society: Towards a New Modernity.* London: Sage.

Beck, U. (1997). 'Democratization of the family.' *Childhood* 4(2): 151–168.

Beishon, S., T. Modood, et al. (1998). *Ethnic Minority Families.* London: Policy Studies Institute.

Bennett, T. and E. B. Silva (2004). *Contemporary Culture and Everyday Life.* Durham: Sociologypress.

Berger, P. L. and T. Luckmann (1991). *The Social Construction of Reality: A Treatise in the Sociology of Knowledge.* Hammondsworth: Penguin.

Berthoud, R. (2000). 'Family formation in multi-cultural Britain: Three patterns of diversity.' *Working Papers of the Institute for Social and Economic Research* Paper 2000-34.

Bhatti, G. (1999). *Asian Children at Home and at School: An Ethnographic Study.* London: Routledge.

Borgers, N., E. de Leeuw, et al. (2000). 'Children as respondents in survey research: Cognitive development and response quality.' *Bulletin de Methodologie Sociologique* 66: 60–75.

Bose, R. (2000). Families in transition. *South Asian Children and Adolescents in Britain.* A. Lau. London: Whurr: 47–60.

Bourdieu, P. (1984). *Distinction: A Social Critique of the Judgement of Taste.* London: Routledge.

Bourdieu, P. (1990). *The Logic of Practice.* Cambridge: Polity Press.

Brannen, J. (1988). 'The study of sensitive subjects.' *The Sociological Review* 36: 552–563.

Brannen, J. (1996). Discourses of adolescence: Young people's independence and autonomy within families. *Children in Families.* J. Brannen and M. O'Brien. London: The Falmer Press: 114–129.

Brannen, J., K. Dodd, et al. (1994). *Young People, Health and Family Life.* Buckingham: Open University Press.

Brannen, J. and M. O'Brien (1996). Introduction. *Children in Families.* J. Brannen and M. O'Brien. London: Falmer: 1–12.

Bulmer, M. (1979). 'Concepts in the analysis of qualitative data.' *Sociological Review* 27(4): 651–677.

Burgess, T. F. (2003). *A General Introduction to the Design of Questionnaires for Survey Research.* Leeds: Information Systems Services, University of Leeds.

Burton, L. and R. Jarrett (2000). 'In the mix, yet on the margins: The place of families in urban neighborhood and child development research.' *Journal of Marriage & Family* 62(4): 1114–1135.

Butt, J. and L. Box (1998). *Family Centred: A Study of the Use of Family Centres by Black Families.* London: REU.

Chamberlain, M. (1999). Brothers and sisters, uncles and aunts: A lateral perspective on Caribbean families. *The New Family?* E. B. Silva and C. Smart. London, Sage: 129–142.

Charmaz, K. (1995). Grounded theory. *Rethinking Methods in Psychology.* J. A. Smith, R. Harré and L. Van Langenhove. London: Sage.

Charmaz, K. (2000). Grounded theory: Objectivist and constructivist methods. *Handbook of Qualitative Research (2nd ed).* N. K. Denzin and Y. S. Lincoln. Thousand Oaks, CA: Sage.

Chatters, L. M. and R. J. Taylor (2004). Religion and families. *Sourcebook of Family Theory and Research.* V. Bengtson, A. Acock, K. Allen, P. Dilworth-Anderson and D. Klein. Thousand Oaks, CA, Sage: 517–541.

Chattoo, S., K. Atkin, et al. (2004). Young people of Pakistani origin and their families: Implications for providing support to young people and their families. Leeds: University of Leeds.

Coffey, A. and P. Atkinson (1996). *Making Sense of Qualitative Data.* London: Sage.

Coley, R. L. and J. E. Morris (2002). 'Comparing father and mother reports of father involvement among low-income minority families.' *Journal of Marriage & Family* 64: 982–997.

Collingwood Bakeo, A. and L. Clarke (2004). Child population (chapter 1). *The Health of Children and Young People.* ONS.

Coltrane, S. (2004). Fathering: Paradoxes, contradictions & dilemmas. *Handbook of Contemporary Families: Considering the Past, Contemplating the Future.* M. Coleman and L. H. Ganong. London: Sage: 224–239.

Costigan, C. and M. Cox (2001). 'Fathers' participation in family research: Is there a self-selection bias?' *Journal of Family Psychology* 15(4): 706–720.

Crossley, M. L. (2000). *Introducing Narrative Psychology: Self, Trauma and the Construction of Meaning.* Buckingham: Open University Press.

Daly, K. (1993). 'Reshaping fatherhood: Finding the models.' *Journal of Family Issues* 14: 510–530.

Daly, K. (1996). *Families and Time: Keeping Pace in a Hurried Culture.* London: Sage.

Daly, K. (2001a). 'Deconstructing family time: From ideology to lived experience.' *Journal of Marriage & Family* 63: 283–294.

Daly, K. (ed.) (2001b). *Minding the Time in Family Experience: Emerging Perspectives and Issues.* London: JAI.

Daly, K. (2003). 'Family theory versus the theories families live by.' *Journal of Marriage & Family* 65: 771–784.

Daly, K. and J. Beaton (2004). Through the lens of time: How families live in and through time. *Sourcebook of Family Theory and Research.* V. Bengtson, A. Acock, K. Allen, P. Dilworth-Anderson and D. Klein. Thousand Oaks, Calif.: Sage.

Deacon, A. and F. Williams (2004). 'Introduction: Themed section on care, values and the future of welfare.' *Social Policy & Society* 3(4): 385–390.

Deutsch, F. M. (1999). *Halving It All: How Equally Shared Parenting Works.* Cambridge, MA: Harvard University Press.

Dollahite, D. C. (1999). *Faithful Fathering: How Religion Fosters Responsible and Meaningful Father Involvement (conference paper).* World Conference of Families, Geneva.

Dollahite, D. C. and L. D. Marks (2004). How highly religious families strive to fulfill sacred purposes. *Sourcebook on Family Theories and Methods*. V. Bengtson, D. Klein, A. Acock, D. Allen and P. Dilworth-Anderson. Thousand Oaks, CA: Sage.

Dollahite, D. C., L. D. Marks, et al. (2004). Families and religious beliefs, practices, and communities: Linkages in a diverse and dynamic cultural context. *Handbook of Contemporary Families: Considering the Past, Contemplating the Future*. M. Coleman and L. H. Ganong. Thousand Oaks, CA, Sage: 411–431.

Dosanjh, J. and P. Ghuman (1996). *Child-Rearing in Ethnic Minorities*. Clevedon, Avon: Multilingual Matters.

Dosanjh, J. and P. Ghuman (1998). 'Child-rearing practices of two generations of Punjabis: Development of personality and independence.' *Children & Society* 12(1): 25–37.

Douglas, M. (ed.) (1984). *Food in the Social Order: Studies of Food and Festivities in Three American Communities*. New York: Russell Sage Foundation.

Douglas, M. (1996). On not being seen dead: Shopping as protest. *Thought Styles: Critical Essays on Good Taste*. London: Sage: 77–105.

Dowd, N. E. (2000). *Redefining Fatherhood*. New York: New York University Press.

Downey, D., P. Braboy Jackson, et al. (1994). 'Sons versus daughters: Sex composition of children and maternal views on socialization.' *Sociological Quarterly* 35: 33–50.

Duffield, M. (2002). 'Trends in female employment 2002.' *Labour Market Trends* (November 2002).

Edgell, S., K. Hetherington, et al. (eds) (1996). *Consumption Matters*. Oxford: Blackwell.

Edwards, R., J. Franklin, et al. (2003). Families and social capital: Exploring the issues. *Families and Social Capital ESRC Research Group Working Paper No. 1*. London: South Bank University.

Eliade, M. (1959). *The Sacred and the Profane: The Nature of Religion; Translated from the French by Willard R. Trask*. New York: Harcourt Brace Jovanovich.

Esterberg, K. G. (2002). *Qualitative Methods in Social Research*. New York: McGraw-Hill.

Feinberg, M. E. (2003). 'The internal structure and ecological context of co-parenting: A framework for research and intervention.' *Parenting: Science and Practice* 3(2): 95–131.

Fiese, B. H. and T. J. Tomcho (2001). 'Finding meaning in religious practices: The relation between religious holiday rituals and marital satisfaction.' *Journal of Family Psychology* 15(4): 597–609.

Finch, J. (1983). *Married to the Job: Wives' Incorporation into Men's Work*. London: George Allen & Unwin.

Finch, J. and J. Mason (1993). *Negotiating Family Responsibilities*. London: Routledge.

Finch, J. and J. Mason (2000). *Passing On: Kinship and Inheritance in England*. London: Routledge.

Flor, D. L. and N. F. Knapp (2001). 'Transmission and transaction: Predicting adolescents' internationalization of parental religious values.' *Journal of Family Psychology* 15(4): 627–645.

Franklin, J. (2004). Social capital: Critical perspectives. *Politics, Trust and Networks: Social Capital in Critical Perspective. Families & Social Capital E.S.R.C.*

Research Group Working Paper No. 7. J. Franklin. London: South Bank University.

Frosh, S., A. Phoenix, et al. (2002). *Young Masculinities: Understanding Boys in Contemporary Society.* Basingstoke: Palgrave.

Gardner, K. and R. Grillo (2002). 'Transnational households and ritual: An overview.' *Global Networks* 2(3): 179–190.

Geertz, C. (1973). *The Interpretation of Cultures.* New York: Basic Books.

Ghate, D. and N. Hazel (2002). *Parenting in Poor Environments: Stress, Support and Coping.* London: Jessica Kingsley.

Giddens, A. (1979). *Central Problems in Social Theory: Action, Structure and Contradiction in Social Analysis.* London: Macmillan.

Giddens, A. (1984). *The Constitution of Society.* Cambridge: Polity Press.

Giddens, A. (1991). *Modernity and Self-Identity: Self and Society in the Late Modern Age.* Cambridge: Polity.

Gillespie, M. (1995). *Television, Ethnicity and Cultural Change.* London: Routledge.

Gillies, V. (2005). 'Meeting parents' needs? Discourses of "support" and "inclusion" in family policy.' *Critical Social Policy* 25(1): 70–90.

Gillis, J. R. (2001). Never enough time: Some paradoxes of modern family time(s) – Diversity, past and present in experiences and expectations of family time. *Minding the Time in Family Experience: Emerging Perspectives and Issues.* K. Daly. London: JAI. 3: 19–36.

Glaser, B. G. (1978). *Theoretical Sensitivity: Advances in the Methodology of Grounded Theory.* CA: The Sociology Press.

Glaser, B. G. and A. L. Strauss (1967). *The Discovery of Grounded Theory: Strategies for Qualitative Research.* London: Weidenfeld and Nicolson.

Golafshani, N. (2003). 'Understanding reliability and validity in qualitative research.' *The Qualitative Report* 8(4): 597–607.

Goldman, R. (2005). *Fathers' Involvement in their Children's Education: A Review of Research and Practice.* London: National Family & Parenting Institute.

Gordon, S., P. Benner, et al. (eds) (1996). *Caregiving: Readings in Knowledge, Practice, Ethics, and Politics.* Philadelphia: University of Pennsylvania Press.

Goulbourne, H. (1999). The transnational character of Caribbean kinship in Britain. *Changing Britain, Families and Households in the 1990s.* S. McRae. Oxford: Oxford University Press: 176–197.

Gregg, P. and J. Wadsworth (2000). Two sides to every story: Measuring worklessness and polarisation at household level, Centre for Economic Performance, Working paper no. 1076.

Gronow, J. and A. Warde (eds) (2001). *Ordinary Consumption.* London: Routledge.

Grover, S. (2004). 'Why won't they listen to us? On giving power and voice to children participating in social research.' *Childhood* 11(1): 81–93.

Grundy, E., M. Murphy, et al. (1999). 'Looking beyond the household: Intergenerational perspectives on living kin and contacts with kin in Great Britain.' *Population Trends* 97: 19–27.

Gunter, B. and A. Furnham (1998). *Children as Consumers: A Psychological Analysis of the Young People's Market.* London: Routledge.

Gunter, B. and J. McAleer (1997). *Children and Television (2nd edition).* London: Routledge.

Hägerstrand, T. (1975). Space, time and human conditions. *Dynamic Allocation of Urban Spaces.* A. Karlqvist. Farnborough: Saxon House.

Halstead, M. (1994). 'Between two cultures? Muslim children in a western liberal society.' *Children & Society* 8(4): 312–326.

Hammersley, M. (1992). Deconstructing the qualitative-quantitative divide. *Mixing Methods: Qualitative and Quantitative Research.* J. Brannen. Aldershot: Avebury: 39–55.

Hammersley, M. (1996). The relationship between qualitative and quantitative research: Paradigm loyalty versus methodological eclecticism. *Handbook of Qualitative Research Methods for Psychology and the Social sciences.* J. T. E. Richardson. Leicester: BPS Books: 159–174.

Handel, G. (1996). 'Family worlds and qualitative family research: Emergence and prospects of whole-family methodology.' *Marriage & Family Review* 24(3/4): 335–348.

Harbottle, L. (1996). 'Bastard' chicken or *ghormeh-sabzi?* Iranian women guarding the health of the migrant family. *Consumption Matters.* S. Edgell, K. Hetherington and A. Warde. Oxford: Blackwell: 204–226.

Henley, A. (1986). The Asian Community in Britain. *Race and Social Work: A Guide to Training.* V. Coombe and A. Little. London: Tavistock.

Henley, K. (2004). *Issues of Gender and Power in Identity Theory: Creating a Mid-Range Model of Maternal Gatekeeping and Father Involvement.* 34th Theory Construction and Research Methodology Workshop, Orlando, Florida: November 2004.

Henricson, C., I. Katz, et al. (2001). *National Mapping of Family Services in England and Wales – A Consultation Document,* National Family and Parenting Institute.

Hobson, B. and D. Morgan (2002). Introduction: Making men into fathers. *Making men into fathers: Men, masculinities and the social politics of fatherhood.* B. Hobson. Cambridge: Cambridge University Press.

Hochschild, A. (1989). *The Second Shift.* New York: Viking Press.

Holden, G. W. (2001). 'Psychology, religion, and the family: It's time for a revival.' *Journal of Family Psychology* 15(4): 657–662.

Home Office (2002). *Secure Borders, Safe Haven: Integration with Diversity in Modern Britain.* London: The Stationary Office.

Home Office (2004). Working together: Co-operation between government and Faith Communities. London: Home Office Faith Communities Unit.

Hood, S. (2004). *State of London's Children (2nd Report).* London: Greater London Authority.

Husain, F. and M. O'Brien (1999). *Muslim Families in Europe: Social Existence and Social Care.* London: University of North London.

Husain, F. and M. O'Brien (2000). 'Muslim communities in Europe: Reconstruction and transformation.' *Current Sociology* 48(4): 1–13.

Husain, F. and M. O'Brien (2001). South Asian Muslims in Britain: Faith, family and community. *Maintaining Our Differences: Minority Families in Multicultural Societies.* C. D. H. Harvey. Aldershot: Ashgate: 15–28.

Hyde, K. E. (1990). *Religion in Childhood and Adolescence: A Comprehensive Review of the Research.* Birmingham, Ala.: Religious Education Press.

Jackson, R. and E. Nesbitt (1993). *Hindu Children in Britain.* Stoke-on-Trent, Trentham.

Jacobson, J. (1997). 'Religion and ethnicity: Dual and alternative sources of identity among young British Pakistanis.' *Ethnic and Racial Studies* 20(2): 238–256.

James, A. and A. Prout (1997). *Constructing and Reconstructing Childhood: Contemporary Issues in the Sociological Study of Childhood.* London: Falmer.

Jensen, A.-M. and L. McKee (2003). Introduction: Theorising childhood and family change. *Children and the Changing Family: Between Transformation and Negotiation.* A.-M. Jensen and L. McKee. London: RoutledgeFalmer: 1–14.

Jerrome, D. (1992). *Good Company: An Anthropological Study of Old People in Groups.* Edinburgh: Edinburgh University Press.

Josselson, R. and A. Leiblich (eds) (1993). *The Narrative Study of Lives.* Newbury Park, CA: Sage.

King, V. (2003). 'The influence of religion on fathers' relationships with their children.' *Journal of Marriage & Family* 65: 382–395.

La Fontaine, J. S. (1979). *Sex and Age as Principles of Social Differentiation.* London: Academic Press.

Lamb, M., J. H. Pleck, et al. (1987). A biosocial perspective on paternal behaviour and involvement. *Parenting Across the Lifespan: Biosocial Dimensions.* J. B. Lancaster, J. Altmann, A. S. Rossi and L. R. Sherrod. Hawthorne, NY: Aldine: 111–142.

Lareau, A. (2000). 'Social class and the daily lives of children: A study from the United States.' *Childhood* 7(2): 155–171.

Lareau, A. (2004). *Unequal Childhoods: Class, Race, and Family Life.* Berkeley, CA: University of California Press.

Larson, H. (2000). 'We don't celebrate Christmas, we just give gifts': Adaptations to migration and social change among Hindu, Muslim and Sikh children in England. *Family, Religion and Social Change in Diverse Societies.* S. K. Houseknecht and J. G. Pankhurst. New York: Oxford University Press: 283–302.

Larson, R. (2001). Mother's time in two-parent and one-parent families: The daily organization of work, time for oneself and parenting. *Minding the Time in Family Experience: Emerging Perspectives and Issues.* K. Daly. London: JAI. 3: 85–109.

Lau, A. (ed.) (2000). *South Asian Children and Adolescents in Britain.* London: Whurr.

Leach, R. (2003). 'Children's participation in family decision-making.' *National Children's Bureau Research Highlights* no. 196.

Lee, R. (1993). *Doing Research on Sensitive Topics.* London: Sage.

Lefebvre, H. (1991). *The Production of Space.* Oxford: Blackwell.

Lindley, J., A. Dale, et al. (2004). 'Ethnic differences in womens' demographic, family characteristics and economic activity profiles, 1992 to 2002.' *Labour Market Trends* (April 2004).

Longhurst, B., G. Bagnall, et al. (2001). Ordinary consumption and personal identity: Radio and the middle classes in the North West of England. *Ordinary Consumption.* J. Gronow and A. Warde. London: Routledge.

Longhurst, B. and M. Savage (1996). Social class, consumption and the influence of Bourdieu: Some critical issues. *Consumption Matters.* S. Edgell, K. Hetherington and A. Warde. Oxford: Blackwell.

Macfarlane, A., M. Stafford, et al. (2004). Social inequalities (Chapter 8). *The Health of Children and Young People.* ONS.

Madge, N. (2001). *Understanding Difference: The Meaning of Ethnicity for Young Lives.* London: National Children's Bureau.

Mahoney, A., K. I. Pargament, et al. (2001). 'Religion in the home in the 1980s and 1990s: A meta-analytic review and conceptual analysis of links between religion, marriage, and parenting.' *Journal of Family Psychology* 15(4): 559–597.

Mahoney, A., K. I. Pargament, A. Murray-Swank and N. Murray-Swank (2003). 'Religion and the sanctification of religious relationships.' *Review of Religious Research* **44**(3): 300–312.

Marks, L. D. (2004). 'Sacred practices in highly religious families: Christian, Jewish, Mormon, and Muslim perspectives.' *Family Process* **43**(2): 217–231.

Marsiglio, W., P. Amato, et al. (2000). 'Scholarship on fatherhood in the 1990s and beyond.' *Journal of Marriage & Family* **62**: 1173–1191.

Mason, J. (2000). *Researching Morality*. E.S.R.C. Research Group on Care, Values and the Future of Welfare: Workshop 4, Methodology for researching moral agencies, Leeds.

Mason, J. (2002). *Qualitative Researching (2nd ed)*. London: Sage.

Mason, J. (2004). 'Managing kinship over long distances: The significance of "the visit".' *Social Policy & Society* **3**(4): 421–429.

Mason, J. and V. May (2004). *Meshing Qualitative and Quantitative Methods in Family Research*. Paper presented at E.S.R.C. Research Methods Festival, Thursday 1st July 2004, Oxford.

Massey, D. (1994). *Space, Place and Gender*. Cambridge: Polity Press.

Matthews, H. (1987). 'Gender, home range and environmental cognition.' *Transactions of the Institute of British Geographers* **12**: 43–56.

Maughan, B., A. Brock, et al. (2004). Mental health (Chapter 12). *The Health of Children and Young People*. ONS.

Mayall, B. (ed.) (1994). *Children's Childhoods: Observed and Experienced*. London: Falmer.

Mayall, B. (1996). *Children, Health and the Social Order*. Buckingham: Open University Press.

Mayall, B. (2002). *Towards a Sociology for Childhood: Thinking from Children's Lives*. Buckingham: Open University Press.

Mayall, B. and H. Zeiher (2003). *Childhood in Generational Perspective*. London: Institute of Education.

McGlone, F., A. Park, et al. (1999). Kinship and friendship: Attitudes and behaviour in Britain, 1986–1995. *Changing Britain: Families and Households in the 1990's*. S. McRae. Oxford: Oxford University Press.

McKee, L. and M. O'Brien (1982). The father figure: Some current orientations and historical perspectives. *The Father Figure*. M. O'Brien and L. McKee. London: Tavistock: 3–25.

McKenzie Leiper, J. (2001). Gendered views of time and time crunch stress: Women lawyers' responses to professional and personal demands. *Minding the Time in Family Experience: Emerging Perspectives and Issues*. K. Daly. London: JAI. **3**: 251–280.

Mills, C. W. (1959). *The Sociological Imagination*. New York: Oxford University Press.

Modood, T. (2004). 'Capitals, ethnic identity and educational qualifications.' *Cultural Trends* **13**(2): 87–105.

Modood, T., R. Berthoud, et al. (1997). *Ethnic Minorities in Britain*. London: Policy Studies Institute.

Morgan, D. (1975). *Social Theory and the Family*. London: Routledge & Kegan Paul.

Morgan, D. (1996). *Family Connections: An Introduction to Family Studies*. Cambridge: Polity Press.

Morgan, D. (1999). Risk and family practices: Accounting for change and fluidity in family life. *The new family?* E. B. Silva and C. Smart. London: Sage: 13–30.

Morgan, D. (2003). Men in families and households. *The Blackwell Companion to the Sociology of Families.* J. Scott, J. Treas and M. Richards. Oxford: Blackwell: 374–393.

Morgan, D. (2004). Everyday life and family practices. *Contemporary Culture and Everyday Life.* T. Bennett and E. B. Silva. Durham, sociologypress: 37–51.

Morrow, V. (1994). Responsible children? Aspects of children's work and employment outside school in contemporary U.K. *Children's Childhoods: Observed and Experienced.* B. Mayall. London: The Falmer Press.

Newson, E. and J. Newson (1976). *Seven Years Old in the Home Environment.* London: Allen & Unwin.

Newson, J. and E. Newson (1968). *Four Years Old in an Urban Community.* London: Allen & Unwin.

O'Brien, M. (1995). 'Allocation of resources in households: Children's perspectives.' *The Sociological Review* 43(3): 501–517.

O'Brien, M. (2003). Social science and public policy perspectives on fatherhood in the European Union. *The Role of the Father in Child Development.* M. Lamb. New York: Chichester, Wiley.

O'Brien, M. and L. McKee (eds) (1982). *The Father Figure.* London: Tavistock.

O'Connell, D. C. and S. Kowal (1995). Basic principles of transcription. *Rethinking Methods in Psychology.* J. A. Smith, R. Harré and L. Van Langenhove. London: Sage: 93–105.

ODPM (2003). Learning to listen: Action plan for children and young people, Office for the Deputy Prime Minister: available at www.odpm.gov.uk/stellent/groups/odpm_about_022929.hcsp.

ONS (2004). *Focus on Religion.* London: Office for National Statistics.

Østberg, S. (2003). *Pakistani Children in Norway: Islamic Nurture in a Secular Context,* Department of Theology and Religious Studies, University of Leeds.

Palkovitz, R. (1997). 'Reconstructing involvement': Expanding conceptualizations of men's caring in contemporary families. *Generative Fathering: Beyond Deficit Perspectives.* A. J. Hawkins and D. C. Dollahite. Thousand Oaks, CA: Sage.

Pankaj, V. (2000). Family mediation services for minority ethnic families in Scotland. Edinburgh: The Scottish Executive Central Research Unit.

Parke, R. D. (1996). *Fatherhood.* Cambridge, MA: Harvard University Press.

Parke, R. D. (2001). 'Introduction to the special section on families and religion: A call for a recommitment by researchers, practitioners, and policymakers.' *Journal of Family Psychology* 15(4): 555–558.

Parke, R. D. (2004). Fathers and families. *Handbook of Parenting.* M. Bornstein. Mahwah NJ: Lawrence Erlbaum Associates.

Patton, M. Q. (1990). *Qualitative Evaluation and Research Methods.* Thousand Oaks, CA: Sage.

Pels, T. (2000). 'Muslim families from Morocco in the Netherlands: Gender dynamics and fathers' roles in a context of change.' *Current Sociology* 48(4).

Phillipson, C., G. Allan, et al. (eds) (2004). *Social Networks and Social Exclusion: Sociological and Policy Issues.* Aldershot: Ashgate.

Pleck, J. H. and J. L. Stueve (2001). Time and paternal involvement. *Minding the Time in Family Experience: Emerging Perspectives and Issues. Contemporary Perspectives on Family Research.* K. Daly. Connecticut: JAI Press. **3**.

Prout, A. (2000). 'Children's participation: Control and self-realisation in British late modernity.' *Children & Society* **14**(4): 151–168.

Putnam, R. (2000). *Bowling Alone: The Collapse and Revival of American Community.* New York; London: Simon & Schuster.

Qureshi, T., D. Berridge, et al. (2000). *Where to Turn? Family Support for South Asian Communities – A Case Study.* London: National Children's Bureau and Joseph Rowntree Foundation.

Qvortrup, J. (1990). A voice for children in statistical and social accounting: A plea for children's rights to be heard. *Constructing and Reconstructing Childhood: Contemporary Issues in the Sociological Study of Childhood.* A. James and A. Prout. London: Falmer.

Qvortrup, J. (1994). Childhood matters: An introduction. *Childhood Matters: Social Theory, Practice and Politics.* J. Qvortrup, M. Bardy, G. Sgritta and H. Windersberger. Brookfield, Avebury: 1–23.

Qvortrup, J., M. Bardy, et al. (eds) (1994). *Childhood Matters: Social Theory, Practice and Politics.* Brookfield, Avebury.

Reynolds, T. (2004). *Caribbean Families, Social Capital and Young People's Diasporic Identities. Families & Social Capital E.S.R.C. Research Group Working Paper No. 11.* London: South Bank University.

Ribbens-McCarthy, J., R. Edwards, et al. (2001). 'Moral tales of the child and the adult: Narratives of contemporary family lives under changing circumstances.' *Sociology* **34**(4): 785–803.

Riessman, C. K. (1993). *Narrative Analysis.* Newbury Park, CA: Sage.

Robinson, M., I. Butler, et al. (2003). Children's experiences of their parents' divorce. *Children and the Changing Family: Between Transformation and Negotiation.* A.-M. Jensen and L. McKee. London: RoutledgeFalmer: 76–89.

Sandelowski, M. (2002). 'Reembodying qualitative inquiry.' *Qualitative Health Research* **12**(1): 104–115.

Scott, A., D. Pearce, et al. (2001). 'The sizes and characteristics of the minority ethnic populations of Great Britain – Latest estimates.' *Population Trends* **105**: 6–15.

Scott, J. (2000). Children as respondents: The challenge for quantitative methods. *Research with Children: Perspectives and Practices.* P. Christensen and A. James. London: Falmer Press: 98–135.

Scott, J. (2003). Children's families. *The Blackwell Companion to the Sociology of Families.* J. Scott, J. Treas and M. Richards. Oxford: Blackwell: 109–141.

Scottish Executive (2004). *Parents' Access To and Demand for Childcare in Scotland: Final Report.*

Shaw, A. (1994). The Pakistani community in Oxford. *Desh Pardesh: The South Asian Presence in Britain.* R. Ballard. London: Hurst: 35–57.

Shaw, A. (2000). *Kinship and Continuity: Pakistani Families in Britain.* Amsterdam: Harwood Academic.

Shaw, A. (2003). Immigrant families in the U.K. *The Blackwell Companion to the Sociology of Families.* J. Scott, J. Treas and M. Richards. Oxford: Blackwell: 270–285.

Sherif-Trask, B. (2004). Muslim families in the United States. *Handbook of Contemporary Families: Considering the Past, Contemplating the Future.* M. Coleman and L. H. Ganong. Thousand Oaks, CA: Sage: 394–408.

Sherkat, D. and C. Ellison (1999). 'Recent developments and current controversies in the sociology of religion.' *Annual Review of Sociology* 25: 363–394.

Silva, E. B. (2004). Materials and morals: Families and technologies in everyday life. *Contemporary Culture and Everyday Life*. T. Bennett and E. B. Silva. Durham: Sociologypress.

Smalley, S. M. V. (2002). Islamic nurture in the west: Approaches to parenting amongst second generation Pakistanis and Khojas in Peterborough (unpublished PhD thesis). *Dept of Theology and Religious Studies*. Leeds: University of Leeds.

Snarey, J. R. and D. C. Dollahite (2001). 'Varieties of religion-family linkages.' *Journal of Family Psychology* 15(4): 646–651.

Soja, E. (1989). *Postmodern Geographies: The Reassertion of Space in Critical Social Theory*. London: Verso.

Song, M. (1996). 'Helping out': Children's labour participation in Chinese takeaway businesses in Britain. *Children in Families*. J. Brannen and M. O'Brien. London: The Falmer Press: 101–113.

Song, M. (1997). '"You're becoming more and more English": Investigating Chinese siblings' cultural identities.' *New Community* 23(3): 343–362.

Sonuga-Barke, E. J. S. and M. Mistry (2000). 'The effect of extended family living on the mental health of three generations within two Asian communities.' *British Journal of Clinical Psychology* 39: 129–141.

Southerton, D. (2003). '"Squeezing time": Allocating practices, coordinating networks and scheduling society.' *Time & Society* 12(1): 5–25.

Southerton, D. (2004). Cultural capital, social networks and social contexts: Cultural orientations toward spare time practices in a New Town. *Social Networks and Social Exclusion: Sociological and Policy Issues*. C. Phillipson, G. Allan and D. Morgan. Aldershot: Ashgate.

Strauss, A. L. and J. Corbin (1998). *Basics of Qualitative Research (2nd ed)*. London: Sage.

Swidler, A. (1986). 'Culture in action: Symbols and strategies.' *American Sociological Review* 51(2): 273–286.

Temple, B. and R. Edwards (2002). 'Interpreters/translators and cross-language research: Reflexivity and border crossings.' *International Journal of Qualitative Methods* 1(2): Article 1. Retrieved 03/03/05 from http://www.ualberta.ca/~ijqm.

Thomas, N. (2000). *Children, Family and the State: Decision-Making and Child Participation*. Macmillan.

Thompson, J. (1989). The theory of structuration. *Social Theory of Modern Societies: Anthony Giddens and his Critics*. D. Held and J. Thompson. Cambridge: Cambridge University Press.

Townsend, N. (2003). Cultural contexts of father involvement. *Handbook of Father Involvement*. C. S. Tamis-LeMonda and N. Cabrera. Mahwah, NJ: Laurence Erlbaum Associates: 249–278.

Valentine, G. (1997). '"My son's a bit dizzy." "My wife's a bit soft": Gender, children and cultures of parenting.' *Gender, Place and Culture: A Journal of Feminist Geography* 4(1): 37–62.

Van der Veer, P. (2004). 'South Asian Islam in Britain.' *Ethnicities* 4(1): 135–146.

Walzer, S. (2004). Encountering oppositions: A review of scholarship about motherhood. *Handbook of Contemporary Families: Considering the Past, Contemplating the Future*. M. Coleman and L. H. Ganong. London: Sage: 209–223.

Warde, A., L. Martens, et al. (1999). 'Consumption and the problem of variety: Cultural omnivorousness, social distinction and dining out.' *Sociology* **33**(1): 105–127.

Warner, M. (1976). *Alone of All Her Sex: The Myth and Cult of the Virgin Mary.* London: Vintage.

Weber, L. R., A. Miracle, et al. (1994). 'Interviewing early adolescents: Some methodological considerations.' *Human Organisation* **53**(1): 42–47.

Werbner, P. (1996). The enigma of Christmas: Symbolic violence, compliant subjects and the flow of English kinship. *Consumption Matters*. S. Edgell, K. Hetherington and A. Warde. Oxford, Blackwell: 135–162.

West, C. and D. H. Zimmerman (1987). 'Doing gender.' *Gender and Society* **1**: 125–151.

Willis, G. B. (2004). *Cognitive Interviewing: A Tool for Improving Questionnaire Design.* London: Sage.

Woollett, A. and H. Marshall (2001). Motherhood and mothering. *Handbook of the Psychology of Women and Gender.* R. Unger. New York: Wiley.

Young, M. and P. Willmott (1957). *Family and Kinship in East London.* London: Routledge & Kegan Paul.

Index

226 *Index*